American Mining Code

Embracing the United States, State and Territorial Mining Laws
and the General Land Office Regulations

by Henry N. Copp

with an introduction by Kerby Jackson

This work contains material that was originally published in 1905.

This publication was created and published for the public benefit,
utilizing public funding and is within the Public Domain.

This edition is reprinted for educational purposes
and in accordance with all applicable Federal Laws.

Introduction Copyright 2018 by Kerby Jackson

Introduction

It has often been said that "*gold is where you find it*", but even beginning prospectors understand that their chances for finding something of value in the earth or in the streams of the Golden West are dramatically increased by going back to those places where gold and other minerals were once mined by our forerunners. Despite this, much of the contemporary information on local mining history that is currently available is mostly a result of mere local folklore and persistent rumors of major strikes, the details and facts of which, have long been distorted. Long gone are the old timers and with them, the days of first hand knowledge of the mines of the area and how they operated. Also long gone are most of their notes, their assay reports, their mine maps and personal scrapbooks, along with most of the surveys and reports that were performed for them by private and government geologists. Even published books such as this one are often retired to the local landfill or backyard burn pile by the descendents of those old timers and disappear at an alarming rate. Despite the fact that we live in the so-called "Information Age" where information is supposedly only the push of a button on a keyboard away, true insight into mining properties remains illusive and hard to come by, even to those of us who seek out this sort of information as if our lives depend upon it. Without this type of information readily available to the average independent miner, there is little hope that our metal mining industry will ever recover.

This important volume and others like it, are being presented in their entirety again, in the hope that the average prospector will no longer stumble through the overgrown hills and the tailing strewn creeks without being well informed enough to have a chance to succeed at his ventures.

Kerby Jackson
Josephine County, Oregon
May 2018

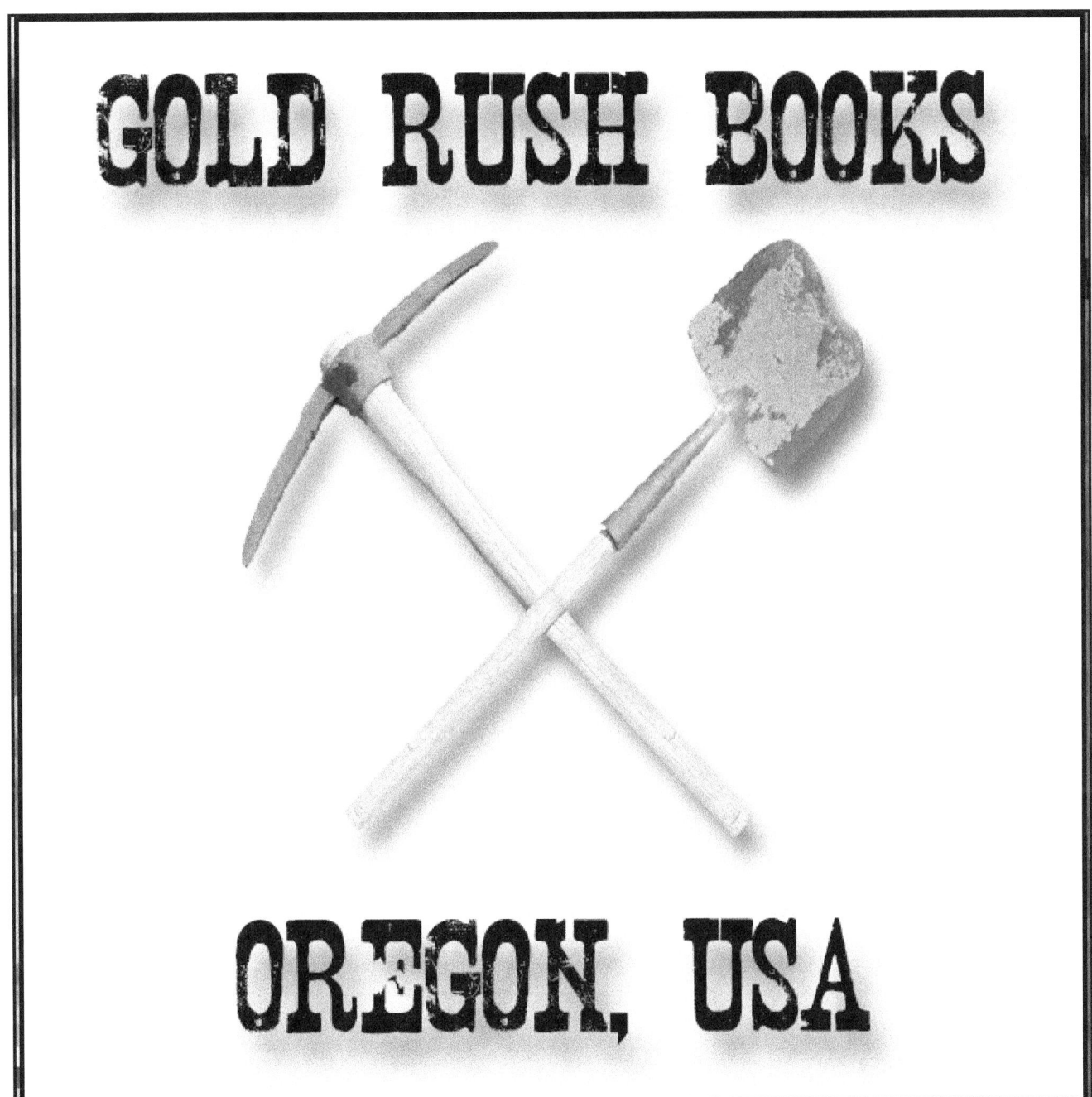

www.GoldMiningBooks.com

CONTENTS.

	PAGE
UNITED STATES LAWS AND INSTRUCTIONS.	
Revised Statutes and Regulations—General Law	1-26
Water Rights	26
Revised Statutes—Act of March 3, 1891—Town Sites	28
Easements	28
Homestead and Pre-emption Claims	29
Certain States Excepted	29
Alaska	41
Revised Statutes—Coal Lands	30
Mineral Entries within Forest Reserves	35
Act of June 3, 1878—Timber Cutting	36
Act of June 3, 1878—Timber and Stone	37
Act of January 31, 1901—Salt and Saline Lands	40
Perjury, Penalty therefor	41
Miscellaneous Provisions	41
Building Stone and Mineral Oils	17
Oil Mining Claims	48
Mineral Deposits	48
FORMS.	
1. Notice of Location	49
2. Proof of Labor	49
3. Notice of Forfeiture	49
4. Affidavit of Failure to Contribute	50
5. Miner's Lien	50
6. Application for Survey	51
7. Application for Patent	51
8. Proof of Posting Notice and Diagram	52
9. Proof that Plat and Notice remained Posted during Period of Publication	52
10. Register's Certificate of Posting for 60 days	53
11. Notice for Publication in Newspaper	53
12. Agreement of Publisher	53
13. Proof of Publication	54
14. Affidavit of $500 Improvement	54
15. Statement of Fees and Charges	54
16. Proof of Ownership and Possession where Records are Lost	54
17. Affidavit of Citizenship	55

CONTENTS.

	PAGE
18. Certificate that no Suit is Pending	55
19. Power of Attorney to Apply for Patent	56
20. Proof of No Known Vein in Placer Claims	56
21. Protest and Adverse Claim	56
22. Tunnel Claim—Location Certificate	59
23. Power of Attorney to Locate and Sell	59
24. Notice of Right to Water	60
25. Pre-emption of Ditch Right of Way, Location of Water Claim	60
26. Mining Deed	60
27. Title Bond to Mining Property	61
28. Escrow Agreement	62
29. Mining Lease	62

LOCAL LAWS.

Arizona	65
California	77
Colorado	81
Idaho	97
Montana	107
Nevada	111
New Mexico	121
Oregon	136
South Dakota	140
Utah	149
Washington	158
Wyoming	168
Canada and Northwest Territory	179

UNITED STATES MINING LAWS

AND

REGULATIONS THEREUNDER.

Reserved from Sale under the Pre-emption and Homestead Laws.

UNITED STATES LAW.—SEC 2318. In all cases lands valuable for minerals shall be reserved from sale, except as otherwise expressly directed by law.

License to Explore, Occupy, and Purchase.

SEC. 2319. All valuable mineral deposits in lands belonging to the United States, both surveyed and unsurveyed, are hereby declared to be free and open to exploration and purchase, and the lands in which they are found to occupation and purchase, by citizens of the United States and those who have declared their intention to become such, under regulations prescribed by law, and according to the local customs or rules of miners in the several mining districts, so far as the same are applicable and not inconsistent with the laws of the United States.

Lode Claims.

SEC. 2320. Mining claims upon veins or lodes of quartz or other rock in place, bearing gold, silver, cinnabar, lead, tin, copper, or other valuable deposits heretofore located, shall be governed as to length along the vein or lode by the customs, regulations, and laws in force at the date of their location. A mining claim located after the tenth day of May, eighteen hundred and seventy-two, whether located by one or more persons, may equal, but shall not exceed, one thousand five hundred feet in length along the vein or lode; but no location of a mining claim shall be made until the discovery of the vein or lode within the limits of the claim located. No claim shall extend more than three hundred feet on each side of the middle of the vein at the surface, nor shall any claim be limited by any mining regulation to less than twenty-five feet on each side of the middle of the vein at the surface, except where adverse rights existing on the tenth day of May, eighteen hundred and seventy-two, render such limitation necessary. The end lines of each claim shall be parallel to each other.

SEC. 2322. The locators of all mining locations heretofore made or which shall hereafter be made, on any mineral vein, lode, or ledge, situated on the public domain, their heirs and assigns, where no adverse claim exists on the tenth day of May, eighteen hundred and seventy-two, so long as they comply with the laws of the United States, and with state, territorial, and local regulations not in conflict with the laws of the United States governing their possessory title, shall have the exclusive right of possession and enjoyment of all the surface included within the lines of their locations, and of all veins, lodes, and ledges throughout their entire depth, the top or apex of which lies inside of such surface lines extended downward vertically, although such veins, lodes, or ledges may so far depart from a perpendicular in their course downward as to extend outside the vertical side lines of such surface locations. But their right of possession to such outside parts of such veins or ledges shall be confined to such portions thereof as lie between vertical planes drawn downward as above described, through the end lines of their locations, so continued in their own direction that such planes will intersect such exterior parts of such veins or ledges. And nothing in this section shall authorize the locator or possession of a vein or lode which extends in its downward course beyond the vertical lines of his claim to enter upon the surface of a claim owned or possessed by another.

Nature and Extent of Mining Claims.

LAND OFFICE REGULATIONS.—1. Mining claims are of two distinct classes: Lode claims and placers.

LODE CLAIMS.

2. The status of lode claims located or patented previous to the 10th day of May, 1872, is not changed with regard to their extent along the lode or width of surface; but the claim is enlarged by sections 2322 and 2328, by investing the locator, his heirs or assigns, with the right to follow, upon the conditions stated therein, all veins, lodes, or ledges, the top or apex of which lies inside of the surface lines of his claim.

3. It is to be distinctly understood, however, that the law limits the possessory right to veins, lodes, or ledges, *other* than the one named in the original location, to such as were not *adversely claimed on May 10, 1872*, and that where such other vein or ledge was so adversely claimed at that date the right of the party so adversely claiming is in no way impaired by the provisions of the Revised Statutes.

4. From and after the 10th May, 1872, any person who is a citizen of the United States, or who has declared his intention to become a citizen, may locate, record, and hold a mining claim of *fifteen hundred linear feet* along the course of any mineral vein or lode subject to location ; or an association of persons, severally qualified as above, may make joint location of such claim of *fifteen hundred feet*, but in no event can a location of a vein or lode made after the 10th day of May, 1872, exceed fifteen hundred feet along the course thereof, whatever may be the number of persons composing the association.

5. With regard to the extent of surface-ground adjoining a vein or lode, and claimed for the convenient working thereof, the Revised Statutes provide that the lateral extent of locations of veins or lodes made after May 10, 1872, shall in no case *exceed three hundred feet on each side of the middle of the vein at the surface*, and that no such surface rights shall be limited by any mining regulations to less than twenty-five feet on each side of the middle of the vein at the surface, except where adverse rights existing on the 10th May, 1872, may render such limitation necessary; the end lines of such claims to be in all cases parallel to each other. Said lateral meas-

urements cannot extend beyond three hundred feet on *either* side of the middle of the vein at the surface, or such distance as is allowed by local laws. For example: 400 feet cannot be taken on one side and two hundred feet on the other. If, however, 300 feet on each side are allowed, and by reason of prior claims but 100 feet can be taken on one side, the locator will not be restricted to less than 300 feet on the other side, and when the locator does not determine by exploration *where* the middle of the vein at the surface is, his discovery shaft must be assumed to mark such point.

6. By the foregoing it will be perceived that no lode claim located after the 10th May, 1872, can exceed a parallelogram fifteen hundred feet in length by 600 feet in width, but whether surface-ground of that width can be taken depends upon the local regulations or State or Territorial laws in force in the several mining districts: and that no such local regulations or State or Territorial laws shall limit a vein or lode claim to less than fifteen hundred feet along the course thereof, whether the location is made by one or more persons, nor can surface rights be limited to less than fifty feet in width unless adverse claims existing on the 10th day of May, 1872, render such lateral limitation necessary.

7. The rights granted to locators under section 2322, Revised Statutes, are restricted to such locations on veins, lodes, or ledges as may be "situated on the public domain." In applications for patent to lode claims where the survey conflicts with the survey or location lines of another lode claim and the ground in such conflict is excluded, the applicant not only has no right to the excluded ground, but he has no right to that portion of any vein or lode the top or apex of which lies within such excluded ground, unless his location was prior to May 10, 1872. His right to the lode claimed terminates where the lode, in its onward course or strike, intersects the exterior boundary of such excluded ground and passes within it.

8. Where, however, the lode claim for which survey is being made was located prior to the conflicting claim, and such conflict is to be excluded, in order to include all ground not so excluded the end line of the survey may be established within the conflicting lode claim, but the line must be so run as not to extend any farther into such conflicting claim than may be necessary to make such end line parallel to the other end line and at the same time embrace the ground so held and claimed. The useless practice in such cases of extending *both* the side lines of a survey into the conflicting claim and establishing an end line wholly within it, beyond a point necessary under the rule just stated, will be discontinued. [This paragraph abolished June 1, 1900]

Patents for Veins or Lodes Heretofore Issued.

UNITED STATES LAW.—SEC. 2328. Applications for patents for mining claims under former laws now pending may be prosecuted to a final decision in the General Land Office; but in such cases where adverse rights are not affected thereby, patents may issue in pursuance of the provisions of this chapter; and all patents for mining-claims upon veins or lodes heretofore issued shall convey all the rights and privileges conferred by this chapter where no adverse rights existed on the tenth day of May, eighteen hundred and seventy-two.

District Rules, Locations, and Annual Expenditures.

UNITED STATES LAW.—SEC. 2324. The miners of each mining district may make regulations not in conflict with the laws of the United States, or with the laws of the state or territory in which the district is situated, governing the location, manner of recording, amount of work necessary to hold possession of a mining claim, subject to the following requirements : The location must be distinctly marked on the ground, so that its boundaries can be readily traced. All records of mining claims hereafter made shall contain the name or names of the locators, the date of the location, and such a description of the claim or claims located by reference to some natural object or permanent monument as will identify the claim. On each claim located after the tenth day of May, eighteen hundred and seventy-two, and until a patent has been issued therefor, not less than one hundred dollars' worth of labor shall be performed or improvements made during each year. On all claims located prior to the tenth day of May, eighteen hundred and seventy-two, ten dollars' worth of labor shall be performed or improvements made by the tenth day of June, eighteen hundred and seventy-four, and each year thereafter, for each one hundred feet in length along the vein, until a patent has been issued therefor ; but where such claims are held in common, such expenditure may be made upon any one claim ; and upon a failure to comply with these conditions, the claim or mine upon which such failure occurred shall be opened to re-location in the same manner as if no location of the same had ever been made : *Provided*, That the original locators, their heirs, assigns, or legal representatives, have not resumed work upon the claim after failure and before such location. Upon the failure of any one of several co-owners to contribute his proportion of the expenditures required hereby, the co-owners who have performed the labor or made the improvements may, at the expiration of the year, give such delinquent co-owner personal notice in writing or notice by publication in the newspaper published nearest the claim, for at least once a week for ninety days, and if at the expiration of ninety days after such notice in writing or by publication such delinquent should fail or refuse to contribute his proportion of the expenditure required by this section, his interest in the claim shall become the property of his co-owners, who have made the expenditures.

How to Locate Claims on Veins or Lodes.

LAND OFFICE REGULATIONS.—9. Locators cannot exercise too much care in defining their locations at the outset, inasmuch as the law requires that all records of mining locations made subsequent to May 10, 1872, shall contain the name or names of the locators, the date of the location, and such a *description of the claim or claims* located, by reference to some natural object or permanent monument, as will identify the claim.

10. No lode claim shall be located until after the discovery of a vein or lode within the limits of the claim, the object of which provision is evidently to prevent the appropriation of presumed mineral ground for speculative purposes, to the exclusion of *bona fide* prospectors, before sufficient work has been done to determine whether a vein or lode really exists.

11. The claimant should, therefore, prior to locating his claim, unless the vein can be traced upon the surface, sink a shaft or run a tunnel or drift to a sufficient depth therein to discover and develop a mineral-bearing vein, lode, or crevice ; should determine, if possible, the general course of such vein in either direction from the point of discovery, by which direction he will be governed in marking the boundaries of his claim on the surface. His location notice should give the course and distance as nearly as practi-

cable from the discovery shaft on the claim to some permanent, well-known points or objects, such, for instance, as stone monuments, blazed trees, the confluence of streams, point of intersection of well-known gulches, ravines, or roads, prominent buttes, hills, etc., which may be in the immediate vicinity, and which will serve to perpetuate and fix the *locus* of the claim and render it susceptible of identification from the description thereof given in the record of locations in the district, and should be duly recorded.

12. In addition to the foregoing data, the claimant should state the names of adjoining claims, or, if none adjoin, the relative positions of the nearest claims; should drive a post or erect a monument of stones at each corner of his surface ground, and at the point of discovery or discovery shaft should fix a post, stake, or board, upon which should be designated the name of the lode, the name or names of the locators, the number of feet claimed, and in which direction from the point of discovery; it being essential that the location notice filed for record, in addition to the foregoing description, should state whether the entire claim of fifteen hundred feet is taken on one side of the point of discovery, or whether it is partly upon one and partly upon the other side thereof, and in the latter case, how many feet are claimed upon each side of such discovery point.

13. The location notice must be filed for record in all respects as required by the State or Territorial laws and local rules and regulations, if there be any.

14. In order to hold the possessory title to a mining claim located prior to May 10, 1872, and for which a patent has not been issued, the law requires that *ten dollars* shall be expended annually in labor or improvements on each claim of *one hundred feet* on the course of the vein or lode until a patent shall have been issued therefor; but where a number of such claims are held in common upon the same vein or lode, the aggregate expenditure that would be necessary to hold all the claims, at the rate of ten dollars per hundred feet, may be made upon any one claim. The first annual expenditure upon claims of this class should have been performed subsequent to May 10, 1872, and prior to January 1, 1875. From and after January 1, 1875, the required amount must be expended *annually* until patent issues.

15. In order to hold the possessory right to a location made since May 10, 1872, not less than one hundred dollars' worth of labor must be performed or improvements made thereon annually until entry shall have been made. Under the provisions of the act of Congress approved January 22, 1880, the first annual expenditure becomes due and must be performed during the calendar year succeeding that in which the location was made. Expenditure made or labor performed prior to the first day of January succeeding the date of location will not be considered as a part of or applied upon the first annual expenditure required by law.

16. Failure to make the expenditure or perform the labor required upon a location made before or since May 10, 1872, will subject a claim to relocation, unless the original locator, his heirs, assigns, or legal representatives have resumed work after such failure and before relocation.

17. Annual expenditure is not required subsequent to entry, the date of issuing the patent certificate being the date contemplated by statute.

18. Upon the failure of any one of several co-owners of a vein, lode, or ledge, which has not been entered, to contribute his proportion of the expenditures necessary to hold the claim or claims so held in ownership in common, the co-owners, who have performed the labor or made the improvements as required by said Revised Statutes, may, at the expiration of the year, give such delinquent co-owner personal notice in writing, or notice by publication in the newspaper published nearest the claim for at least once a week for ninety days; and if upon the expiration of ninety days after such notice in writing, or upon the expiration of one hundred and eighty days after the first newspaper publication of notice, the delinquent co-owner shall have failed to contribute his proportion to meet such expenditures or improvements, his interest in the claim by law passes to his co-owners who have made the expenditures or improvements as aforesaid.

Where a claimant alleges ownership of a forfeited interest under the foregoing provision, the sworn statement of the publisher as to the facts of publication, giving dates and a printed copy of the notice published, should be furnished, and the claimant must swear that the delinquent co-owner failed to contribute his proper proportion within the period fixed by the statute.

Cross Lodes.

UNITED STATES LAW.—SEC. 2336. Where two or more veins intersect or cross each other, priority of title shall govern, and such prior location shall be entitled to all ore or mineral contained within the space of intersection; but the subsequent location shall have the right of way through the space of intersection for the purposes of the convenient working of the mine. And where two or more veins unite, the oldest or prior location shall take the vein below the point of union, including all the space of intersection.

How to Apply for a Patent.

UNITED STATES LAW.—SEC. 2335. A patent for any land claimed and located for valuable deposits may be obtained in the following manner: Any person, association, or corporation authorized to locate a claim under this chapter, having claimed and located a piece of land for such purposes, who has, or have, complied with the terms of this chapter, may file in the proper land-office an application for a patent, under oath, showing such compliance, together with a plat and field-notes of the claim or claims in common, made by or under the direction of the United States Surveyor-General, showing accurately the boundaries of the claim or claims, which shall be distinctly marked by monuments on the ground, and shall post a copy of such plat, together with a notice of such application for a patent, in a conspicuous place on the land embraced in such plat previous to the filing of the application for a patent, and shall file an affidavit of at least two persons that such notice has been duly posted, and shall file a copy of the notice in such land-office, and shall thereupon be entitled to a patent for the land, in the manner following: The register of the land-office, upon the filing of such application, plat, field-notes, notices, and affidavits, shall publish a notice that such application has been made, for the period of sixty days, in a newspaper to be by him designated as published nearest to such claim; and he shall also post such notice in his office for the same period. The claimant at the time of filing this application, or at any time thereafter, within the sixty days of publication, shall file with the register a certificate of the United States Surveyor-General that five hundred dollars' worth of labor has been expended or improvements made upon the claim by himself or grantors; that the plat is correct, with such further description by such reference to natural objects or permanent monuments as shall identify the claim, and furnish an accurate description, to be incorporated in the patent. At the expiration of the sixty days of publication the claimant shall file his affidavit, showing that the plat and notice have been posted in a conspicuous place on the claim during such period of publication. If no adverse claim shall have been filed with the register and the receiver of the proper land-office at the expiration of the sixty days of publication, it shall be assumed that the applicant is entitled to a patent, upon the payment to the proper officer of five dollars per acre, and that no adverse claim exists; and thereafter no objection from third parties to the issuance of a patent shall be heard, except it be shown that the applicant has failed to comply with the terms of this chapter.

LAND OFFICE REGULATIONS.—37. As a condition for making of application for patent according to section 2325, there must be a preliminary showing of work or expenditure upon each location, either by showing the full amount sufficient to the maintenance of possession under section 2324 for the pending year, or, if there has been failure, it should be shown that work has been resumed so as to prevent relocation by adverse parties after abandonment.

The "pending year" means the calendar year in which application is made, and has no reference to a showing of work at date of the final entry.

38. This preliminary showing may, where the matter is unquestioned, consist of the affidavit of two or more witnesses familiar with the facts.

39. The claimant is required, in the first place, to have a correct survey of his claim made under authority of the surveyor-general of the State or Territory in which the claim lies, such survey to show with accuracy the exterior surface boundaries of the claim, which boundaries are required to be distinctly marked by monuments on the ground. Four plats and one copy of the original field-notes in each case will be prepared by the surveyor-general; one plat and the original field-notes to be retained in the office of the surveyor-general, one copy of the plat to be given the claimant for posting upon the claim, one plat and a copy of the field-notes to be given the claimant for filing with the proper register, to be finally transmitted by that officer, with other papers in the case, to this office, and one plat to be sent by the surveyor-general to the register of the proper land district, to be retained on his files for future reference. As there is no resident surveyor-general for the State of Arkansas, applications for the survey of mineral claims in said State should be made to the Commissioner of this office, who, under the law, is *ex officio* the U. S. surveyor-general.

40. The survey and plat of mineral claims required to be filed in the proper land office with application for patent must be made subsequent to the recording of the location of the claim (if the laws of the State or Territory or the regulations of the mining district require the notice of location to be recorded), and when the original location is made by survey of a United States deputy surveyor such location survey cannot be substituted for that required by the statute, as above indicated.

41. The surveyors-general should designate all surveyed mineral claims by a progressive series of numbers, beginning with survey No. 37, irrespective as to whether they are situated on surveyed or unsurveyed lands, the claim to be so designated at date of issuing the order therefor, in addition to the local designation of the claim; it being required in all cases that the plat and field-notes of the survey of a claim must, in addition to the reference to permanent objects in the neighborhood, describe the locus of the claim with reference to the lines of public surveys by a line connecting a corner of the claim with the nearest public corner of the United States surveys, unless such claim be on unsurveyed lands at a distance of more than two miles from such public corner, in which latter case it should be connected with a United States mineral monument. Such connecting line must not be more than *two miles* in length and should be measured on the ground direct between the points, or calculated from actually surveyed traverse lines if the nature of the country should not permit direct measurement. If a regularly established survey corner is within two miles of a claim situated on unsurveyed lands, the connection should be made with

such corner in preference to a connection with a United States mineral monument. The connecting line must be surveyed by the deputy mineral surveyor at the time of his making the particular survey, and be made a part thereof.

42. Upon the approval of the survey of a mining claim made upon surveyed lands the surveyor-general will prepare and transmit to the local land office and to this office a diagram tracing showing the portions of legal 40-acre subdivisions made fractional by reason of the mineral survey, designating each of such portions by the proper lot number, beginning with No. 1 in each section, and giving the area of each lot.

43. The following particulars should be observed in the survey of every mining claim:

(1) The exterior boundaries of the claim, the number of feet claimed along the vein, and, as nearly as can be ascertained, the direction of the vein, and the number of feet claimed on the vein in each direction from the point of discovery or other well defined place on the claim should be represented on the plat of survey and in the field-notes.

(2) The intersection of the lines of the survey with the lines of conflicting prior surveys should be noted in the field-notes and represented upon the plat.

(3) Conflicts with unsurveyed claims, where the applicant for survey does not claim the area in conflict, should be shown by actual survey.

(4) The total area of the claim embraced by the exterior boundaries should be stated, and also the area in conflict with each intersecting survey, substantially as follows:

	Acres.
Total area of claim	10.50
Area in conflict with survey No. 302	1.56
Area in conflict with survey No. 948	2.33
Area in conflict with Mountain Maid lode mining claim, unsurveyed	1.48

It does not follow that because mining surveys are required to exhibit all conflicts with prior surveys the areas of conflict are to be excluded. The field-notes and plat are made a part of the application for patent, and care should be taken that the description does not inadvertently exclude portions intended to be retained. It is better that the application for patent should state the portions to be excluded in express terms.

44. The claimant is then required to post a copy of the plat of such survey in a conspicuous place upon the claim, together with notice of his intention to apply for a patent therefor, which notice will give the date of posting, the name of the claimant, the name of the claim, the number of the survey, the mining district and county, and the names of adjoining and conflicting claims as shown by the plat survey. Too much care cannot be exercised in the preparation of this notice, inasmuch as the data therein are to be repeated in the other notices required by the statute, and upon the accuracy and completeness of these notices will depend in a great measure the regularity and validity of the proceedings for patent.

45. After posting the said plat and notice upon the premises, the claimant will file with the proper register and receiver a copy of such plat and the field-notes of survey of the claim, accompanied by the affidavit of at least two credible witnesses that such plat and notice are posted conspicuously upon the claim, giving the date and place of such posting; a copy of the *notice* so posted to be attached to and form a part of said affidavit.

46. Accompanying the field-notes so filed must be the sworn statement of the claimant that he has the possessory right to the premises therein described, in virtue of a compliance by himself (and by his grantors, if he claims by purchase) with the mining rules, regulations, and customs of the mining district, State, or Territory in which the claim lies, and with the mining laws of Congress; such sworn statement to narrate briefly, but as clearly as possible, the facts constituting such compliance, the origin of his possession, and the basis of his claim to a patent.

47. This sworn statement must be supported by a copy of the location notice, certified by the officer in charge of the records where the same is

recorded, and where the applicant for patent claims the interests of others associated with him in making the location, or only as purchaser, in addition to the copy of the location notice, must be furnished a complete abstract of title as shown by the record in the office where the transfers are by law required to be recorded, certified to by the officer in charge of the record, under his official seal. The officer should also certify that no conveyances affecting the title to the claim in question appear of record other than those set forth in the abstract, which abstract shall be brought down to the date of the application for patent. Where the applicant claims as sole locator, his affidavit should be furnished to the effect that he has disposed of no interest in the land located.

48. In the event of the mining records in any case having been destroyed by fire or otherwise lost, affidavit of the fact should be made, and secondary evidence of possessory title will be received, which may consist of the affidavit of the claimant, supported by those of any other parties cognizant of the facts relative to his location, occupancy, possession, improvements, &c.; and in such case of lost records, any deeds, certificates of location or purchase, or other evidence which may be in the claimant's possession and tend to establish his claim, should be filed.

49. Before receiving and filing a mineral application for patent, local officers will be particular to see that it includes no land which is embraced in a prior or pending application for patent or entry, or for any lands embraced in a railroad selection, or for which publication is pending or has been made by any other claimants, and if, in their opinion, after investigation, it should appear that a mineral application should not, for these or other reasons, be accepted and filed, they should formally reject the same, giving the reasons therefor, and allow the applicant thirty days for appeal to this office under the Rules of Practice.

50. Upon the receipt of these papers, if no reason appears for rejecting the application, the register will, at the expense of the claimant (who must furnish the agreement of the publisher to hold applicant for patent alone responsible for charges of publication), publish a notice of such application for the period of sixty days in a newspaper published nearest to the claim, and will post a copy of such notice in his office for the same period. When the notice is published in a *weekly* newspaper, nine consecutive insertions are necessary; when in a *daily* newspaper, the notice must appear in each issue for sixty-one consecutive issues. In both cases the first day of issue must be excluded in estimating the period of sixty days.

51. The notices so published and posted must embrace all the data given in the notice posted upon the claim. In addition to such data the published notice must further indicate the locus of the claim by giving the connecting line, as shown by the field-notes and plat, between a corner of the claim and a United States mineral monument or a corner of the public survey, and thence the boundaries of the claim by courses and distances.

52. The register shall publish the notice of application for patent in a paper of established character and general circulation, to be by him designated as being the newspaper published nearest the land.

53. The claimant at the time of filing the application for patent, or at any time within the sixty days of publication, is required to file with the register a certificate of the surveyor-general that not less than five hundred dollars' worth of labor has been expended or improvements made, by the applicant or his grantors, upon each location embraced in the application, or if the application embraces several locations held in common, that an amount equal to five hundred dollars for each location has been so expended upon, and for the benefit of, the entire group; that the plat filed by the claimant is correct; that the field-notes of the survey, as filed, furnish such an accurate description of the claim as will if incorporated in a patent serve to fully identify the premises and that such reference is made therein to natural objects or permanent monuments as will perpetuate and fix the locus thereof: *Provided,* That as to all applications for patent made and passed to entry before July 1, 1898, or which are by protests or adverse

claims prevented from being passed to entry before that time, where the application embraces several locations held in common, proof of an expenditure of five hundred dollars upon the group will be sufficient and an expenditure of that amount need not be shown to have been made upon, or for the benefit of, each location embraced in the application.

54. The surveyor-general may derive his information upon which to base his certificate as to the value of labor expended or improvements made from his deputy who makes the actual survey and examination upon the premises, and such deputy should specify with particularity and full detail the character and extent of such improvements.

55. It will be the more convenient way to have this certificate indorsed by the surveyor-general, both upon the plat and field-notes of survey filed by the claimant as aforesaid.

56. After the sixty days' period of newspaper publication has expired, the claimant will furnish from the office of publication a sworn statement that the notice was published for the statutory period, giving the first and last day of such publication, and his own affidavit showing that the plat and notice aforesaid remained conspicuously posted upon the claim sought to be patented during said sixty days' publication, giving the dates.

57. Upon the filing of this affidavit the register will, if no adverse claim was filed in his office during the period of publication, permit the claimant to pay for the land according to the area given in the plat and field-notes of survey aforesaid, at the rate of five dollars for each acre and five dollars for each fractional part of an acre, except as otherwise provided by law, the receiver issuing the usual duplicate receipt therefor. The claimant will also make a sworn statement of all charges and fees paid by him for publication and surveys, together with all fees and money paid the register and receiver of the land office, after which the complete record will be forwarded to the Commissioner of the General Land Office and a patent issued thereon if found regular.

58. At any time prior to the issuance of patent, protest may be filed against the patenting of the claim as applied for, upon any ground tending to show that the applicant has failed to comply with the law in a matter which would avoid the claim. Such protest cannot, however, be made the means of preserving a surface conflict lost by failure to adverse or lost by the judgment of the court in an adverse suit. One holding a present joint interest in a mineral location included in an application for patent who is excluded from the application, so that his interest would not be protected by the issue of patent thereon, may protest against the issuance of a patent as applied for, setting forth in such protest the nature and extent of his interest in such location, and such a protestant will be deemed a party in interest entitled to appeal. This results from the holding that a co-owner excluded from an application for patent does not have an "adverse" claim within the meaning of sections 2325 and 2326 of the Revised Statutes. See Turner *v.* Sawyer, 150 U. S., 578–586.

59. Any party applying to make entry as *trustee* must disclose fully the nature of the trust and the name of the *cestui que trust;* and such trustee, as well as the beneficiaries, must furnish satisfactory proof of citizenship; and the names of beneficiaries, as well as that of the trustee, must be inserted in the final certificate of entry.

73. In sending up the papers in the case the register must not omit certifying to the fact that the notice was posted in his office for the full period of sixty days, such certificate to state distinctly when such posting was done and how long continued. The plat forwarded as part of the proof should not be *folded*, but *rolled*, so as to prevent creasing, and either transmitted in a separate package or so enclosed with the other papers that it may pass through the mails without creasing or mutilation. If forwarded separately, the letter transmitting the papers should state the fact.

74. No entry will be allowed until the register has satisfied himself, by a careful examination, that proper proofs have been filed upon all the points

indicated in official regulations in force, and that they show a sufficient *bona fide* compliance with the laws and such regulations.

75. The consecutive series of numbers of mineral entries must be continued, whether the same are of lode or placer claims or mill sites.

Surveys to be Adjusted to the Public Surveys.

UNITED STATES LAW.—SEC. 2327. The description of vein or lode claims, upon surveyed lands, shall designate the location of the claim with reference to the lines of the public surveys, but need not conform therewith; but where a patent shall be issued for claims upon unsurveyed lands, the surveyor-general, in extending the surveys, shall adjust the same to the boundaries of such patented claim, according to the plat or description thereof, but so as in no case to interfere with or change the location of any such patented claim.

Annual Expenditure.

ACT OF CONGRESS OF JANUARY 22, 1880.—An Act to amend sections twenty-three hundred and twenty-four and twenty-three hundred and twenty-five of the Revised Statutes of the United States concerning mineral lands.

Be it enacted, etc., That section twenty-three hundred and twenty-five of the Revised Statutes of the United States be amended by adding thereto the following words: "*Provided*, That where the claimant for a patent is not a resident of or within the land district wherein the vein, lode, ledge or deposit sought to be patented is located, the application for patent and the affidavits required to be made in this section by the claimant for such patent may be made by his, her, or its authorized agent, where said agent is conversant with the facts sought to be established by said affidavits: *And provided*, That this section shall apply to all applications now pending for patents to mineral lands."

SEC. 2. That section twenty-three hundred and twenty-four of the Revised Statutes of the United States be amended by adding the following words: "*Provided*, That the period within which the work required to be done annually on all unpatented mineral claims shall commence on the first day of January succeeding the date of location of such claim, and this section shall apply to all claims located since the tenth day of May, anno Domini eighteen hundred and seventy-two."

ACT OF CONGRESS OF FEBRUARY 11, 1875.—An act to amend section two thousand three hundred and twenty-four of the Revised Statutes, relating to the development of the mining resources of the United States.

Be it enacted, etc., That section two thousand three hundred and twenty-four of the Revised Statutes be, and the same is hereby, amended so that where a person or company has or may run a tunnel for the purpose of developing a lode or lodes, owned by said person or company, the money so expended in said tunnel shall be taken and considered as expended on said lode or lodes, whether located prior to or since the passage of said act, and such person or company shall not be required to perform work on the surface of said lode or lodes in order to hold the same as required by said act.

Tunnel Rights.

UNITED STATES LAW.—SEC. 2323. Where a tunnel is run for the development of a vein or lode, or for the discovery of mines, the owners of such tunnel shall have the right of possession of all veins or lodes within three thousand feet from the face of such tunnel on the line thereof, not previously known to exist, discovered in such tunnel, to the same extent as if discovered from the surface: and locations on the line of such tunnel of veins or lodes, not appearing on the surface, made by other parties after the commencement of the tunnel, and while the same is being prosecuted with reasonable diligence, shall be invalid; but failure to prosecute the work on the tunnel for six months shall be considered as an abandonment of the right to all undiscovered veins on the line of such tunnel.

LAND OFFICE REGULATIONS.—19. The effect of section 2323, Revised Statues, is simply to give the proprietors of a mining tunnel run in good faith the possessory right to fifteen hundred feet of any blind lodes cut, discovered, or intersected by such tunnel, which were not previously known to exist, within three thousand feet from the face or point of commencement of such tunnel, and to prohibit other parties, after the commencement of the tunnel, from prospecting for and making locations of lodes on the *line thereof* and within said distance of three thousand feet, unless such lodes appear upon the surface or were previously known to exist.

20. The term "face," as used in said section, is construed and held to mean the first working face formed in the tunnel, and to signify the point at which the tunnel actually enters cover; it being from this point that the three thousand feet are to be counted upon which prospecting is prohibited as aforesaid.

21. To avail themselves of the benefits of this provision of law, the proprietors of a mining tunnel will be required, at the time they enter cover as aforesaid, to give proper notice of their tunnel location by erecting a substantial post, board, or monument at the face or point of commencement thereof, upon which should be posted a good and sufficient notice, giving the names of the parties or company claiming the tunnel right; the actual or proposed course or direction of the tunnel; the height and width thereof, and the course and distance from such face or point of commencement to some permanent well-known objects in the vicinity by which to fix and determine the locus in manner heretofore set forth applicable to locations of veins or lodes, and at the time of posting such notice they shall, in order that miners or prospectors may be enabled to determine whether or not they are within the lines of the tunnel, establish the boundary lines thereof, by stakes or monuments placed along such lines at proper intervals, to the terminus of the three thousand feet from the face or point of commencement of the tunnel, and the lines so marked will define and govern as to the specific boundaries within which prospecting for lodes not previously known to exist is prohibited while work on the tunnel is being prosecuted with reasonable diligence.

22. At the time of posting notice and marking out the lines of the tunnel as aforesaid, a full and correct copy of such notice of location defining the tunnel claim must be filed for record with the mining recorder of the district, to which notice must be attached the sworn statement or declaration of the owners, claimants, or projectors of such tunnel, setting forth the facts in the case; stating the amount expended by themselves and their predecessors in interest in prosecuting work thereon; the extent of the

work performed, and that it is *bona fide* their intention to prosecute work on the tunnel so located and described with reasonable diligence for the development of a vein or lode, or for the discovery of mines, or both as the case may be. This notice of location must be duly recorded, and with the said sworn statement attached, kept on the recorder's files for future reference.

23. By a compliance with the foregoing much needless difficulty will be avoided, and the way for the adjustment of legal rights acquired in virtue of said section 2323 will be made much more easy and certain.

24. This office will take particular care that no improper advantage is taken of this provision of law by parties making or professing to make tunnel locations, ostensibly for the purposes named in the statute, but really for the purpose of monopolizing the lands lying in front of their tunnels, to the detriment of the mining interests and to the exclusion of *bona fide* prospectors or miners, but will hold such tunnel claimants to a strict compliance with the terms of the statutes; and a *reasonable diligence* on their part in prosecuting the work is one of the essential conditions of their implied contract. Negligence or want of due diligence will be construed as working a forfeiture of their right to all undiscovered veins on the line of such tunnel.

Placer Claims.

UNITED STATES LAW.—SEC. 2329. Claims usually called "placers," including all forms of deposit, excepting veins of quartz, or other rock in place, shall be subject to entry and patent, under like circumstances and conditions, and upon similar proceedings, as are provided for vein or lode claims; but where the lands have been previously surveyed by the United States, the entry in its exterior limits shall conform to the legal subdivisions of the public lands.

LAND OFFICE REGULATIONS.—25. But one discovery of mineral is required to support a placer location, whether it be of twenty acres by an individual, or of one hundred and sixty acres or less by an association of persons.

26. The act of August 4, 1892, extends the mineral land laws so as to bring lands chiefly valuable for building stone within the provisions of said law, by authorizing a placer entry of such lands. It does not operate, however, to withdraw lands chiefly valuable for building stone from entry under any existing law applicable thereto. Registers and receivers should therefore make a reference to said act on the entry papers in the case of all placer entries made for lands containing stone chiefly valuable for building purposes. It will be noted that lands reserved for the benefit of public schools or donated to any State are not subject to entry under said act.

27. It is to be observed that the provisions of the mineral laws relating to placers are extended by the act of February 11, 1897, so as to allow the location and entry thereunder of public lands chiefly valuable for petroleum or other mineral oils, and entries of that nature made prior to the passage of said act are to be considered as though made thereunder.

36. The regulations hereinbefore given as to the manner of marking locations on the ground, and placing the same on record, must be observed in the case of placer locations so far as the same are applicable, the law requiring, however, that where placer claims are upon *surveyed* public lands the locations must hereafter be made to conform to legal subdivisions thereof as near as practicable.

Legal Subdivisions—Ten-Acre Lots.

UNITED STATES LAW.—SEC. 2330. Legal subdivisions of forty acres may be subdivided into ten-acre tracts; and two or more persons, or associations of persons, having contiguous claims of any size, although such claims may be less than ten acres each, may make joint entry thereof; but no location of a placer claim, made after the ninth day of July, eighteen hundred and seventy, shall exceed one hundred and sixty acres for any one person or association of persons, which location shall conform to the United States surveys; and nothing in this section contained shall defeat or impair any *bona fide* pre-emption or homestead claim upon agricultural lands, or authorize the sale of the improvements of any *bona fide* settler to any purchaser.

LAND OFFICE REGULATIONS.—28. By section 2330 authority is given for the subdivision of forty-acre legal subdivisions into *ten-acre* lots, which is intended for the greater convenience of miners in segregating their claims both from one another and from intervening agricultural lands.

29. It is held, therefore, that under a proper construction of the law these ten-acre lots in mining districts should be considered and dealt with, to all intents and purposes, as legal subdivisions, and that an applicant having a legal claim which conforms to one or more of these ten-acre lots, either adjoining or cornering, may make entry thereof, after the usual proceedings, without further survey or plat.

30. In cases of this kind, however, the notice given of the application must be very specific and accurate in description, and as the forty-acre tracts may be subdivided into ten-acre lots, either in the form of squares, of ten by ten chains, or, if parallelograms, five by twenty chains, so long as the lines are parallel and at right angles with the lines of the public surveys, it will be necessary that the notice and application state specifically what ten-acre lots are sought to be patented in addition to the other *data* required in the notice.

31. Where the ten-acre subdivision is in the form of a square it may be described, for instance, as the "SE. $\frac{1}{4}$ of the SW. $\frac{1}{4}$ of the NW. $\frac{1}{4}$," or, if in the form of a parallelogram as aforesaid, it may be described as the "W. $\frac{1}{2}$ of the W. $\frac{1}{2}$ of the SW. $\frac{1}{4}$ of the NW. $\frac{1}{4}$ (or the N. $\frac{1}{2}$ of the S. $\frac{1}{2}$ of the NE. $\frac{1}{4}$ of the SE. $\frac{1}{4}$) of section ——, township ——, range ——," as the case may be; but, in addition to this description of the land, the notice must give all the other *data* that is required in a mineral application, by which parties may be put on inquiry as to the premises sought to be patented. The proofs submitted with applications for claims of this kind must show clearly the character and the extent of the improvements upon the premises.

32. The proof of improvements must show their value to be not less than *five hundred dollars* and that they were made by the applicant for patent or his grantors. The annual expenditure to the amount of $100, required by section 2324, Revised Statutes, must be made upon placer claims as well as lode claims.

33. By section 2330 it is declared that no location of a placer claim, made after July 9, 1870, shall exceed one hundred and sixty acres for any one person or association of persons, which location shall conform to the United States surveys.

34. Section 2331 provides that all placer-mining claims located after May 10, 1872, shall conform as nearly as practicable with the United States systems of public surveys, and the subdivisions of such surveys, and no such locations shall include more than twenty acres for each individual claimant.

35. The foregoing provisions of law are construed to mean that after the 9th day of July, 1870, no location of a placer claim can be made to exceed one hundred and sixty acres, whatever may be the number of locators associated together, or whatever the local regulations of the district may allow; and that from and after May 10, 1872, no location can exceed twenty acres for each individual participating therein: that is, a location by two persons

cannot exceed forty acres, and one by three persons cannot exceed sixty acres.

SEC. 2331. Where placer claims are upon surveyed lands, and conform to legal subdivisions, no further survey or plat shall be required, and all placer-mining claims located after the tenth day of May, eighteen hundred and seventy-two, shall conform as near as practicable with the United States system of public land surveys, and the rectangular subdivisions of such surveys, and no such location shall include more than twenty acres for each individual claimant; but where placer claims cannot be conformed to legal subdivisions, survey and plat shall be made as on unsurveyed lands; and where by the segregation of mineral lands in any legal subdivision a quantity of agricultural land less than forty acres remains, such fractional portions of agricultural land may be entered by any party qualified by law, for homestead or pre-emption purposes.

LAND OFFICE REGULATIONS.—60. The proceedings to obtain patents for claims usually called placers, including all forms of deposit, excepting veins of quartz or other rock in place, are similar to the proceedings prescribed for obtaining patents for vein or lode claims; but where said placer claim shall be upon surveyed lands, and conforms to legal subdivisions, no further survey or plat will be required ; and all placer mining claims located after May 10, 1872, shall conform as nearly as practicable with the United States system of public-land surveys and the rectangular subdivisions of such surveys, and no such location shall include more than twenty acres for each individual claimant; but where placer claims cannot be conformed to legal subdivisions, survey and plat shall be made as on unsurveyed lands. But where such claims are located previous to the public surveys, and do not conform to legal subdivisions, survey, plat and entry thereof may be made according to the boundaries thereof, provided the location is in all respects legal.

61. The proceedings for obtaining patents for veins or lodes having already been fully given, it will not be necessary to repeat them here, it being thought that careful attention thereto by applicants and the local officers will enable them to act understandingly in the matter, and make such slight modifications in the notice, or otherwise, as may be necessary in view of the different nature of the two classes of claims; placer claims being fixed, however, at two dollars and fifty cents per acre, or fractional part of an acre.

62. The first care in recognizing an application for patent upon a placer claim must be exercised in determining the exact classification of the lands. To this end the clearest evidence of which the case is capable should be presented.

(1) If the claim be all placer ground, that fact must be stated in the application and corroborated by accompanying proofs; if of mixed placers and lodes, it should be so set out, with a description of all known lodes situated within the boundaries of the claim. A specific declaration, such as is required by section 2333, Revised Statutes, must be furnished as to each lode intended to be claimed. All other known lodes are, by the silence of the applicant, excluded by law from all claim by him, of whatsoever nature, possessory or otherwise.

(2) Deputy surveyors shall, at the expense of the parties, make full examination of all placer claims surveyed by them, and duly note the facts as specified in the law, stating the quality and composition of the soil, the kind and amount of timber and other vegetation, the locus and size of streams, and such other matters as may appear upon the surface of the claim. This examination should include the character and extent of all

surface and underground workings, whether placer or lode, for mining purposes.

(3) In addition to these data, which the law requires to be shown in all cases, the deputy should report with reference to the proximity of centers of trade or residence; also of well-known systems of lode deposit or of individual lodes. He should also report as to the use or adaptability of the claim for placer mining; whether water has been brought upon it in sufficient quanity to mine the same, or whether it can be procured for that purpose; and, finally, what works or expenditures have been made by the claimant or his grantors for the development of the claim, and their situation and location with respect to the same as applied for.

(4) This examination should be reported by the deputy under oath to the surveyor-general, and duly corroborated; and a copy of the same should be furnished with the application for patent to the claim, constituting a part thereof, and included in the oath of the applicant.

(5) Applications awaiting entry, whether published or not, must be made to conform to these regulations, with respect to examination as to the character of the land. Entries already made will be suspended for such additional proofs as may be deemed necessary in each case.

Placer Claims Containing Lodes.

UNITED STATES LAW.—SEC. 2333. Where the same person, association or corporation is in possession of a placer claim, and also a vein or lode included within the boundaries thereof, application shall be made for a patent for the placer claim, with the statement that it includes such vein or lode, and in such case a patent shall issue for a placer claim, subject to the provisions of this chapter, including such vein or lode, upon the payment of five dollars per acre for such vein or lode claim, and twenty-five feet of surface on each side thereof. The remainder of the placer claim, or any placer claim not embracing any vein or lode claim, shall be paid for at the rate of two dollars and fifty cents per acre, together with all costs of proceedings; and where a vein or lode, such as is described in section twenty-three hundred and twenty, is known to exist within the boundaries of a placer claim, an application for a patent for such placer claim which does not include an application for the vein or lode claim shall be construed as a conclusive declaration that the claimant of the placer claim has no right of possession of the vein or lode claim; but where the existence of a vein or lode in a placer claim is not known, a patent for the placer claim shall convey all valuable mineral and other deposits within the boundaries thereof.

LAND OFFICE REGULATIONS.—32. Applicants for patent to a placer claim, who are also in possession of a known vein or lode included therein, must state in their application that the placer includes such vein or lode. The published and posted notices must also include such statement. If veins or lodes lying within a placer location are owned by other parties, the fact should be distinctly stated in the application for patent, and in all the notices. But in all cases, whether the lode is claimed or excluded, it must be surveyed and marked upon the plat, the field-notes and plat giving the area of the lode claim or claims and the area of the placer separately. It should be remembered that an application which omits to include an application for a known vein or lode therein must be construed as a conclusive declaration that the applicant has no right of possession to the vein or lode. Where there is no known lode or vein, the fact must appear by the affidavit of two or more witnesses.

Building Stone and Mineral Oils.

ACT OF CONGRESS OF AUGUST 4, 1892.—An act to authorize the entry of lands chiefly valuable for building stone under the placer-mining laws.

Be it enacted, etc., That any person authorized to enter lands under the mining laws of the United States may enter lands that are chiefly valuable for building stone under the provisions of the law in relation to placer mineral claims : *Provided*, That lands reserved for the benefit of the public schools or donated to any State shall not be subject to entry under this act.

SEC. 2. That an act entitled "An act for the sale of timber lands in the States of California, Oregon, Nevada, and Washington Territory," approved June third, eighteen hundred and seventy-eight, be, and the same is hereby, amended by striking out the words "States of California, Oregon, Nevada, and Washington Territory" where the same occur in the second and third lines of said act, and insert in lieu thereof the words, "public-land States," the purpose of this act being to make said act of June third, eighteen hundred and seventy-eight, applicable to all the public-land States.

SEC. 3. That nothing in this act shall be construed to repeal section twenty-four of the act entitled "An act to repeal timber-culture laws, and for other purposes," approved March third, eighteen hundred and ninety-one.

ACT OF CONGRESS, FEBRUARY 11, 1897.—An act to authorize the entry and patenting of lands containing petroleum and other mineral oils under the placer-mining laws of the United States.

Be it enacted, etc., That any person authorized to enter lands under the mining laws of the United States may enter and obtain patent to lands containing petroleum or other mineral oils, and chiefly valuable therefor, under the provisions of the laws relating to placer-mineral claims : *Provided*, That lands containing such petroleum or other mineral oils which have heretofore been filed upon, claimed or improved as mineral, but not patented, may be held and patented under the provisions of this Act the same as if such filing, claim or improvement were subsequent to the date of the passage hereof.

Possessory Right.

UNITED STATES LAW.—SEC. 2332. Where such person or association, they and their grantors, have held and worked their claims for a period equal to the time prescribed by the statute of limitations for mining claims of the State or Territory where the same may be situated, evidence of such possession and working of the claims for such period shall be sufficient to establish a right to a patent thereto under this chapter, in the absence of any adverse claim; but nothing in this chapter shall be deemed to impair any lien which may have attached in any way whatever to any mining claim or property thereto attached prior to the issuance of a patent.

LAND OFFICE REGULATIONS.—76. The provisions of section 2332, Revised Statutes, will greatly lessen the burden of proof, more especially in the case of old claims located many years since, the records of which, in many cases, have been destroyed by fire, or lost in other ways during the lapse of time, but concerning the possessory right to which all controversy or litigation has long been settled.

77. When an applicant desires to make his proof of possessory right in accordance with this provision of law, he will not be required to produce evidence of location, copies of conveyances, or abstracts of title, as in other cases, but will be required to furnish a duly certified copy of the statute of limitation of mining claims for the State or Territory, together with his sworn statement giving a clear and succinct narration of the facts as to the origin of his title, and likewise as to the continuation of his possession of the mining ground covered by his application; the area thereof; the nature and extent of the mining that has been done thereon; whether there has been any opposition to his possession, or litigation with regard to his claim and, if so, when the same ceased; whether such cessation was caused by compromise or by judicial decree, and any additional facts within the claimant's knowledge having a direct bearing upon his possession and *bona fides* which he may desire to submit in support of his claim.

78. There should likewise be filed a certificate, under seal of the court having jurisdiction of mining cases within the judicial district embracing the claim, that no suit or action of any character whatever involving the right of possession to any portion of the claim applied for is pending, and that there has been no litigation before said court affecting the title to said claim or any part thereof for a period equal to the time fixed by the statute of limitations for mining claims in the State or Territory as aforesaid, other than that which has been finally decided in favor of the claimant.

79. The claimant should support his narrative of facts relative to his possession, occupancy, and improvements by corroborative testimony of any disinterested person or persons of credibility who may be cognizant of the facts in the case and are capable of testifying understandingly in the premises.

Proof of Citizenship of Mining Claimants.

UNITED STATES LAW.—SEC. 2321. Proof of citizenship, under this chapter, may consist, in the case of an individual, of his own affidavit thereof; in the case of an association of persons unincorporated, of the affidavit of their authorized agent, made on his own knowledge, or upon information and belief; and in the case of a corporation organized under the laws of the United States, or of any State or Territory thereof, by the filing of a certified copy of their charter or certificate of incorporation.

LAND OFFICE REGULATIONS.—68. The proof necessary to establish the citizenship of applicants for mining patents must be made in the following manner: In case of an incorporated company, a certified copy of their charter or certificate of incorporation must be filed. In case of an association of persons unincorporated, the affidavit of their duly authorized agent, made upon his own knowledge or upon information and belief, setting forth the residence of each person forming such association, must be submitted. This affidavit must be accompanied by a power of attorney from the parties forming such association, authorizing the person who makes the affidavit of citizenship to act for them in the matter of their application for patent.

69. In case of an individual or an association of individuals who do not appear by their duly authorized agent, you will require the affidavit of each applicant, showing whether he is a native or naturalized citizen, when and where born and his residence.

70. In case an applicant has declared his intention to become a citizen or has been naturalized, his affidavit must show the date, place, and the court before which he declared his intention, or from which his certificate of citizenship issued, and present residence.

71. The affidavit of the claimant as to his citizenship may be taken before the register or receiver, or any other officer authorized to administer oaths within the land district; or, if the claimant is residing beyond the limits of the district, the affidavit may be taken before the clerk of any court of record or before any notary public of any State or Territory.

72. If citizenship is established by the testimony of disinterested persons, such testimony may be taken at any place before any person authorized to administer oaths, and whose official character is duly verified.

Mill Sites.

UNITED STATES LAW.—SEC. 2337. Where non-mineral land not contiguous to the vein or lode is used or occupied by the proprietor of such vein or lode for mining or milling purposes, such non-adjacent surface-ground may be embraced and included in an application for a patent for such vein or lode, and the same may be patented therewith, subject to the same preliminary requirements as to survey and notice as are applicable to veins or lodes; but no location hereafter made of such non-adjacent land shall exceed five acres, and payment for the same must be made at the same rate as fixed by this chapter for the superficies of the lode. The owner of a quartz mill or reduction works, not owning a mine in connection therewith, may also receive a patent for his mill site, as provided in this section.

LAND OFFICE REGULATIONS.—63. Land entered as a mill site must be shown to be non-mineral. Mill sites are simply auxiliary to the working of mineral claims, and as section 2337, which provides for the patenting of mill sites, is embraced in the chapter of the Revised Statutes relating to mineral lands, they are therefore included in this circular.

64. To avail themselves of this provision of law parties holding the possessory right to a vein or lode, and to a piece of non-mineral land not contiguous thereto for mining or milling purposes, not exceeding the quantity allowed for such purpose by section 2337, or prior laws, under which the land was appropriated, the proprietors of such vein or lode may file in the proper land office their application for a patent, under oath, in manner already set forth herein, which application, together with the plat and field-notes, may include, embrace, and describe, in addition to the vein or lode, such non-contiguous mill site, and after due proceedings as to notice, etc., a patent will be issued conveying the same as one claim. The owner of a patented lode may, by an independent application, secure a mill site if good faith is manifest in its use or occupation in connection with the lode and no adverse claim exists.

65. Where the original survey includes a lode claim and also a mill site the lode claim should be described in the plat and field-notes as "Sur. No. 37, A," and the mill site as "Sur. No. 37, B," or whatever may be its appropriate numerical designation; the course and distance from a corner of the mill site to a corner of the lode claim to be invariably given in such plat and field-notes, and a copy of the plat and notice of application for patent must be conspicuously posted upon the mill site as well as upon the vein or lode for the statutory period of sixty days. In making the entry no separate receipt or certificate need be issued for the mill site, but the whole area of both lode and mill site will be embraced in one entry, the price being five dollars for each acre and fractional part of an acre embraced by such lode and mill-site claim.

66. In case the owner of a quartz mill or reduction works is not the owner or claimant of a vein or lode the law permits him to make application therefor in the same manner prescribed herein for mining claims, and after due notice and proceedings, in the absence of a valid adverse filing, to enter and receive a patent for his mill site at said price per acre.

67. In every case there must be satisfactory proof that the land claimed as a mill site is not mineral in character, which proof may, where the matter is unquestioned, consist of the sworn statement of two or more persons capable, from acquaintance with the land, to testify understandingly.

Appointment of Deputy Surveyors of Mining Claims—Charges for Surveys and Publications—Fees for Registers and Receivers, etc.

UNITED STATES LAW.—SEC. 2334. The surveyor-general of the United States may appoint in each land-district containing mineral lands as many competent surveyors as shall apply for appointment to survey mining claims. The expenses of the survey of vein or lode claims, and the survey and subdivision of placer claims into smaller quantities than one hundred and sixty acres, together with the cost of publication of notices, shall be paid by the applicants, and they shall be at liberty to obtain the same at the most reasonable rates, and they shall also be at liberty to employ any United States deputy surveyor to make the survey. The Commissioner of the General Land Office shall also have power to establish the maximum charges for surveys and publication of notices under this chapter; and, in case of excessive charges for publication, he may designate any newspaper published in a land district where mines are situated for the publication of mining notices in such district, and fix the rates to be charged by such paper; and, to the end that the Commissioner may be fully informed on the subject, each applicant shall file with the register a sworn statement of all charges and fees paid by such applicant for publication and surveys, together with all fees and money paid the register and the receiver of the land office, which statement shall be transmitted, with the other papers in the case, to the Commissioner of the General Land Office.

LAND OFFICE REGULATIONS.—91. Section 2334 provides for the appointment of surveyors of mineral claims, and authorizes the Commissioner of the General Land Office to establish the rates to be charged for surveys and for newspaper publications. Under this authority of law the following rates have been establised as the maximum charges for newspaper publications in mining cases:

(1) Where a daily newspaper is designated the charge shall not exceed seven dollars for each ten lines of space occupied, and where a weekly newspaper is designated as the medium of publication five dollars for the same space will be allowed. Such charge shall be accepted as full payment for publication in each issue of the newspaper for the entire period required by law.

It is expected that these notices shall not be so abbreviated as to curtail the description essential to a perfect notice, and the said rates established upon the understanding that they are to be in the usual body type used for advertisements.

(2) For the publication of citations in contests or hearings involving the character of lands the charges shall not exceed eight dollars for five publications in weekly newspapers or ten dollars for publications in daily newspapers for thirty days.

92. The surveyors-general of the several districts will, in pursuance of said law, appoint in each land district as many *competent* deputies for the survey of mining claims as may seek such appointment, it being distinctly understood that all expenses of these notices and surveys are to be borne by the mining claimants and not by the United States. The claimant may

employ *any* deputy surveyor within such district to do his work in the field. Each deputy mineral surveyor before entering upon the duties of his office or appointment shall be required to enter into such bond for the faithful performance of his duties as may be prescribed by the regulations of the land department in force at that time.

93. With regard to the *platting* of the claim and other *office work* in the surveyor-general's office, that officer will make an estimate of the cost thereof, which amount the claimant will deposit with any assistant United States treasurer or designated depository in favor of the United States Treasurer, to be passed to the credit of the fund created by "individual depositors for surveys of the public lands," and file with the surveyor-general duplicate certificates of such deposit in the usual manner.

94. The surveyor-general will endeavor to appoint mineral deputy surveyors, so that one or more may be located in each mining district for the greater convenience of miners.

95. The usual oaths will be required of these deputies and their assistants as to the correctness of each survey executed by them.

The duty of the deputy mineral surveyor ceases when he has executed the survey and returned the field-notes and preliminary plat thereof with his report to the surveyor-general. He will not be allowed to prepare for the mining claimant the papers in support of an application for patent or otherwise perform the duties of an attorney for the land office in connection with a mining claim.

The surveyors-general and local land officers are expected to report any infringement of this regulation to this office.

96. Should it appear that excessive or exorbitant charges have been made by any surveyor or any publisher, prompt action will be taken with the view of correcting the abuse.

97. The fees payable to the register and receiver for filing and acting upon applications for mineral-land patents are five dollars to each officer, to be paid by the applicant for patent at the time of filing, and the like sum of five dollars is payable to each officer by an adverse claimant at the time of filing his adverse claim. (Sec. 2238, R. S., paragraph 9.)

98. At the time of payment of fee for mining application or adverse claim the receiver will issue his receipt therefor in duplicate, one to be given the applicant or adverse claimant, as the case may be, and one to be forwarded to the Commissioner of the General Land Office *on the day of issue*. The receipt for mining application should have attached the certificate of the register that the lands included in the application are vacant lands subject to such appropriation.

99. The register and receiver will, at the close of each month, forward to this office an abstract of mining applications filed, and a register of receipts, accompanied with an abstract of mineral lands sold, and an abstract of adverse claims filed.

100. The fees and purchase-money received by registers and receivers must be placed to the credit of the United States in the receiver's monthly and quarterly account, charging up in the disbursing account the sums to which the register and receiver may be respectively entitled as fees and commissions, with limitations in regard to the legal maximum.

Adverse Claims.

UNITED STATES LAW.—SEC. 2326. Where an adverse claim is filed during the period of publication, it shall be upon oath of the person or persons making the same, and shall show the nature, boundaries, and extent of such adverse claim, and all proceedings, except the publication of notice and making and filing of the affidavit thereof, shall be stayed until the controversy shall have been settled or decided by a court of competent jurisdiction, or the adverse claim waived. It shall be the duty of the adverse claimant, within thirty days after filing his claim, to commence proceedings in a court of competent jurisdiction, to determine the question of the right of possession, and prosecute the same with reasonable diligence to final judgment ; and a failure so to do shall be a waiver of his adverse claim. After such judgment shall have been rendered, the party entitled to the possession of the claim, or any portion thereof, may, without giving further notice, file a certified copy of the judgment-roll with the register of the land office, together with the certificate of the surveyor-general that the requisite amount of labor has been expended or improvements made thereon, and the description required in other cases, and shall pay to the receiver five dollars per acre for his claim, together with the proper fees, whereupon the whole proceedings and the judgment-roll shall be certified by the register to the Commissioner of the General Land Office, and a patent shall issue thereon for the claim, or such portion thereof as the applicant shall appear, from the decision of the court, to rightly possess. If it appears from the decision of the court that several parties are entitled to separate and different portions of the claim, each party may pay for his portion of the claim with the proper fees, and file the certificate and description by the surveyor-general, whereupon the register shall certify the proceedings and judgment-roll to the Commissioner of the General Land Office, as in the preceding case, and patents shall issue to the several parties according to their respective rights. Nothing herein contained shall be construed to prevent the alienation of a title conveyed by a patent for a mining claim to any person whatever.

ACT OF CONGRESS OF APRIL 26, 1882.—An act to amend section twenty-three hundred and twenty-six of the Revised Statutes, in regard to mineral lands, and for other purposes.

Be it enacted, etc., That the adverse claim required by section twenty-three hundred and twenty-six of the Revised Statutes may be verified by the oath of any duly authorized agent or attorney-in-fact of the adverse claimant cognizant of the facts stated, and the adverse claimant, if residing or at the time being beyond the limits of the district wherein the claim is situated, may make oath to the adverse claim before the clerk of any court of record of the United States or the State or Territory where the adverse claimant may then be, or before any notary public of such State or Territory.

SEC. 2. That applicants for mineral patents, if residing beyond the limits of the district wherein the claim is situated, may make any oath or affidavit required for proof of citizenship before the clerk of any court of record, or before any notary public of any State or Territory.

ACT OF CONGRESS OF MARCH 3, 1881.—An Act to amend section twenty-three hundred and twenty-six of the Revised Statutes, relating to suits at law affecting the title to mining claims.

Be it enacted, etc., That if, in any action brought pursuant to section twenty-three hundred and twenty-six of the Revised Statutes, title to the ground in controversy shall not be established by either party, the jury shall so find, and judgment shall be entered according to the verdict. In such case costs shall not be allowed to either party, and the claimant shall not proceed in the land office, or be entitled to a patent for the ground in controversy, until he shall have perfected his title.

LAND OFFICE REGULATIONS —80. An adverse mining claim must be filed with the register and receiver of the land office where the application for patent was filed, or with the register and receiver of the district in which the land is situated at the time of filing the adverse claim. It must be on the oath of the adverse claimant, or it may be verified by the oath of any duly authorized agent or attorney-in-fact of the adverse claimant cognizant of the facts stated.

81. Where an agent or attorney-in-fact verifies the adverse claim, he must distinctly swear that he is such agent or attorney, and accompany his affidavit by proof thereof.

82. The agent or attorney-in-fact must make the affidavit in verification of the adverse claim within the land district where the claim is situated.

83. The adverse notice must fully set forth the nature and extent of the interference or conflict; whether the adverse party claims as a purchaser for valuable consideration or as a locator; if the former, a certified copy of the original location, the original conveyance, a duly certified copy thereof, or an abstract of title from the office of the proper recorder should be furnished, or if the transaction was a merely verbal one he will narrate the circumstances attending the purchase, the date thereof, and the amount paid, which facts should be supported by the affidavit of one or more witnesses, if any were present at the time, and if he claims as a locator he must file a duly certified copy of the location from the office of the proper recorder.

84. In order that the "*boundaries*" and "*extent*" of the claim may be shown, it will be incumbent upon the adverse claimant to file a plat showing his entire claim, its relative situation or position with the one against which he claims, and the extent of the conflict: *Provided, however*, That if the application for patent describes the claim by legal subdivisions, the adverse claimant, if also claiming by legal subdivisions, may describe his adverse claim in the same manner without further survey or plat. If the claim is not described by legal subdivisions, it will generally be more satisfactory if the plat thereof is made from an actual survey by a deputy mineral surveyor, and its correctness officially certified thereon by him.

85. Upon the foregoing being filed within the sixty days' publication, the register, or in his absence the receiver, will give notice in writing to *both parties* to the contest that such adverse claim has been filed, informing them that the party who filed the adverse claim will be required within thirty days from the date of such filing to commence proceedings in a court of competent jurisdiction to determine the question of right of possession, and to prosecute the same with reasonable diligence to final judgment, and that, should such adverse claimant fail to do so, his adverse claim will be considered waived, and the application for patent be allowed to proceed upon its merits.

86. When an adverse claim is filed as aforesaid, the register or receiver will indorse upon the same the precise date of filing, and preserve a record of the date of notifications issued thereon; and thereafter all proceedings on the application for patent will be suspended, with the exception of the completion of the publication and posting of notices and plat, and the filing of the necessary proof thereof, until the controversy shall have been adjudicated in court, or the adverse claim waived or withdrawn.

87. Where an adverse claim has been filed and suit thereon commenced within the statutory period, and final judgment determining the right of possession rendered in favor of the applicant, it will not be sufficient for

him to file with the register a certificate of the clerk of the court, setting forth the facts as to such judgment, but he must, before he is allowed to make entry, file a certified copy of the judgment, together with the other evidence required by section 2326 Revised Statutes.

88. Where such suit has been dismissed, a certificate of the clerk of the court to that effect or a certified copy of the order of dismissal will be sufficient.

89. After an adverse claim has been filed and suit commenced, a relinquishment or other evidence of abandonment will not be accepted, but the case must be terminated and proof thereof furnished as required by the last two paragraphs.

90. Where an adverse claim has been filed, but no suit commenced against the applicant for patent within the statutory period, a certificate to that effect by the clerk of the State court having jurisdiction in the case, and also by the clerk of the circuit court of the United States for the district in which the claim is situated, will be required.

Affidavits—Hearings to Establish the Character of Lands.

UNITED STATES LAW.—SEC. 2335. All affidavits required to be made under this chapter may be verified before any officer authorized to administer oaths within the land district where the claims may be situated, and all testimony and proofs may be taken before any such officer, and, when duly certified by the officer taking the same, shall have the same force and effect as if taken before the register and receiver of the land office. In cases of contest as to the mineral or agricultural character of land, the testimony and proofs may be taken as herein provided on personal notice of at least ten days to the opposing party; or if such party cannot be found, then by publication of at least once a week for thirty days in a newspaper, to be designated by the register of the land office as published nearest to the location of such land; and the register shall require proof that such notice has been given.

LAND OFFICE REGULATIONS.—101. The Rules of Practice in cases before the United States district land offices, the General Land Office, and the Department of the Interior will, so far as applicable, govern in all cases and proceedings arising in contests and hearings to determine the mineral character of lands.

102. No public land shall be withheld from entry as agricultural land on account of its mineral character, except such as is returned by the surveyor-general as mineral; and the presumption arising from such a return may be overcome by testimony taken in the manner hereinafter described.

103. Hearings to determine the character of lands are practically of two kinds, as follows:

(1) Lands returned as mineral by the surveyor-general.

When such lands are sought to be entered as agricultural under laws which require the submission of final proof after due notice by publication and posting, the filing of the proper non-mineral affidavit in the absence of allegations that the land is mineral will be deemed sufficient as a preliminary requirement. A satisfactory showing as to character of land must be made when final proof is submitted.

In case of application to enter, locate, or select such lands as agricultural, under laws in which the submission of final proof after due publication and posting is *not* required, notice thereof must first be given by publication for sixty days and posting in the local office during the same period, and affirmative proof as to the character of the land submitted. In the absence of allegations that the land is mineral, and upon compliance with this requirement, the entry, location, or selection will be allowed, if otherwise regular.

(2) Lands returned as agricultural and alleged to be mineral in character.

Where as against the claimed right to enter such lands as agricultural it is alleged that the same are mineral, or are applied for as mineral lands, the proceedings in this class of cases will be in the nature of a contest, and the practice will be governed by the rules in force in contest cases.

104. Where a railroad company seeks to select lands not returned as mineral, but within six miles of any mining location, claim, or entry, or where in the case of a selection by a State, the lands sought to be selected are within a township in which there is a mining location, claim, or entry, publication must be made of the lands selected at the expense of the railroad company or State for a period of sixty days, with posting for the same period, in the land office for the district in which the lands are situated, during which period of publication the local land officers will receive protests or contests for any of said tracts or subdivisions of lands claimed to be more valuable for mining than for agricultural purposes.

105. At the expiration of the period of publication the register and receiver will forward to the Commissioner of the General Land Office the published list, noting thereon any protests, or contests, or suggestions as to the mineral character of any such lands, together with any information they may have received as to the mineral character of any of the lands mentioned in said list, when a hearing may be ordered.

106. At the hearings under either of the aforesaid classes, the claimants and witnesses will be thoroughly examined with regard to the character of the land; whether the same has been thoroughly prospected; whether or not there exists within the tract or tracts claimed any lode or vein of quartz or other rock in place, bearing gold, silver, cinnabar, lead, tin, or copper, or other valuable deposit which has ever been claimed, located, recorded, or worked; whether such work is entirely abandoned, or whether occasionally resumed; if such lode does exist, by whom claimed, under what designation, and in which subdivision of the land it lies; whether any placer mine or mines exist upon the land; if so, what is the character thereof—whether of the shallow-surface description, or of the deep cement, blue lead, or gravel deposits; to what extent mining is carried on when water can be obtained, and what the facilities are for obtaining water for mining purposes; upon what particular ten-acre subdivisions mining has been done, and at what time the land was abandoned for mining purposes, if abandoned at all.

107. The testimony should also show the agricultural capacities of the land, what kind of crops are raised thereon, and the value thereof; the number of acres actually cultivated for crops of cereals or vegetables, and within which particular ten-acre subdivision such crops are raised; also which of these subdivisions embrace the improvements, giving in detail the extent and value of the improvements, such as house, barn, vineyard, orchard, fencing, etc., and mining improvements.

108. The testimony should be as full and complete as possible; and in addition to the leading points indicated above, where an attempt is made to prove the mineral character of lands which have been entered under the agricultural laws, it should show at what date, if at all, valuable deposits of mineral were first known to exist on the lands.

109. When the case comes before this office such decision will be made as the law and the facts may justify; in cases where a survey is necessary to set apart the mineral from the agricultural land, the proper party *at his own expense* will be required to have the work done, at his option, either by United States deputy, county, or other local surveyor; application therefor must be made to the register and receiver, accompanied by a description of the land to be segregated, and the evidence of service upon the opposite party of notice of his intention to have such segregation made; the register and receiver will forward the same to this office, when the necessary instructions for the survey will be given. The survey in such case, where the claims to be segregated are vein or lode claims, must be executed in such manner as will conform to the requirements in section 2320, United States Revised Statutes, as to length and width and parallel end lines.

110. Such survey when executed must be properly sworn to by the surveyor, either before a notary public, officer of a court of record, or before the register or receiver, the deponent's character and credibility to be properly certified to by the officer administering the oath.

111. Upon the filing of the plat and field-notes of such survey with the register and receiver, duly sworn to as aforesaid, they will transmit the same to the surveyor-general for his verification and approval; who, if he finds the work correctly performed, will properly mark out the same upon the original township plat in his office, and furnish authenticated copies of such plat and description both to the proper local land office and to this office, to be affixed to the duplicate and triplicate township plats respectively.

112. With the copy of plat and description furnished the local office and this office must be a diagram tracing, verified by the surveyor-general, showing the claim or claims segregated, and designating the separate fractional agricultural tracts in each 40-acre legal subdivision by the proper lot number, beginning with No. 1 in each section, and giving the area in each lot, the same as provided in paragraph 45, in the survey of mining claims on surveyed lands.

113. The fact that a certain tract of land is decided upon testimony to be mineral in character is by no means equivalent to an award of the land to a miner. In order to secure a patent for such land he must proceed as in other cases, in accordance with the foregoing regulations.

Blank forms for proofs in mineral cases are not furnished by the General Land Office. [Land Office blanks are for sale by Henry N. Copp, Washington, D. C.—EDITOR.]

Water Rights.

UNITED STATES LAW.—SEC. 2339. Whenever, by priority of possession, rights to the use of water for mining, agricultural, manufacturing, or other purposes, have vested and accrued, and the same are recognized and acknowledged by the local customs, laws, and decisions of courts, the possessors and owners of such vested rights shall be maintained and protected in the same; and the right of way for the construction of ditches and canals for the purposes herein specified is acknowledged and confirmed; but whenever any person, in the construction of any ditch or canal, injures or damages the possession of any settler on the public domain, the party committing such injury or damage shall be liable to the party injured for such injury or damage.

SEC. 2340. All patents granted, or pre-emption or homesteads allowed, shall be subject to any vested and accrued water rights, or rights to ditches and reservoirs, used in connection with such water rights, as may have been acquired under or recognized by the preceding section.

SEC. 17. ACT OF CONGRESS MARCH 3, 1891.—An act to repeal timber culture laws and for other purposes. That reservoir sites located or selected and to be located and selected under the provisions of "An act making appropriations for sundry civil expenses of the government for the fiscal year ending June 30, 1889, and for other purposes," and amendments thereto, shall be restricted to and shall contain only so much land as is actually necessary for the construction and maintenance of reservoirs; excluding so far as practicable lands occupied by actual settlers at the date of the location of said reservoirs, and that the provision of "An act making appropriations for sundry civil expenses of the government for the fiscal year ending June 30, 1891, and for other purposes," which reads as follows, namely: "No person who shall, after the passage of this act, enter upon any of the public lands with a view to occupation, entry, or settlement under any of the land laws, shall be permitted to acquire title to more than 320 acres in the aggregate under all said laws," shall be construed to include in the maximum amount of lands the title to which is permitted to be acquired by one person only agricultural lands, and not to include lands entered or sought to be entered under mineral land laws.

Sec. 18. That the right of way through the public lands and reservations of the United States is hereby granted to any canal or ditch company, formed for the purpose of irrigation and duly organized under the laws of any State or Territory, which shall have filed, or may hereafter file, with the Secretary of the Interior, a copy of its articles of incorporation, and due proofs of its organization under the same, to the extent of the ground occupied by the water of the reservoir, and of the canal and its laterals, and 50 feet on each side of the marginal limits thereof; also the right to take from the public lands adjacent to the line of the canal or ditch, material, earth, and stone necessary for the construction of such canal or ditch; *Provided*, That no such right of way shall be located as to interfere with the proper occupation by the government of any such reservation; and all maps of location shall be subject to the approval of the department of the government having jurisdiction of such reservation, and the privilege herein granted shall not be construed to interfere with the control of water for irrigation and other purposes under authority of the respective States and Territories.

Sec. 19. That any canal or ditch company desiring to secure the benefits of this act shall, within twelve months after location of 10 miles of its canal, if the same be upon surveyed lands, and if upon unsurveyed lands, within twelve months after the survey thereof by the United States, file with the register of the land office for the district where such land is located a map of its canal or ditch and reservoir; and upon the approval thereof by the Secretary of the Interior the same shall be noted upon the plats in said office, and thereafter all such lands over which such rights of way shall pass shall be disposed of subject to such right of way. Whenever any person or corporation, in the construction of any canal, ditch or reservoir, injures or damages the possession of any settler on the public domain, the party committing such injury or damage shall be liable to the party injured for such injury or damage.

Sec. 20. That the provisions of this act shall apply to all canals, ditches, or reservoirs, heretofore or hereafter constructed, whether constructed by corporations, individuals, or associations of individuals, on the filing of the certificates and maps herein provided for. If such ditch, canal or reservoir has been or shall be constructed by an individual or association of individuals it shall be sufficient for such individual or association of individuals to file with the Secretary of the Interior, and with the register of the land office where said land is located, a map of the line of such canal, ditch or reservoir, as in case of a corporation, with the name of the individual owner or owners thereof, together with the articles of association, if any there be. Plats heretofore filed shall have the benefits of this act from the date of their filing, as though filed under it: *Provided*, That if any section of said canal or ditch shall not be completed within five years after the location of said section, the rights herein granted shall be forfeited as to any uncompleted section of said canal, ditch, or reservoir, to the extent that the same is not completed at the date of the forfeiture.

SEC. 23. That nothing in this act shall authorize such canal or ditch company to occupy such right of way except for the purpose of said canal or ditch, and then only so far as may be necessary for the construction, maintenance, and care of said canal or ditch.

Townsites on Mineral Lands.

UNITED STATES LAW.—SEC. 2386. Where mineral veins are possessed, which possession is recognized by local authority, and to the extent so possessed and recognized, the title to town lots to be acquired shall be subject to such recognized possession and the necessary use thereof; but nothing contained in this section shall be so construed as to recognize any color of title in possessors for mining purposes, as against the United States.

ACT OF CONGRESS OF MARCH 3, 1891.—An Act to repeal timber-culture laws, and for other purposes.

SEC. 16. That townsite entries may be made by incorporated towns and cities on the mineral lands of the United States, but no title shall be acquired by such towns or cities to any vein of gold, silver, cinnabar, copper, or lead, or to any valid mining claim or possession held under existing law. When mineral veins are possessed within the limits of an incorporated town or city, and such possession is recognized by local authority or by the laws of the United States, the title to town lots shall be subject to such recognized possession and the necessary use thereof and when entry has been made or patent issued for such townsites to such incorporated town or city, the possessor of such mineral vein may enter and receive patent for such mineral vein, and the surface ground appertaining thereto: *Provided*, That no entry shall be made by such mineral-vein claimant for surface ground where the owner or occupier of the surface ground shall have had possession of the same before the inception of the title of the mineral-vein applicant.

Easements.

UNITED STATES LAW.—SEC. 2338. As a condition of sale, in the absence of necessary legislation by Congress, the local legislature of any State or Territory may provide rules for working mines, involving easements, drainage, and other necessary means to their complete development; and those conditions shall be fully expressed in the patent.

Homestead and Pre-emption Claims.

UNITED STATES LAW.—SEC. 2341. Whenever, upon the lands heretofore designated as mineral lands, which have been excluded from survey and sale, there have been homesteads made by citizens of the United States, or persons who have declared their intention to become citizens, which homesteads have been made, improved, and used for agricultural purposes, and upon which there have been no valuable mines of gold, silver, cinnabar, or copper discovered, and which are properly agricultural lands, the settlers or owners of such homesteads shall have a right of pre-emption thereto, and shall be entitled to purchase the same at the price of one dollar and twenty-five cents per acre, and in quantity not to exceed one hundred and sixty acres; or they may avail themselves of the provisions of chapter five of this title, relating to "HOMESTEADS."

SEC. 2342. Upon the survey of the lands described in the preceding section, the Secretary of the Interior may designate and set apart such portions of the same as are clearly agricultural lands, which lands shall thereafter be subject to pre-emption and sale as other public lands, and be subject to all the laws and regulations applicable to the same.

Certain States Excepted.

UNITED STATES LAW.—SEC. 2345. The provisions of the preceding sections of this chapter shall not apply to the mineral lands situated in the States of Michigan, Wisconsin, and Minnesota, which are declared free and open to exploration and purchase, according to legal subdivisions, in like manner as before the tenth day of May, eighteen hundred and seventy-two. And any *bona fide* entries of such lands within the States named since the tenth of May, eighteen hundred and seventy-two, may be patented without reference to any of the foregoing provisions of this chapter. Such lands shall be offered for public sale in the same manner, at the same minimum price, and under the same rights of pre-emption, as other public lands.

ACT OF CONGRESS OF MAY 5, 1876.—An Act to exclude the States of Missouri and Kansas from the provisions of the act of Congress entitled "An act to promote the development of the mining resources of the United States," approved May tenth, eighteen hundred and seventy-two.

Be it enacted, etc., That within the States of Missouri and Kansas deposits of coal, iron, lead, or other mineral be, and they are hereby, excluded from the operation of the act entitled "An act to promote the development of the mining resources of the United States," approved May tenth, eighteen hundred and seventy-two, and all lands in said States shall be subject to disposal as agricultural lands.

ACT OF CONGRESS OF MARCH 3, 1883.—An Act to exclude the public lands in Alabama from the operation of the laws relating to mineral lands.

Be it enacted, etc., That within the State of Alabama all public lands, whether mineral or otherwise, shall be subject to disposal only as agricultural lands: *Provided, however,* That all lands which have heretofore been reported to the General Land Office as containing coal and iron shall first be offered at public sale: *And provided further,* That any *bona fide* entry under the provisions of the homestead law of lands within said State heretofore made may be patented without reference to an act approved May tenth, eighteen hundred and seventy-two, entitled, "An act to promote the development of the mining resources of the United States," in cases where the persons making application for such patents have in all other respects complied with the homestead law relating thereto.

Coal Lands.

UNITED STATES REVISED STATUTES.—SEC. 2347. Every person above the age of twenty-one years, who is a citizen of the United States, or who has declared his intention to become such, or any association of persons severally qualified as above, shall, upon application to the register of the proper land office, have the right to enter by legal subdivisions any quantity of vacant coal lands of the United States not otherwise appropriated or reserved by competent authority, not exceeding one hundred and sixty acres to such individual person, or three hundred and twenty acres to such association, upon payment to the receiver of not less than ten dollars per acre for such lands where the same shall be situated more than fifteen miles from any completed railroad, and not less than twenty dollars per acre for such lands as shall be within fifteen miles of such road.

SEC. 2348. Any person or association of persons severally qualified as above provided, who have opened and improved, or shall hereafter open and improve any coal mine or mines upon the public lands, and shall be in actual possession of the same, shall be entitled to a preference-right of entry under the preceding section, of the mines so opened and improved: *Provided,* That when any association of not less than four persons, severally qualified as above provided, shall have expended not less than five thousand dollars in working and improving any such mine or mines, such association may enter not exceeding six hundred and forty acres, including such mining improvements.

SEC. 2349. All claims under the preceding section must be presented to the register of the proper land district within sixty days after the date of actual possession and the commencement of improvements on the land, by the filing of a declaratory statement therefor; but when the township plat is not on file at the date of such improvement, filing must be made within sixty days from the receipt of such plat at the district office, and where the improvements shall have been made prior to the expiration of three months from the third day of March, eighteen hundred and seventy-three, sixty days from the expiration of such three months shall be allowed for the filing of a declaratory statement, and no sale under the provisions of this section shall be allowed until the expiration of six months from the third day of March, eighteen hundred and seventy-three.

SEC. 2350. The three preceding sections shall be held to authorize only one entry by the same person or association of persons; and no association of persons, any member of which shall have taken the benefit of such sections, either as an individual or as a member of any other association, shall enter or hold any other lands under the provisions thereof; and no member of any association which shall have taken the benefit of such section shall enter or hold any other lands under their provisions; and all persons claiming under section twenty-three hundred and forty-eight shall be required to prove their respective rights and pay for the lands filed upon within one year from the time prescribed for filing their respective claims; and upon failure to file the proper notice or to pay for the land within the required period, the same shall be subject to entry by any other qualified applicant.

SEC. 2351. In case of conflicting claims upon coal lands where the improvements shall be commenced after the third day of March, eighteen hundred and seventy-three, priority of possession and improvement, followed by proper filing and continued good faith, shall determine the preference-right to purchase. And also where improvements have already been made prior to the third day of March, eighteen hundred and seventy-three, division of the land claimed may be made by legal subdivisions, to include as near as may be the valuable improvements of the respective parties. The Commissioner of the General Land Office is authorized to issue all needful rules and regulations for carrying into effect the provisions of this and the four preceding sections.

LAND OFFICE REGULATIONS.—Under the authority conferred by said section 2351 the following rules and regulations are issued for carrying into effect the provisions of said law:

1. Sale of coal lands is provided for—

By ordinary *private entry* under section 2347.

By granting a *preference-right* of purchase, based on priority of possession and improvement, under section 2348.

2. The land entered under either section must be *by legal subdivisions*, as made by the regular United States survey. Entry is confined to surveyed lands; to such as are vacant, not otherwise appropriated, reserved by competent authority, or containing valuable minerals other than coal.

3. Individuals and associations may purchase. If an individual, he must be twenty-one years of age and a citizen of the United States, or have declared his intention to become such citizen.

4. If an association of persons each person must be qualified as above.

5. A person is not disqualified by the ownership of any quantity of other land, nor by having removed from his own land in the same State or Territory.

6. Any individual may enter by legal subdivisions as aforesaid any area not exceeding one hundred and sixty acres.

7. Any association may enter not to exceed three hundred and twenty acres.

8. Any association of not less than four persons, duly qualified, who shall have expended not less than $5,000 in working and improving any coal mine or mines, may enter under section 2348 not exceeding six hundred and forty acres, including such mining improvements.

9. One person can have the benefit of one entry or filing *only*. He is disqualified by having made such entry or filing alone or as a member of an association. No entry can be allowed an association which has in it a single person thus disqualified, as the law prohibits the entry or holding of more than one claim either by an individual or an association.

10. Lands that are sufficiently valuable for gold, silver, or copper to prevent their entry as agricultural lands cannot be entered as coal lands; and you will not allow any entry to be made under the above-named provisions of law of lands valuable for their deposits of said minerals.

11. The present rules relative to "hearings to establish the character of lands," contained in General Land Office regulations of October 31, 1881, issued under the mining laws, will, as far as applicable, govern your action in determining the character of lands sought to be entered as coal lands.

12. The price per acre is $10 where the land is situated *more* than fifteen miles from any completed railroad, and $20 per acre where the land is *within* fifteen miles of such road. The price of the land, however, must be determined by its distance from a completed railroad at the date of payment and entry irrespective of the preference-right of entry.

13. When application is made to purchase coal land at the rate of $10 per acre you will in all cases require satisfactory proof that the land applied for is at date of entry situated more than fifteen miles from any completed railroad. This proof may consist of the affidavit of the applicant, or that of his duly authorized agent, corroborated by the affidavit of some disinterested credible party showing personal knowedge of the facts.

14. Where the land lies *partly within* fifteen miles of such road and in *part outside* such limit, the *maximum* price must be paid for all legal subdivisions the greater part of which lie within fifteen miles of such road.

15. The term "completed railroad" is held to mean one which is actually constructed on the face of the earth; and lands within fifteen miles of any point of a railroad so constructed will be held and disposed of at $20 per acre.

16. Any duly qualified person or association must be preferred as purchasers of those public lands on which they have opened and improved or shall open and improve any coal mine or mines, and which they shall have in actual possession.

17. Possession by agent is recognized as the possession of the principal. The clearest proof on the point of agency must, however, be required in every case, and a clearly-defined possession must be established.

18. The *opening and improving* of a coal mine, in order to confer a preference-right of purchase, must not be considered as a mere matter of form; the labor expended and improvements made must be such as to clearly indicate the good faith of the claimant.

19. These lands are intended to be sold, where there are adverse claimants therefor, to the party who, by substantial improvements, actual possession, and a reasonable industry, shows an intention to continue his development of the mines, in preference to those who would purchase for speculative purposes only. With this view you will require such proof of compliance with the law, when lands are applied for under section 2348 by adverse claimants, as the circumstances of each case may justify.

20. In conflicts where improvements have been or shall hereafter be commenced, priority of possession and improvement shall govern the award when the law has been fully complied with by each party. A mere possession, however, without satisfactory improvements, will not secure the tract to the first occupant when a subsequent claimant shows his full compliance with the law.

21. After an entry has been allowed to one party, you will make no investigation concerning it at the instance of any person except on instructions from this office. You will, however, receive all affidavits concerning such case and forward the same to this office, accompanied by a statement of the facts as shown by your records.

22. Prior to entry it is competent for you to order an investigation, on sufficient grounds set forth under oath of a party in interest and substantiated by the affidavits of disinterested and credible witnesses.

MANNER OF OBTAINING TITLE.

23. When title is sought by *private entry* the party will himself make oath to the following application, which must be presented to the register:

I, —— ——, hereby apply, under the provisions of the Revised Statutes of the United States relating to the sale of coal lands of the United States, to purchase the —— quarter of section ——, in township ——, of range ——, in the district of lands subject to sale at the land office at ——, and containing —— acres; and I solemnly swear that no portion of said tract is in the possession of any other party; that I am twenty-one years of age, a citizen of the United States (or have declared my intention to become a citizen of the United States), and have never held nor purchased lands under said act, either as an individual or as a member of an association; and I do further swear that I am well acquainted with the character of said described land, and with each and every legal subdivision thereof, having frequently passed over the same; that my knowledge of said land is such as to enable me to testify understandingly with regard thereto; that said land contains large deposits of coal and is chiefly valuable therefor; that there is not to my knowledge within the limits thereof any vein or lode of quartz or other rock in place bearing gold, silver, or copper, and that there is not within the limits of said land, to my knowledge, any valuable deposit of gold, silver, or copper. So help me God.

24. Thereupon the register if the tract is vacant will so certify to the receiver, stating the price, and the applicant or his duly authorized agent must then pay the amount of purchase-money.

25. The receiver will then issue to the purchaser a duplicate receipt, and at the close of the month the register and receiver will make returns of the sale to the General Land Office, from whence, when the proceedings are found regular, a patent or complete title will be issued; and on surrender of the duplicate receipt such patent will be delivered, at the option of the patentee, either by the Commissioner at Washington or by the register at the district land office.

26. This disposition at private entry will be subject to any valid prior adverse right which may have attached to the same land and which is protected by section 2348.

27. *Second.* When the application to purchase is based on a priority of possession, &c., as provided for in section 2348, the claimant must, when the township plat is on file in your office, file his declaratory statement for the tract claimed sixty days from and after the first day of his actual possession, and improvement. Sixty days, exclusive of the first day of possession, &c., must be allowed.

28. The declaratory statement must be substantially as follows, to wit:

I, —— ——, do solemnly swear that I am —— years of age, and a citizen of the United States (or have declared my intention to become a citizen of the United States); that I never have, either as an individual or as a member of an association, held or purchased any coal lands under the provisions of the Revised Statutes of the United States relating to the sale of coal lands of the United States, and I do hereby declare my intention to purchase, under the provisions aforesaid, the —— quarter of section ——, in township ——, of range ——, of lands subject to sale at the district land office at ——, and that I came into possession of said tract on the —— day of ——, A. D. 18—, and have ever since remained in actual possession continuously; that I have located and opened a valuable mine of coal thereon, and have expended in labor and improvements on said mine the sum of —— dollars, the labor and improvements being as follows: [here describe the nature and character of the improvements]; and I do furthermore solemnly swear that I am well acquainted with the character of said described land, and with each and every legal subdivision thereof, having frequently passed over the same; that my knowledge of said land is such as to enable me to testify understandingly with regard thereto; that there is not, to my knowledge, within the limits thereof any vein or lode of quartz or other rock in place bearing gold, silver, or copper, and that there is not within the limits of said land, to my knowledge, any valuable deposit of gold, silver or copper. So help me God.

29. When the township p'at is not on file at date of claimant's first possession the declaratory statement must be filed within sixty days from the filing of such plat in your office.

30. One year from and after the expiration of the period allowed for filing the declaratory statement is given within which to make proof and payment; but you will allow no party to make final proof and payment except on notice to all others who appear on your records as claimants to the same tract.

31. A party who otherwise complies with the law may enter *after* the expiration of said year, *provided* no valid adverse right shall have intervened. He postpones his entry beyond said year at his own risk, and the government cannot thereafter protect him against another who complies with the law, and the value of his improvements can have no weight in his favor.

32. Each claimant at the time of actual purchase must make affidavit as follows:

I, ―― ――, claiming under the provisions of the Revised Statutes of the United States relating to the sale of coal lands of the United States, the right of purchase to the ―― quarter of section ――, in township ―― of range ――, subject to sale at ――, do solemnly swear that I have never had the right of purchase under the aforesaid provisions of law either as an individual or as a member of an association, and that I have never held any other lands under its provisions; I further swear that I have expended in developing coal mines on said tract in labor and improvements the sum of ―― dollars, the nature of such improvements being as follows: ―― ―― ――; that I am now in the actual possession of said mines, and make the entry for my own use and benefit, and not directly or indirectly for the use and benefit of any other party; and I do furthermore swear that I am well acquainted with the character of said described land, and with each and every legal subdivision thereof, having frequently passed over the same; that my knowledge of said land is such as to enable me to testify understandingly with regard thereto; that the same is chiefly valuable for coal; that there is not, to my knowledge, within the limits thereof any vein or lode of quartz or other rock in place bearing gold, silver, or copper, and that there is not within the limits of said land, to my knowledge, any valuable deposit of gold, silver, or copper. So help me God.

―― ――.

33. The application, declaratory statement, and the affidavit required at the time of actual purchase, the forms of which are given above under paragraphs 23, 28, and 32, may be sworn to before any officer authorized by law to administer oaths, but the authority of such officer must be properly shown.

34. Any party duly qualified under the law, *after* swearing to his application or declaratory statement, may, by a sufficient power of attorney duly executed under the laws of the State or Territory in which such party may then be residing, empower an agent to file with the register of the proper land office the application, declaratory statement, or affidavit required at the time of actual purchase, and also authorize him to make payment for an entry of the land in the name of such qualified party; and when such power of attorney shall have been filed in your office you will permit such agent to act thereunder as above indicated.

35. Where a claimant shows by affidavit that he is not personally acquainted with the character of the land, his duly authorized agent who possesses such knowledge may make the required affidavit as to its character; but whether this affidavit is made by principal or agent it must be corroborated by the affidavits of two disinterested and credible witnesses having knowledge of its character.

36. Nothing in these regulations shall be so construed as to prevent a party from proving his citizenship or age, or establishing the status of the lands sought to be entered, in accordance with ordinary rules of evidence; and any proof regularly introduced for that purpose that would be competent in a court or before a commissioner charged with the ascertainment of facts may be considered.

37. Assignments of the right to purchase will be recognized when properly executed. Proof and payment must be made, however, within the prescribed period, which dates from the first day of the possession of the assignor who initiated the claim.

38. The "Rules of Practice in cases before the United States district land offices, the General Land Office, and the Department of the Interior," ap-

proved December 20, 1880, will, as far as applicable, govern all cases and proceedings arising under the sections of the Revised Statutes above quoted providing for the sale of coal lands of the United States.

Coal Claimants' Applications.

[From circular instructions issued August 7, 1895, relative to deposits by individuals for the survey of public lands under section 2401, Revised Statutes, as amended by the act of August 20, 1894.—21 L. D., 77.]

LAND OFFICE REGULATIONS.—In addition to the rights of settlers, referred to in the foregoing portions of this circular, sections 2401, 2402, and 2403, United States Revised Statutes, as amended by the act of August 20, 1894, embrace provisions in favor of "persons and associations lawfully possessed of coal lands and otherwise qualified to make entry thereof."

The coal-land laws contained in sections 2347 to 2352, United States Revised Statutes, provide methods by which persons properly qualified may become lawfully possessed of coal lands even before the survey of the lands, and be entitled to enter the same after survey. For particular information in regard thereto, reference is made to Departmental circular of July 31, 1882, entitled "Coal-Land Laws and Regulations Thereunder." Such parties, in cases where the tracts of which they are lawfully possessed are still unsurveyed, may, under said sections 2401, 2402, and 2403, as amended by act of August 20, 1894, apply to the surveyor-general for the surveying district in which the lands are included, for a survey of the township or townships including the land according to the provisions of said sections. Such an application must be accompanied by the affidavit of the applicant or applicants substantially as prescribed for declaratory statements on page 7 of the said circular of July 31, 1882, corroborated by the testimony of two or more witnesses, in which the qualifications of the applicants, the character and location of the land, indicating the township or townships in which it is included as nearly as practicable, and other essential facts must be so set forth as to satisfy the surveyor-general that the case comes properly within the provisions of the law as above given. He will, thereupon, if he approves the application, transmit the same to this office, with the required proofs and his report.

Mineral Entries Within Forest Reserves.

The law provides that "any mineral lands in any forest reservation which have been or which may be shown to be such, and subject to entry under the existing mining laws of the United States and the rules and regulations applying thereto, shall continue to be subject to such location and entry," notwithstanding the reservation. This makes mineral lands in the forest reserves subject to location and entry under the general mining laws in the usual manner.

Owners of valid mining locations made and held in good faith under the mining laws of the United States and the regulations thereunder are authorized and permitted to fell and remove from such mining claims any timber growing thereon, for actual mining purposes in connection with the particular claim from which the timber is felled or removed.

The law provides that "The Secretary of the Interior may permit under regulations to be prescribed by him, the use of timber and stone found upon such reservations, free of charge, by *bona fide* settlers, miners, residents, and prospectors for minerals, for firewood, fencing, buildings, mining, prospecting, and other domestic purposes, as may be needed by such persons for such purposes; such timber to be used within the State or Territory, respectively, where such reservations may be located."

This provision is limited to persons resident in forest reservations who have not a sufficient supply of timber or stone on their own claims or lands for the purposes enumerated, or for necessary use in developing the mineral or other natural resources of the lands owned or occupied by them. Such persons, therefore, are permitted to take timber and stone from public lands in the forest reservations under the terms of the law above quoted, strictly for their individual use on their own claims or lands owned or occupied by them, but not for sale or disposal, or use on other lands, or by other persons: *Provided*, That where the stumpage value exceeds one hundred dollars, application must be made to and permission given by the Department.

Timber Cutting.

ACT OF CONGRESS OF JUNE 3, 1878.—An Act authorizing the citizens of Colorado, Nevada, and the Territories, to fell and remove timber on the public domain for mining and domestic purposes.

Be it enacted, etc., That all citizens of the United States and other persons, *bona fide* residents of the State of Colorado or Nevada, or either of the Territories of New Mexico, Arizona, Utah, Wyoming, Dakota, Idaho, or Montana, and all other mineral districts of the United States, shall be and are hereby, authorized and permitted to fell and remove, for building, agricultural, mining, or other domestic purposes, any timber or other trees growing or being on the public lands, said lands being mineral, and not subject to entry under existing laws of the United States, except for mineral entry, in either of said States, Territories, or districts, of which such citizens or persons may be at the time *bona fide* residents, subject to such rules and regulations as the Secretary of the Interior may prescribe for the protection of the timber and of the undergrowth growing upon such lands, and for other purposes: *Provided*, The provisions of this act shall not extend to railroad corporations.

SEC. 2. That it shall be the duty of the register and the receiver of any local land office in whose district any mineral land may be situated, to ascertain from time to time whether any timber is being cut or used upon any such lands, except for the purposes authorized by this act, within their respective land districts; and, if so, they shall immediately notify the Commissioner of the General Land Office of that fact; and all necessary expenses incurred in making such proper examinations shall be paid and allowed such register and receiver in making up their next quarterly accounts.

SEC. 3. Any person or persons who shall violate the provisions of this act, or any rules and regulations in pursuance thereof made by the Secretary of the Interior, shall be deemed guilty of a misdemeanor, and, upon conviction, shall be fined in any sum not exceeding five hundred dollars, and to which may be added imprisonment for any term not exceeding six months.

LAND OFFICE REGULATIONS.—1. The act applies to the States of Colorado, Nevada, Montana, Idaho, Wyoming, North Dakota, South Dakota, and Utah, and the Territories of New Mexico and Arizona, and all other mineral districts of the United States.

2. The land from which timber may be felled or removed under the provisions of this act must be known to be of a *strictly mineral* character and "not subject to entry under existing laws of the United States, except for mineral entry." Parties who take timber from the public lands under assumed authority of this act must stand prepared to show that their acts are within the prescribed terms of the law granting such privilege, the burden being upon such parties of proving by a preponderance of evidence that the land from which the timber is taken is "mineral" within the meaning of the act.

3. The privileges granted are confined to citizens of the United States and other persons, *bona fide* residents of the States, Territories, and other mineral districts, provided for in the act.

4. The uses for which timber may be felled or removed are limited by the wording of the act to "building, agricultural, mining, or other domestic purposes."

5. No timber is permitted to be felled or removed for purposes of sale or traffic, or to manufacture the same into lumber or other timber product as an article of merchandise, or for any other use whatsoever, except as defined in section.4 of these rules and regulations.

6. No timber cut or removed under the provisions of this act may be transported out of the State or Territory where procured.

7. No timber is permitted to be used for smelting purposes, smelting being a separate and distinct industry from that of mining.

8. No growing trees of any kind whatsoever less than eight inches in diameter are permitted to be cut.

9. Persons felling or removing timber under the provisions of this act must utilize all of each tree cut that can be profitably used, and must dispose of the tops, brush, and other refuse in such manner as to prevent the spread of forest fires.

Timber and Stone.

ACT OF CONGRESS OF JUNE 3, 1878.—An act for the sale of timber lands in the States of California, Oregon, Nevada, and in Washington Territory.

Be it enacted, etc., That surveyed public lands of the United States within the States of California, Oregon, and Nevada, and in Washington Territory, not included within military, Indian, or other reservations of the United States, valuable chiefly for timber, but unfit for cultivation, and which have not been offered at public sale according to law, may be sold to citizens of the United States, or persons who have declared their intention to become such, in quantities not exceeding one hundred and sixty acres to any one person or association of persons, at the minimum price of two dollars and fifty cents per acre; and lands valuable chiefly for stone may be sold on the same terms as timber lands: *Provided*, That nothing herein contained shall defeat or impair any *bona fide* claim under any law of the United States, or authorize the sale of any mining claim, or the improvements of any *bona fide* settler, or lands containing gold, silver, cinnabar, copper, or coal, or lands selected by the said States under any law of the United States donating lands for internal improvements, education, or other purposes: *And provided further*, That none of the rights conferred by the act approved July twenty-sixth, eighteen hundred and sixty-six, entitled "An Act granting the right of way to ditch and canal owners over the public lands, and for other purposes," shall be abrogated by this act; and all patents granted shall be subject to any vested and accrued water-rights, or rights to ditches and reservoirs used in connection with such water-rights as may have been acquired under and by the provisions of said act; and such rights shall be expressly reserved in any patent issued under this act.

SEC. 2. That any person desiring to avail himself of the provisions of this act shall file with the register of the proper district a written statement in duplicate, one of which is to be transmitted to the General Land Office, designating by legal subdivisions the particular tract of land he desires to purchase, setting forth that the same is unfit for cultivation, and valuable chiefly for its timber or stone; that it is uninhabited; contains no mining or other improvements, except for ditch or canal purposes, where any such do exist, save such as were made by or belong to the applicant, nor as deponent verily believes, any valuable deposit of gold, silver, cinnabar, copper, or coal; that deponent has made no other application under this act; that he does not apply to purchase the same on speculation, but in good faith to appropriate it to his own exclusive use and benefit; and that he has not, directly or indirectly, made any agreement or contract, in any way or manner, with any person or persons whatsoever, by which the title which he might acquire from the Government of the United States should inure, in whole or in part, to the benefit of any person except himself; which statement must be verified by the oath of the applicant before the register or the receiver of the land office within the district where the land is situated; and if any person taking such oath shall swear falsely in the premises, he shall be subject to all the pains and penalties of perjury, and shall forfeit the money which he may have paid for said lands, and all right and title to the same; and any grant or conveyance which he may have made, except in the hands of *bona fide* purchasers, shall be null and void.

SEC. 3. That upon the filing of said statement, as provided in the second section of this act, the register of the land office shall post a notice of such application, embracing a description of the land by legal subdivisions, in his office, for a period of sixty days, and shall furnish the applicant a copy of the same for publication, at the expense of such applicant, in a newspaper published nearest the location of the premises, for a like period of time; and after the expiration of the said sixty days, if no adverse claim shall have been filed, the person desiring to purchase shall furnish to the register of the land office satisfactory evidence, first, that said notice of the application prepared by the register as aforesaid was duly published in a newspaper as herein required; secondly, that the land is of the character contemplated in this act, unoccupied and without improvements, other than those excepted, either mining or agricultural, and that it apparently contains no valuable deposits of gold, silver, cinnabar, copper, or coal; and upon payment to the proper officer of the purchase-money of said land, together with the fees of the register and the receiver, as provided for in case of mining claims in the twelfth section of the act approved May tenth, eighteen hundred and seventy-two, the applicant may be permitted to enter said tract, and, on the transmission to the General Land Office of the papers and testimony in the case, a patent shall issue thereon : *Provided*, That any person having a valid claim to any portion of the land may object, in writing, to the issuance of a patent to lands so held by him, stating the nature of his claim thereto ; and evidence shall be taken, and the merits of said objection shall be determined by the officers of the land office, subject to appeal, as in other land cases. Effect shall be given to the foregoing provisions of this act by regulations to be prescribed by the Commissioner of the General Land Office.

SEC. 6. That all acts and parts of acts inconsistent with the provisions of this act are hereby repealed.

LAND OFFICE REGULATIONS.—The first, second and third sections provide for the sale of surveyed lands in California, Oregon, Nevada, and in Washington Territory [all public land States—see Act of August 4, 1892,] not yet proclaimed and offered at public sale, valuable chiefly for timber and stone, unfit for cultivation, and consequently for disposal under the preemption and homestead laws. When a party applies to purchase a tract thereunder, the register and receiver will require him to make affidavit that he is a citizen of the United States by birth or naturalization, or that he has declared his intention to become a citizen under the naturalization laws. If native born, parol evidence of that fact will be received; if not native born, record evidence of the prescribed qualification must be furnished. In connection herewith, he will be required to make the sworn statement in duplicate, according to the attached form, as provided for in the second section of the act. One of the duplicate statements filed in each is by the act required to be transmitted to this office, and the registers and receivers will accordingly send up with their monthly returns the duplicate statements to be transmitted for the month.

The evidence in regard to the publication of notice required to be furnished, in the third section of the act, must consist of the affidavit of the publisher or other person having charge of the newspaper in which the notice is published, with a copy of the notice attached thereto, setting forth the nature of his connection with the paper, and that the notice was duly published for the prescribed period. The evidence required in the same section with regard to the non-mineral character of the land, and its unoccupied and unimproved condition, must consist of the testimony of at least two disinterested witnesses, to the effect that they know the facts to which they testify from personal inspection of the land and of each of its smallest legal subdivisions, as per form attached. This testimony may be taken before the register or receiver, or any officer using an official seal and authorized to administer oaths in the land district in which the land lies. Upon such proof being produced, if no adverse claim shall have been filed, the entry applied for may be allowed in pursuance of the provisions of the act. The receiver will issue his receipt for the purchase-money, and the register his certificate of purchase, numbering the entry in the regular cash series. The register and receiver will enter the sale on their books, and make the usual returns therefor to this office, noting on the monthly extracts, opposite the entry, and on the entry papers, a reference to the act of Congress under which allowed. They will forward all the papers in the case with their returns to this office, except the retained duplicate statement filed under the second section of the act, to which the register will give the same number with the other papers for the entry, and retain it on the appropriate file with the former application in his office.

The register and receiver will be entitled to a fee of five dollars each for allowing an entry under said act, and jointly at the rate of twenty-two cents and a half per hundred words for testimony reduced by them to writing for claimants, which will be accounted for as other fees.

If, at the expiration of the sixty days' notice provided for in the third section of the act, an adverse claim should be found to exist calling for an investigation, the register and receiver will allow the parties a hearing according to the rules of practice.

In case of an association of persons making application for such an entry, each of the persons must prove the requisite qualifications, and their names must appear in and be subscribed to the sworn statement, as in case of an individual person. They must also unite in the regular application for entry, which will be made in their joint names as in other cases of joint cash entry. The forms prescribed for cases of applications by individual persons may be adapted for use in applications of this class.

Salt Springs and Salt Deposits.

ACT OF CONGRESS OF JANUARY 31, 1901.—An act extending the mining laws to saline lands.

Be it enacted, etc., That all unoccupied lands of the United States containing salt springs, or deposits of salt in any form, and chiefly valuable therefor, are hereby declared to be subject to location and purchase under the provisions of the law relating to placer-mining claims: *Provided*, That the same person shall not locate or enter more than one claim hereunder.

LAND OFFICE REGULATIONS.—1. Under this act the provisions of the law relating to placer-mining claims are extended to all States and Territories and the district of Alaska, so as to permit the location and purchase thereunder of all unoccupied public lands containing salt springs, or deposits of salt in any form, and chiefly valuable therefor, with the *proviso*, "That the same person shall not locate or enter more than one claim hereunder."

2. Rights obtained by location under the placer-mining laws are assignable and the assignee may make the entry in his own name; so under this act a person holding as assignee may make entry in his own name, *provided* he has not held under this act, at any time, either as locator, assignee or entryman, any other lands; his right is exhausted by having held under this act any particular tract, either as locator, assignee or entryman, either as an individual or as a member of an association. It follows, therefore, that no application for patent or entry, made under this act, shall embrace more than one single location.

3. In order that the conditions imposed by the proviso, as set forth in the above paragraph, may duly appear, the notice of location presented for record, the application for patent and the application to purchase must each contain a specific statement under oath by each person whose name appears therein that he never has, either as an individual or as a member of an association, located, applied for, entered, or held any other lands under the provisions of this act. Assignments made by persons who are not severally qualified as herein stated will not be recognized.

Perjury—Penalty Thereof.

UNITED STATES LAW.—SEC. 5392. Every person who, having taken an oath before a competent tribunal, officer, or person, in any case in which a law of the United States authorizes an oath to be administered, that he will testify, declare, depose, or certify truly, or that any written testimony, declaration, deposition, or certificate by him subscribed is true, willfully and contrary to such oath states or subscribes any material matter which he does not believe to be true, is guilty of perjury, and shall be punished by a fine of not more than two thousand dollars, and by imprisonment at hard labor not more than five years, and shall, moreover, thereafter, be incapable of giving testimony in any court of the United States until such time as the judgment against him is reversed.

Miscellaneous Provisions.

UNITED STATES LAW.—SEC. 2343. The President is authorized to establish additional land districts, and to appoint necessary officers under existing laws, wherever he may deem the same necessary for the public convenience in executing the provisions of this chapter.

SEC. 2344. Nothing contained in this chapter shall be construed to impair, in any way, rights or interests in mining property acquired under existing laws; or to affect the provisions of the act entitled "An act granting to A. Sutro the right of way and other privileges to aid in the construction of a draining and exploring tunnel to the Comstock lode, in the State of Nevada," approved July twenty-five, eighteen hundred and sixty-six.

SEC. 2346. No act passed at the first session of the thirty-eighth Congress, granting lands to States or corporations to aid in the construction of roads or for other purposes, or to extend the time of grants made prior to the thirtieth day of January, eighteen hundred and sixty-five, shall be so construed as to embrace mineral lands, which in all cases are reserved exclusively to the United States, unless otherwise specially provided in the act or acts making the grant.

ALASKA.

ACT OF CONGRESS OF MAY 17, 1884.—An Act providing a civil government for Alaska.

SEC. 8. That the said district of Alaska is hereby created a land district, and a United States land office for said district is hereby located at Sitka. The commissioner provided for by this act to reside at Sitka shall be *ex officio* register of said land office, and the clerk provided for by this act shall be *ex officio* receiver of public moneys, and the marshal provided for by this act shall be *ex officio* surveyor-general of said district, and the laws of the United States relating to mining claims, and the rights incident thereto, shall, from and after the passage of this act, be in full force and effect in said district, under the administration thereof herein provided for, subject to such regulations as may be made by the Secretary of the Interior, approved by the President: *Provided*, That the Indians or other persons in said district shall not be disturbed in the possession of any lands actually in their use or occupation or now claimed by them, but the terms under which such persons may acquire title to such lands is reserved for future legislation by Congress: *And provided further*, That parties who have located mines or mineral privileges therein under the laws of the United States applicable to the public domain, or who have occupied and improved or exercised acts of ownership over such claims, shall not be disturbed therein but shall be allowed to perfect their title to such claims by payment as aforesaid: *And provided also*, That the land not exceeding six hundred and forty acres at any station now occupied as missionary stations among the Indian tribes in said section, with the improvements thereon erected by or for such societies, shall be continued in the occupancy of the several religious societies to which said missionary stations respectively belong until action by Congress. But nothing contained in this act shall be construed to put in force in said district the general land laws of the United States.

LAND OFFICE REGULATIONS.—The administration of the mining laws as prescribed by these regulations will be, so far as applicable, adopted for, and extended to Alaska.

[Section 13, Act of May 14, 1898, concerning British subjects is inoperative.—ED.]

Mining Rights.

ACT OF CONGRESS OF JUNE 6, 1900.—Extracts from the law providing a civil government for Alaska.

Establishment of recording districts by the judges of the district courts.

SEC. 13. The judges of the district, or a majority of them, shall, as soon as practicable after their appointment, meet, and by appropriate order, to be thereafter entered in each division of the court, divide the district into three recording divisions, designate the division of the court to supervise each, and also define the boundaries thereof by reference to natural objects and permanent landmarks or monuments, in such manner that the boundaries of each recording division can be readily determined and become generally known from such description, which order shall be given publicity in such manner by posting, publication, or otherwise as the judges or any division of the court may direct, the necessary expense of the publication of such order and description of the recording divisions to be allowed and paid as other court expenses.

At any regular or special term an order may be made by the court establishing one or more recording districts within the recording division under the supervision of such division of the court and defining the boundaries thereof by reference to natural objects and permanent landmarks or monuments, in such manner that the boundaries thereof can be readily determined.

The order establishing a recording district shall designate a commissioner to be *ex officio* recorder thereof, and shall also designate the place where the commissioner shall keep his recording office within the recording district:

Provided, The clerk of the court shall be *ex officio* recorder of all that portion of the recording division under the supervision of his division of the court not embraced within the limits of a recording district established, bounded, and described therein as authorized by this Act, and when any part of the division for which a clerk has been recording shall be embraced in a recording district, such clerk shall transcribe that portion of his records appertaining to such district and deliver the same to the commissioner designated as recorder thereof.

Whenever it appears to the satisfaction of the court that the public interests demand, or that the convenience of the people require, the court may change or modify the boundaries or discontinue a recording district or change the location of a recording office, or remove the commissioner acting as *ex officio* recorder, and appoint another commissioner to fill the office.

SEC. 14. The clerk as *ex officio* recorder must procure such books for records as the business of his office requires and such as may be required by the respective commissioners designated as recorders in his division of the court, but orders for the same must first be obtained from the court or the judge thereof. The respective officers acting as *ex officio* recorders shall have the custody and must keep all the books, records, maps, and papers deposited in their respective offices, and where a recorder is removed or from any cause becomes unable to act, or a recording district is discontinued, the records and all books, papers, and property relating thereto shall be delivered to the clerk or such officer or person as the court or judge thereof may direct.

The record books procured by the clerk, as herein provided, shall be paid for by him, on the order of the court, out of any moneys in his hands, as other court expenses are paid.

Requirement for the recording of notices of mining locations, affidavits of annual work done on mining claims, etc.

SEC. 15. The respective recorders shall, upon the payment of the fees for the same prescribed by the Attorney-General, record separately, in large and well-bound separate books, in fair hand:

First. Deeds, grants, transfers, contracts to sell or convey real estate and mortgages of real estate, releases of mortgages, powers of attorney, leases which have been acknowledged or proved, mortgages upon personal property;

Second. Certificates of marriage and marriage contracts and births and deaths;

Third. Wills devising real estate admitted to probate;

Fourth. Official bonds;

Fifth. Transcripts of judgments which by law are made liens upon real estate;

Sixth. All orders and judgments made by the district court or the commissioners in probate matters affecting real estate which are required to be recorded;

Seventh. Notices and declaration of water rights;

Eighth. Assignments for the benefit of creditors;

Ninth. Affidavits of annual work done on mining claims;

Tenth. Notices of mining location and declaratory statements;

Eleventh. Such other writings as are required or permitted by law to be recorded, including the liens of mechanics, laborers, and others: *Provided*, Notices of location of mining claims shall be filed for record within ninety days from the date of the discovery of the claim described in the notice, and all instruments shall be recorded in the recording district in which the property or subject-matter affected by the instrument is situated, and where the property or subject-matter is not situated in any established recording district the instrument affecting the same shall be recorded in the office of the clerk of the division of the court having supervision over the recording division in which such property or subject-matter is situated.

Miners may make rules and regulations—Mining records heretofore made, legalized.

SEC. 16. Any clerk or commissioner authorized to record any instrument who having collected fees for so doing fails to record such instrument shall account to his successor in office, or to such person as the court may direct, for all the fees received by him for recording any instrument on file and unrecorded at the expiration of his official term, or at the time he is required to transfer his records to another officer under the direction of the court. And any clerk or commissioner who fails, neglects, or refuses to so account for fees received and not actually earned by the recording of instrument shall be deemed guilty of a misdemeanor, and on conviction thereof shall be fined not less than one hundred dollars nor more than one thousand dollars, and imprisoned for not more than one year, or until the fees received and unearned as aforesaid shall have been properly accounted for and paid over by him, as hereinbefore provided. And in addition such fees may be recovered from such clerk or commissioner or the bondsmen of either, in a civil action which shall be brought by the district attorney, in the name of the United States, to recover the same; and the amount when recovered shall be by the court transferred to the successor in office of such recorder, who shall thereupon proceed to record the unrecorded instruments: *Provided*, Miners in any organized mining district may make rules and regulations governing the recording of notices of location of mining claims, water rights, flumes and ditches, mill sites and affidavits of labor, not in conflict with this Act or the general laws of the United States; and nothing in this Act shall be construed so as to prevent the miners in any regularly organized mining district not within any recording district established by the court from electing their own mining recorder to act as such until a recorder therefor is appointed by the court: *Provided further*, All records heretofore regularly made by the United States commissioner at Dyea, Skagway, and the recorder at Douglas City, not in conflict with any records regularly made with the United States commissioner at Juneau, are hereby legalized. And all records heretofore made in good faith in any regularly organized mining district are hereby made public records, and the same shall be delivered to the recorder for the recording district including such mining district within six months from the passage of this Act.

Mining laws extended to the District of Alaska—Tide lands subject to exploration and mining—Rights to dredge and mine below low tide, subject to rules and regulations by Secretary of War—Reservation of sixty-foot roadway by act of May 14, 1898, shall not apply to mineral lands.

SEC. 26. The laws of the United States relating to mining claims, mineral locations, and rights incident thereto are hereby extended to the District of Alaska: *Provided*, That subject only to such general limitations as may be necessary to exempt navigation from artificial obstructions all land and shoal water between low and mean high tide on the shores, bays and inlets of Bering Sea, within the jurisdiction of the United States, shall be subject to exploration and mining for gold and other precious metals by citizens of the United States, or persons who have legally declared their intentions to become such, under such reasonable rules and regulations as the miners in organized mining districts may have heretofore made or may hereafter make governing the temporary possession thereof for exploration and mining purposes until otherwise provided by law: *Provided further*, That the rules and regulations established by the miners shall not be in conflict with the mining laws of the United States; and no exclusive permits shall be granted by the Secretary of War authorizing any person or persons, corporation or company to excavate or mine under any of said waters below low tide, and if such exclusive permit has been granted it is hereby revoked and declared null and void; but citizens of the United States or persons who have legally declared their intention to become such shall have the right to dredge and mine for gold or other precious metals in said waters, below low tide, subject to such general rules and regulations as the Secretary of War may prescribe for the preservation of order and the protection of the interests of commerce; such rules and regulations shall not, however, deprive miners on the beach of the right hereby given to dump tailings into or pump from the sea opposite their claims, except where such dumping would actually obstruct navigation, and the reservation of a roadway sixty feet wide, under the tenth section of the Act of May fourteenth, eighteen hundred and ninety-eight, entitled "An Act extending the homestead laws and providing for right of way for railroads in the

District of Alaska, and for other purposes," shall not apply to mineral lands or town sites.

Rights of Indians and persons conducting schools or missions.

SEC. 27. The Indians or persons conducting schools or missions in the district shall not be disturbed in the possession of any lands now actually in their use or occupation, and the land, at any station not exceeding six hundred and forty acres, now occupied as missionary stations among the Indian tribes in the section, with the improvements thereon erected by or for such societies, shall be continued in the occupancy of the several religious societies to which the missionary stations respectively belong, and the Secretary of the Interior is hereby directed to have such lands surveyed in compact form as nearly as practicable and patents issued for the same to the several societies to which they belong; but nothing contained in this Act shall be construed to put in force in the district the general land laws of the United States.

Coal Lands.

ACT OF CONGRESS OF JUNE 6, 1900.—An Act to extend the coal-land laws to the district of Alaska.

Be it enacted, etc., That so much of the public-land laws of the United States are hereby extended to the district of Alaska as relate to coal lands, namely, sections twenty-three hundred and forty-seven to twenty-three hundred and fifty-two, inclusive, of the Revised Statutes.

LAND OFFICE REGULATIONS.—Under the coal-land law, sections 2347 to 2352, inclusive, of the Revised Statutes, and the regulations thereunder issued July 31, 1882, coal-land filings and entries must be *by legal subdivisions* as made by the regular United States survey.

Section 2401 of the Revised Statutes, as amended by act of August 20, 1894, is as follows:

Section 2401 (as amended by the act of August 20, 1894). When the settlers in any township not mineral or reserved by the Government, or persons and associations lawfully possessed of coal lands and otherwise qualified to make entry thereof, or when the owners or grantees of public lands of the United States, under any law thereof, desire a survey made of the same under the authority of the surveyor-general and shall file an application therefor in writing, and shall deposit in a proper United States depository to the credit of the United States a sum sufficient to pay for such survey, together with all expenditures incident thereto, without cost or claim for indemnity on the United States, it shall be lawful for the surveyor-general, under such instructions as may be given him by the Commissioner of the General Land Office, and in accordance with law, to survey such township or such public lands owned by said grantees of the Government, and make return therefor to the general and proper local land office: *Provided*, That no application shall be granted unless the township so proposed to be surveyed is within the range of the regular progress of the public surveys embraced by existing standard lines or bases for township and subdivisional surveys.

Under said section 2401 as amended, persons and associations lawfully possessed of coal claims upon unsurveyed lands, may have such claims surveyed, provided the township so proposed to be surveyed is within the range of the regular progress of the public surveys embraced by existing standard lines or bases for township and subdivisional surveys.

Although the system of public-land surveys was extended to the district of Alaska by a provision contained in the act of Congress approved March 3, 1899 (30 Stat., 1098), no township or subdivisional surveys have been made, nor have any standard lines or bases for township and subdivisional surveys been established within the district; therefore until the filing in your office of the official plat of survey of the township, no coal filing nor entry can be made.

ACT OF CONGRESS OF APRIL 28, 1904.—An Act to amend the law of June 6, 1900, concerning Alaska coal mines.

Be it enacted, etc., That any person or association of persons qualified to make entry under the coal-land laws of the United States, who shall have opened or improved a coal mine or coal mines on any of the unsurveyed public lands of the United States in the district of Alaska, may locate the lands upon which such mine or mines are situated, in rectangular tracts containing forty, eighty, or one hundred and sixty acres, with north and south boundary lines run according to the true meridian, by marking the four corners thereof with permanent monuments, so that the boundaries thereof may be readily and easily traced. And all such locators shall, within one year from the passage of this act, or within one year from making such location, file for record in the recording district, and with the register and receiver of the land district in which the lands are located or situated, a notice containing the name or names of the locator or locators, the date of the location, the description of the lands located, and a reference to such natural objects or permanent monuments as will readily identify the same.

SEC. 2. That such locator or locators, or their assigns, who are citizens of the United States, shall receive a patent to the lands located by presenting, at any time within three years from the date of such notice, to the register and receiver of the land district in which the lands so located are situated an application therefor, accompanied by a certified copy of a plat of survey and field notes thereof, made by a United States deputy surveyor or a United States mineral surveyor, duly approved by the surveyor-general for the district of Alaska, and a payment of the sum of ten dollars per acre for the lands applied for; but no such application shall be allowed until after the applicant has caused a notice of the presentation thereof, embracing a description of the lands, to have been published in a newspaper in the district of Alaska published nearest the location of the premises for a period of sixty days, and shall have caused copies of such notice, together with a certified copy of the official plat of survey, to have been kept posted in a conspicuous place upon the land applied for and in the land office for the district in which the lands are located for a like period, and until after he shall have furnished proof of such publication and posting, and such other proof as is required by the coal-land laws: *Provided*, That nothing herein contained shall be so construed as to authorize entries to be made or title to be acquired to the shore of any navigable waters within said district.

SEC. 3. That during such period of posting and publication, or within six months thereafter, any person or association of persons having or asserting any adverse interest or claim to the tract of land or any part thereof sought to be purchased shall file in the land office where such application is pending, under oath, an adverse claim, setting forth the nature and extent thereof, and such adverse claimant shall, within sixty days after the filing of such adverse claim, begin an action to quiet title in a court of competent jurisdiction within the district of Alaska, and thereafter no patent shall issue for such claim until the final adjudication of the rights of the parties, and such patent shall then be issued in conformity with the final decree of such court therein.

SEC. 4. That all the provisions of the coal-land laws of the United States not in conflict with the provisions of this act shall continue and be in full force in the district of Alaska.

Oil Mining Claims.

Act of Congress of February 12, 1903.—An Act Defining what shall constitute and providing for assessments on oil mining claims.

Be it enacted, etc.: That where oil lands are located under the provisions of title thirty-two, chapter six, Revised Statutes of the United States, as placer mining claims, the annual assessment labor upon such claims may be done upon any one of a group of claims lying contiguous and owned by the same person or corporration, not exceeding five claims in all : *Provided,* That said labor will tend to the development or to determine the oil-bearing character of such contiguous claims.

Mineral Deposits.

Public lands, outside the States of Michigan, Minnesota, Wisconsin, Missouri and Kansas, valuable for deposits of alum, asphaltum, borax, carbonate and nitrate of soda, fire-clay, gypsum, iron, kaolin, limestone, marble, mica, petroleum, salt, sulphur, and umber, diamonds and precious stones, onyx, cryolite, or any mineral that renders the land more valuable on its account than for agricultural purposes can, generally speaking, be located and patented under the mining laws as hereinbefore described. In view of the varying decisions of courts and the Land Department, it is suggested that the claimant of an unusual deposit should write a full statement of the facts to the Commissioner of the General Land Office and be guided by his advice.

If the deposit is a vein in an original rock in place, the proceeding will be that for lode claims, but where the deposit is in a secondary formation, as are all the deposits above named, the proceeding will be that for placer claims.

Deposits found in the United States in land belonging to private parties, unlike those in most European countries, belong to the owners of the land and can not be disturbed without the consent of such private owners. Deposits found on public lands in the five excepted States are bought in the same manner as adjoining agricultural lands. Land scrip is generally used to enter such deposits but it can not take mineral deposits elsewhere.—[NOTE BY EDITOR.]

PRACTICAL FORMS.

a. FORMS.

FORM 1.

✢ Notice of Location.

Notice is hereby given that the undersigned, having complied with the requirements of Chapter Six of Title Thirty-two of the Revised Statutes of the United States, and the local customs, laws and regulations, has located ——— linear feet on the ——— lode [twenty acres of placer mining ground], situated in ——— Mining District, ——— County, ———, and described as follows:

[*Describe the claim accurately (by courses and distances, if possible,) with reference to some natural object or permanent monument, and mark the boundaries by suitable monuments; if a placer claim is located on surveyed land, describe the legal subdivision.*]

Discovered ———, 188–.   ——— ———, Locator.
Located ———, 188–.   Recorded ———, 188–.
Attest:

———
———

NOTE.—Record of location notices, in absence of a District Recorder, should be made with the proper recorder of deeds for the county wherein the claim is situated. It is advisable to have these notices attested by witnesses, for locators cannot be too careful about their evidence.

In re-locations to increase width of surface ground under the local law, or to more particularly identify or describe the claim, use the above form, but state after the description that it is a re-location, and in addition, where the original location is recorded, in order that the title may revert back to the original discovery.

In locations of abandoned mines, the fact that it is such a location should be stated, and the affidavits of two or more respectable parties that such mine was abandoned and subject to re-location, should be recorded with the location notice.

Where the location is by agent, that fact should be stated after the name of the locator, thus: By Thomas Jones, agent (or attorney).

FORM 2.

✢ Proof of Labor

——— of ———, *County of* ———, ss.

Before me the subscriber personally appeared ———, who being duly sworn says that at least ——— dollars' worth of labor or improvements were performed or made upon [here describe claim], situated in ——— mining district, ——— county, ——— of ——— during the year ending ———, 188–. Such expenditure was made by or at the expense of ——— ———, owners of said claim, for the purpose of holding said claim.

[Jurat]   ——— ——— (Signature).

NOTE.—The record of an affidavit like the above is *prima facie* evidence of the performance of such labor.

FORM 3.

Notice of Forfeiture.

——— County, ——— ———, 188–.

To—(names of all parties who have record title to any portion of the mine). You are hereby notified that I have expended ——— dollars in labor and improvements upon the ——— lode (describe the claim), as will appear by certificate filed ———, 188-, in the office of the Recorder of said county (or district), in order to hold said premises under the provisions of section 2324 Revised Statutes of the United States, being the amount required to hold the same for the year ending ———, 188-. And if within ninety days from the service of this notice (or within ninety days after this notice by publication), you fail or refuse to contribute your proportion of such expenditure as a co-owner, your interest in said claim will become the property of the subscriber under said section 2324.

——— ——— (Signature).

NOTE.—At the expiration of 180 days, this notice should be recorded with the affidavit of the newspaper publisher (see Form 13) that the same was published for the period of ninety days, together with the affidavit (Form 4) of the party signing the notice to the effect that one or more of the co-owners named in the published notice have not paid their share of the expenditure. This completes the record title.

FORM 4.

Affidavit of Failure to Contribute.

——— of ———, County of ———, ss

——— ———, being duly sworn, deposes and says that for the year ending ———, 188-, he expended at least ——— dollars in labor and improvements upon the ——— lode [or ——— placer claim] (here describe the claim), to hold the same under the laws of the United States and of this ——— (district, Territory or State): that due notice thereof was personally served upon ——— ———, co-owners, on the ——— day of ———, 188-, (or was duly published in the ——— ———, as appears from the affidavit of the publisher thereof): and that ——— ——— (of the said) co-owners have failed or refused to contribute their share of said expenditures within the time required by law.

——— ———.

Subscribed and sworn to before me this ——— day of ———, 188-.

——— ———.

FORM 5.

Miner's Lien.

KNOW ALL MEN BY THESE PRESENTS, That I, ———, of the county of ———, ——— of ———, do hereby give notice of my intention to hold and claim a lien, by virtue of the statute in such case made and provided, upon ——— (describe premises), with all improvements and appurtenances, situated in ——— Mining District, County of ———, ——— of ———.

The said lien being claimed and held for and on account of *work and labor done by me as* ——— *for* ———, *owner of said premises* in and upon said premises, from the ——— day of ———, A. D. 188-, to the ——— day of ———, A. D. 188-.

The total value of the said work and labor being ——— dollars, upon which there has been paid the sum of ——— dollars, leaving a balance of ——— dollars still due, owing and unpaid to me, the said claimant.

——— ——— (Signature).

——— of ———, County of ———, ss.

On this ——— day of ———, A. D. 188-, personally appeared before me the above named ———, and who being by me first duly sworn, on ——— oath states that the abstract of indebtedness mentioned and described in the foregoing notice, is true and correct, and that there is still due and owing to ——— from the said ———, for the ——— aforesaid, the sum of ——— dollars and ——— cents.

——— ——— (Signature.)

Subscribed and sworn to before me this ——— day of ———, A. D. 188-.

(Official signature.)

NOTE.—For materials insert "goods furnished and delivered to owners of said premises, for use on said premises, and which were used on said premises." Below substitute "materials furnished, to wit: Powder, lumber, etc., as per bill annexed," in place of "work and labor."

FORMS. 51

FORM 6.
Application for Survey.

———— ————, 188–.

To ————, *United States Surveyor-General for* ————:

SIR—In compliance with the provisions of Chapter Six of Title Thirty-two, Revised Statutes of the United States, ———— herewith make application for an official survey of the mining claim known as the ———— mine, claimed by ————, located in ———— Mining District, in the County of ————, Township No. ————, Range No. ————, ———— base and meridian, in the ———— of ————, and ———— request that you will send to ———— address an estimate of the amount to be deposited, for the work to be done in your office; and that after such deposit shall have been made, you will cause the said mining claim to be surveyed by ————, United States Deputy Surveyor at ————.

Respectfully,

———— ————, Claimant.

P. O. Address, ————, ———— county, ————.

NOTE.—Survey is not required when placer-claims embrace legal subdivisions.

FORM 7.
Application for Patent.

————, *County of* ————, *ss*.

APPLICATION FOR PATENT FOR THE ———— ———— MINING CLAIM.

To the Register and Receiver of the U. S. Land Office at ————.

————, being duly sworn according to law, deposes and says, that in virtue of a compliance with the mining rules, regulations and customs, by himself, the said ————, and his co-claimants (residence of each should be stated), ————, applicants for patent herein ha— become the owner of and ———— in the actual, quiet and undisturbed possession of ———— linear feet of the ———— vein, lode or deposit, bearing ————, together with surface ground ———— feet in width, for the convenient working thereof, as allowed by local rules and customs of miners; said mineral claim, vein, lode or deposit and surface ground being situated in the ———— mining district, county of ————, and ———— of ————, and being more particularly set forth and described in the official field-notes of survey thereof, hereto attached, dated ———— day of ————, A. D. 188–, and in the official plat of said survey, now posted conspicuously upon said mining claim or premises, a copy of which is filed herewith. Deponent further states that the facts relative to the right of possession of himself (and his said co-claimants hereinbefore named) to said mining claim, vein, lode or deposit and surface ground, so surveyed and platted, are substantially as follows, to wit:

(*Trace the history of the lode fully.*)

Which will more fully appear by reference to the copy of the original record of location and the abstract of title hereto attached and made a part of this affidavit; the value of the labor done and improvements made upon said ———— claim, by himself and his grantors, being equal to the sum of five hundred dollars, and said improvements consist of (*describe fully*). In consideration of which facts, and in conformity with the provisions of Chapter Six of Title Thirty-two of the Revised Statutes of the United States, application is hereby made for and in behalf of said ———— for a patent from the Government of the United States for the said ———— mining claim, vein, lode, deposit, and the surface ground so officially surveyed and platted.

———— ————.

Subscribed and sworn to before me this ———— day of ————, A. D. 188–, and I hereby certify that I consider the above deponent a credible and reliable person, and that the foregoing affidavit, to which was attached the field-notes of survey of the ———— mining claim, was read and examined by him before his signature was affixed thereto and the oath made by him.

(*Official Signature.*)

NOTE.—The above is slightly changed in applying for placer mines.

FORM 8.

Proof of Posting Notice and Diagram on the Claim.

———— of ————, County of ————, ss.:

———— aud ————, each for himself, and not one for the other, being first duly sworn according to law, deposes and says, that he is a citizen of the United States, over the age of twenty-one years, and was present on the ———— day of ————, A. D 188-, when a plat representing the ————, and certified to as correct by the United States Surveyor-General of ————, and designated by him as lot No. ————, together with a notice of the intention of ———— and ———— to apply for a patent for the mining claim and premises so platted, was posted in a conspicuous place upon said mining claim, to wit: Upon ————, where the same could be easily seen and examined; the notice so conspicuously posted upon said claim being in words and figures as follows, to wit:

NOTICE OF THE APPLICATION OF ———— AND ———— FOR A UNITED STATES PATENT.

Notice is hereby given that in pursuance of Chapter Six of Title Thirty-two of the Revised Statutes of the United States, ———— and ————, claiming ———— linear feet of the ———— vein, lode or mineral deposit, bearing ————, with surface ground ———— feet in width, lying and being situated within the ———— mining district, county of ————, and ———— of ————, ha- made application to the United States for a patent for the said mining claim, which is more fully described as to metes and bounds by the official plat herewith posted and by the fie d-notes of survey thereof, now filed in the office of the Register of the District of Lands, subject to sale at ————, which field-notes of survey describe the boundaries and extent of said claim on the surface, with magnetic variation at ———— east, as follows, to wit:

(*Full description by courses and distances.*)

the said mining claim being of record in the office of the Recorder of ————, at ————, in the county and ———— aforesaid, the presumed general course of direction of the said ———— vein, lode or mineral deposit bei g shown upon the plat posted herewith, as near as can be determined from present developments; this claim being for ———— linear feet thereof, together with the surface ground shown upon the official plat posted herewith, the said vein, lode and mining premises hereby sought to be patented being bounded on the ———— by the ———— mining claim.

Any and all persons claiming adversely the mining ground, vein, lode, premises, or any portion thereof so described, surveyed, platted and applied for, are hereby notified that unless their adverse claims are duly filed as according to law and the regulations thereunder within sixty days from the date hereof, with the Register of the United States Land Office at ————, in the ———— of ————, they will be barred, in virtue of the provisions of said statute.

———— ———— (Names of applicants.)
Dated on the grounds this ———— day of ————, A. D. 188-.
Witness: (Names of witnesses.) ———— ————.
———— ————.

Subscribed and sworn to before me this ———— day of ————, A. D. 188-, and I hereby certify that I consider the above deponen s credible and reliable witnesses, and that the foregoing affidavit and notice were read by each of them before their signatures were affixed thereto and the o th made by them.

———— ————,

NOTE.—The notice to be posted on the claim with the plat is given in the above form.

FORM 9.

Proof that Plat and Notice Remained Posted on Claim During Period of Publication.

———— of ————, County of ————, ss.:

————, being first duly sworn according to law, deposes and says, that he is claimant (and co-owner with ————) in the ———— mining claim, ————

mining district, ―――― county, the official plat of which premises, designated by the Surveyor-General as lot No. ――――, together with the notice of intention to apply for a patent therefor, was posted thereon, on the ―――― day of ――――, A. D. 188–, as fully set forth and described in the affidavit of ―――― and ――――, dated the ―――― day of ――――, A. D. 188–, which affidavit was duly filed in the office of the Register at ―――― in this case; and that the plat and notice so mentioned and described, remained continuously and conspicuously posted upon said mining claim from the ―――― day of ――――, A. D. 188–, until and including the ―――― day of ―――― ――――. A. D. 188–, including the sixty days period during which notice of said application for patent was published in the newspaper.

[Jurat.]

―――― ――――.
(One of the applicants.)

FORM 10.

Register's Certificate of Posting Notice for Sixty Days.

United States Land Office, at ――――, ――――, 188–.

I hereby certify that the official plat of the ―――― lode designated by the Surveyor-General as lot No. ―――― was filed in this office on the ―――― day of ――――, A. D. 188–, and that the attached notice of the intention of ―――― to apply for a patent for the mining claim or premises embraced by said plat, and described in the field-notes of survey thereof filed in said application, was posted conspicuously in this office on the ―――― day of ――――, A. D. 188–, and remained so posted until the ―――― day of ――――, A. D. 188–, being the full period of sixty consecutive days during the period of publication as required by law; and that said plat remained in this office during that time, subject to examination, and that no adverse claim thereto has been filed.

―――― ――――, *Register*.

NOTE.—The notice posted in the office should be attached to this certificate; a copy of the notice published is the one usually posted in the Register's office.

FORM 11.

Notice for Publication in Newspaper.

Mining Application No.――.

United States Land Office, ―――― ――――, ――――, 188–.

Notice is hereby given that ――――, whose post office address is ――――, has this day filed his application for a patent for ―――― linear feet of the ―――― mine or vein bearing ――――, with surface ground ―――― feet in width, situated in ―――― mining district, county of ――――, and ―――― of ――――, and designated by the field-notes and official plat on file in this office as lot No. ――――, in township ――――, range ――――, of ―――― meridian, ――――. Said lot No. ―――― being described as follows, to wit: Beginning at, etc.

Magnetic variation ――――, containing ―――― acres.

The location of this mine is recorded in the Recorder's office of ――――, in book ―――― of ――――. The adjoining claimants are ――――.

Any and all persons claiming adversely any portion of said ―――― mine or surface ground are required to file their adverse claims with the Register of the United States Land Office at ――――, in the ―――― of ――――, during the sixty days period of publication hereof, or they will be barred by virtue of the provisions of the statute.

―――― ――――, *Register*.

FORM 12.

Agreement of Publisher.

The undersigned, publisher and proprietor of the ――――, a ―――― newspaper, published at ――――, county of ――――, and ―――― of ――――, does hereby agree to publish a notice, dated United States Land Office, ――――, required by Chapter Six of Title Thirty-two, Revised Statutes of the United States, of the intention of ―――― to apply for a patent for his claim on the

—— lode, situated in —— mining district, county of ——, of ——, and to hold the said —— alone responsible for the amount due for publishing the same. And it is hereby expressly stipulated and agreed that no claim shall be made against the Government of the United States, or its officers or agents, for such publication.

Witness my hand and seal this —— day of ——, A. D. 188–.
Witness:
——.
—— ——.

FORM 13.
Proof of Publication.

—— of ——, *County of* ——, *ss.*

Reprint copy of } ——, being first duly sworn, deposes and says,
Notice of Application. } that he is the —— of the ——, a newspaper published at ——, in —— county, in the —— of ——; that the notice of the application for a patent for the —— mining claim, of which a copy is hereto attached, was first published in said newspaper, in its issue dated the —— of ——, 188–. and was published in each [daily or weekly] issue of said newspaper for [sixty consecutive days, or nine consecutive weeks.] thereafter, the full period of sixty days, the last publication thereof being in the issue dated the —— of ——, 188–.

—— ——.

Subscribed and sworn to before me this —— day of ——, A. D. 188–.
[SEAL.] —— ——, *Notary Public.*

FORM 14.
Affidavit of Five Hundred Dollars Improvement.

—— of ——, *County of* ——, *ss.*

—— and ——, of lawful age, being first duly sworn according to law, depose and say that they are acquainted with the —— mining claim in —— mining district, county and —— aforesaid, for which —— has made application for patent under the provisions of Chapter Six of Title Thirty-two, Revised Statutes of the United States and that the labor done and improvements made thereon by the applicant and his grantors exceed five hundred dollars in value, and said improvements consist of (describe fully).

—— ——.

Subscribed and sworn to before me this —— day of ——, A. D. 188–.
—— ——.

FORM 15.
Statement of Fees and Charges

—— of ——, *County of* —— *ss.*

——, being first duly sworn according to law, deposes and says that he is the applicant for patent for the —— lode in —— mining district, county of ——, —— of ——, under the provisions of Chapter Six of Title Thirty-two of the Revised Statutes of the United States, and that in the prosecution of said application he has paid out the following amounts, and no more, viz.: To the credit of the Surveyor-General's office, —— dollars; for surveying, —— dollars; for filing in the local land office, —— dollars; for publication of notice, —— dollars; and for the land embraced in his claim, —— dollars.

—— ——.

Subscribed and sworn to before me this —— day of ——, A. D. 188–.
[SEAL.] —— ——, *Notary Public.*

FORM 16.
Proof of Ownership and Possession in Case of Loss or Absence of Mining Records.

—— of ——, *County of* ——, *ss.*

—— ——, and —— ——, each for himself, and not one for the other, being first duly sworn according to law, deposes and says that he is a citizen of the United States, over the age of twenty-one years, and a resident of —— county, ——, and has resided in —— mining district, wherein the —— mine is situated, since —— day of ——, 18—. That since said date he has been acquainted with the —— mine, and with the possessors and workers thereof. That said mine was located and has been possessed and worked in accordance with the customs and usages of miners in said district, and in conformity with the rules and regulations governing the location, holding and working of mining claims, in force and observed in the (State) of ——. That there are no written records known to deponent existing in said mining district. That affiant is credibly informed and believes that the —— mine was located in the year 18—, and that if any record was made of said location, and of the names of locators, the same has not been in existence for a long number of years past, and that by reason thereof the names of locators cannot now be ascertained, and no abstract of title from locators to the present owner can be made. That the possession of applicant and his predecessors in interest of said —— mine has been actual, notorious and continuous, to the positive knowledge of deponent, since his residence in said mining district, and that such possession has been perfected and maintained in conformity with mining usages and customs, and has been acquiesced in and respected by the miners of said district. That applicant's right to the said —— mine is not in litigation within the knowledge of affiant, and that no action or actions have been commenced affecting the right to said mine since his acquaintance therewith (and that the time for the commencement thereof, as required to be instituted under the provisions of the Statute of Limitations of the —— of ——, has long since elapsed). That applicant and his predecessors in interest have expended in the improvement, development, and working of said mine a sum of money exceeding —— dollars, as follows, to wit :——

—— ——.
—— ——.
—— ——.

Subscribed and sworn to before me this —— day of ——, A. D. 188-, and I certify that the aforenamed —— and —— are credible and respectable persons, to whose affidavits full faith and credit should be given.
[SEAL.]   —— ——.

NOTE.—This should be sworn to by at least two respectable persons.

FORM 17.

Affidavit of Citizenship.

—— of ——, County of ——, ss.

——, being first duly sworn according to law, deposes and says, that he is the applicant for patent for —— mining claim, situated in —— mining district, county of —— ; that he is a native born citizen of the United States, born in ——, county of ——, State of ——, in the year 18—, and is now a resident of ——.

—— ——.

Subscribed and sworn to before me this —— day of ——, A. D. 188-.

—— ——.

NOTE.—If the applicant is a naturalized citizen, or has declared his intention to become a citizen, he should show in his affidavit where, when and before what court he was naturalized or his declaration was made.

FORM 18.

Certificate that No Suit is Pending.

—— of ——, County of ——, ss.

I, ——, clerk of the court in and for —— county, ——, do hereby certify that there is now no suit or action of any character pending in said court involving the right of possession to any portion of —— mining claim, and that there has been no litigation before said court affecting the title to said claim, or any part thereof, for ——— years last past, other than what has been finally decided in favor of ———.

In witness whereof, I have hereunto set my hand and affixed the seal of said court, at my office in ———, this ——— day of ———, A. D. 188–.

[SEAL.] ——— ———, Clerk of the ——— Court, ———.

FORM 19.

Power of Attorney to Apply for Patent.

KNOW ALL MEN BY THESE PRESENTS, that we, ——— and ———, do hereby constitute and appoint ——— as our attorney in fact, for us and in our names, to make application to the United States for the entry and purchase of certain Government lands, in ——— mining district, ——— county, ——— of ———, known as the ——— mining claim and premises; and to have the same surveyed, and to take any and all steps that may be necessary to procure from the Government of the United States a patent to the said lands and premises, granting the same to us. And to do all other acts appertaining to the said survey and entry aforesaid as we ourselves could do by our own act and in our own proper person.

In witness whereof we have hereunto set our hands and affixed our seals the ——— day of ———, A. D. 188–.

——— ———.
——— ———.

——— of ———, County of ———, ss.

On this ——— day of ———, A. D. 188–, before me, ———, a Notary Public in and for the ———, county of ———, personally appeared ———, known to me to be the same person whose name ——— subscribed to the foregoing instrument, and acknowledged to me that ——— executed the same.

In witness whereof I have hereunto set my hand and affixed my official seal at my office, the day and year in this certificate first above written.

[SEAL.] ——— Notary Public.

FORM 20.

Proof that No Known Vein Exists in a Placer Mining Claim.

——— of ———, County of ———, ss.

——— and ———, of the said county and ———, being first duly sworn, each for himself, deposes and says, that he is well acquainted with the ——— placer mining claim, embracing ——— ———, situated in the ——— mining district, in the county of ———, and ——— of ———, owned and worked by ———, applicant for United States patent; that for many years he has resided near, and often been upon the said mining premises, and that no known vein or veins of quartz or other rock in place, bearing gold, silver, cinnabar, lead, tin or copper, exist on said mining claim, or on any part thereof, so far as he knows, and he verily believes that none exist thereon. And further, that he has no interest whatever in the said placer mine of ———.

———.
———.

Subscribed and sworn to before me this ——— day of ———, A. D., 188–.

NOTE.—In case any known mines exist within the exterior boundaries of the placer claim, the names of such known veins should be given.

FORM 21.

Protest and Adverse Claim.

United States Land Office, ——— of ———.

In the matter of the application of ———, for a United States patent for the ——— lode or mining claim and the land and premises appertaining to said mine, situated in the ——— mining district, in ——— county, ——— of ———.

To the Register and Receiver of the United States Land Office at ———, and to the above-named applicants for patent for the ——— lode.

You are hereby notified that ——— of the city of ———, county of ———, and ——— of ———, and a citizen of the United States of America, is the lawful owner, and entitled to the possession of ——— hundred feet of the said ——— lode or mine described in said application, as shown by the diagram posted on said claim, and the copy thereof filed in the land office with said application, and as such owner this contestant, the said ———, does protest against the issuing of a patent thereon to said applicant, and does dispute and contest the right of said applicant therefor.

And this contestant does present the nature of his adverse claim, and does fully set forth the same in the affidavit hereto attached, marked Exhibit A, and the further exhibits thereto attached, and made part of said affidavit.

The said ——— therefore respectfully asks the said Register and Receiver that all further proceedings in the matter be stayed, until a final settlement and adjudication of the rights of this contestant can be had in a court of competent jurisdiction.

(Place and Date.) ——— ———.

EXHIBIT A.

——— of ——— County of ———, ss.

———, being first duly sworn, deposes and says, that he is a citizen of the United States, born in the State of ———, and is now residing in ———; that he is the contestant and protestant named in, and who subscribed the notice and protest hereto annexed. Affiant further says that he is the owner by purchase and in the possession of the (adverse) lode or vein of quartz and other rock in place, bearing ——— and other metals. That the said lode is situated in the ——— mining district, ——— county, ——— of ———.

[*The history of the lode should be given in full; for instance, as follows:*]

This affiant further says, that on the day of location the premises hereinafter described were mineral lands of the public domain, and entirely vacant and unoccupied, and were not owned, held, or claimed by any person or persons as mining ground or otherwise, and that while the same were so vacant and unoccupied, and unclaimed, to wit:

On the ——— ——— day of ———, 18—, (name locators,) each and all of them being citizens of the United States, entered upon and explored the premises, discovered and located the said ——— ——— lode, and occupied the same as mining claims. That the said premises so located and appropriated consist of ——— ——— feet in a ——— erly direction, and ——— ——— ——— feet in a ———erly direction, as will fully appear by reference to the notice of location, a duly certified copy whereof is hereunto annexed, marked Exhibit B, and hereby made a part of this affidavit. That the locators, after the discovery of the said ——— lode, drove a stake on said lode on the discovery claim, erected a monument of stone around said stake, and placed thereon a written notice of location describing the claim so located and appropriated, giving the names of the locators and quantity taken by each, and after doing all the acts and performing all the labor required by the laws and regulations of said ——— mining district and territory of ———, the locators of said lode caused said notice to be filed and recorded in the proper books of record in the Recorder's office in said district on the ——— day of ———, 18—.

Affiant further says, that the said locators remained continuously in possession of said lode, working upon the same, and within ——— months from the date of said location had done and performed work and labor on said location in mining thereon and developing the same, more than ——— days work, and expended on said location more than ——— hundred dollars, and by said labor and money expended upon the said mining location and claim, had developed the same and extracted therefrom more than ——— tons of ore.

And affiant further says, that said locators, in all respects, complied with every custom, rule, regulation and requirement of the mining laws, and every rule and custom established and in force in said —————— mining district, and thereby became and were owners (except as against the paramount title of the United States) and the rightful possessors of said mining claims and premises.

And this affiant further says, that said locators proved and established to the satisfaction of the Recorder of said —————— mining district that they had fully complied with all the rules, customs, regulations, and requirements of the laws of said district, and thereupon the said Recorder issued to the locators of said —————— lode, certificates confirming their titles and rights to said premises.

That the said lode was located and worked by the said locators as tenants in common, and they so continued in the rightful and undisputed possession thereof from the time of said location until on or about the —————— day of ——————, A. D. 18—, at which time the said locators and owners of said lode formed and organized under the laws of the State (or Territory) of ——————, and incorporated under the name of the "——————," and on the —————— day of ——————, A. D. 18—, each of the locators of said lode conveyed said lode and each of their rights, titles, and interest in and to said lode, to said "—————— mining company."

On the said —————— day of ——————, 18—, the said company entered into and upon said —————— lode, and was seized and possessed thereof and every part and parcel of the same, and occupied and mined thereon until the —————— day of ——————, 18—, at which time the said —————— mining company sold and conveyed the same to this affiant, which said several transfers and conveyances will fully appear, by reference to the abstract of title and paper hereto attached, marked Exhibit D, and made a part of this affidavit.

[*In case of individual transfers.*]

And this affiant further says, that the said ——————, who located claim —————— northwesterly of the said —————— lode, and the said —————— who located claim —————— northwesterly thereon, was seized and in possession of said claims, and occupied and mined thereon until the —————— day of ——————, 18—, at which time the said —————— and —————— sold and conveyed the same to ——————, and thereupon the said —————— was seized and possessed of said mining claims and locations, and occupied and mined thereon until the —————— day of ——————, 18—, at which time the said —————— sold and conveyed the same to this affiant, as will fully appear by reference to the abstract of title and paper hereto attached, marked Exhibit D, and which this affiant hereby makes a part of this his affidavit.

Affiant further says, that he is now and has been in the occupation and possession of the said —————— lode since the —————— day of ——————, 18—, and that said lode and mining claims were located, and the title thereto established, several —————— before said (applied for) —————— lode was located.

Affiant further says, that said —————— lode, as shown by the notice and diagram posted on said claim, and the copy thereof filed in the United States Land Office at said —————— with said application for a patent, crosses and overlaps said —————— lode, and embraces about —————— hundred feet in length by —————— hundred feet in width of the said —————— lode, the property of this affiant, as fully appears by reference to the diagram or map duly certified by ——————, United States Deputy Surveyor, hereto attached, marked Exhibit C, and which diagram presents a correct description of the relative locations of the said (adverse) lode, and of the pretended (applied for) lode.

Affiant further says, that he is informed and believes that said applicant for patent well knew that affiant was the owner in possession and entitled to the possession of so much of said mining ground embraced within the survey and diagram of said applications, as is hereinbefore stated, and that this affiant is entitled to all the —————— and other metal in said (adverse) lode, and all that may be contained within a space of —————— feet on each side of said (adverse) lode.

And affiant further says, that this protest is made in entire good faith, and with the sole object of protecting the legal rights and property of this affiant in the said (adverse) lode and mining premises.

Subscribed and sworn to before me this ——— day of ———, A. D. 188–.

SURVEYOR'S CERTIFICATE.

On the diagram marked Exhibit C, the Surveyor must certify in effect, as fol'ows:

I hereby certify that the above diagram correctly represents the conflict claimed to exist between the ——— and ——— lodes, as actually surveyed by me. And I further certify, that the value of the labor and improvements on the (adverse) lode, exceeds five hundred dollars, and said improvements consist of (state in full).

(Place and date.)

——— ———, *U. S. Deputy Surveyor.*

FORM 22*.

Tunnel Claim—Location Certificate.

Know all men by these presents, that the undersigned, citizens of the United States, have this ——— day of ———, 188–, claimed by right of location, a tunnel claim, for the purpose of discovering and working veins, lodes or deposits on the line thereof [cutting the ——— lode, and working the ——— lode]. Said tunnel claim is situated in the ——— mining district, county of ———, State of ———, and the location and bounds of said tunnel are staked on the surface at the place of commencement and termination thereof, as well as along the line thereof. Said claim is more particularly described as follows: [*Describe the commencement and termination by reference to natural objects and permanent monuments, and the line by courses and distances.*]

Dated ———, 188–.

——— ———,
Locator.

FORM 23.

Power of Attorney to Locate and Sell.

Know all men by these presents, that we, the undersigned [*names*], ———, citizens of the United States, have made, constituted and appointed A. B. [*some third person, who will locate and stake*], our true and lawful attorney for us, and in our names to locate, stake and record for us each lode claims and placer mining ground in the ———, ——— county, ——— of ———, and having located the same, to bargain, sell, grant, release and convey the same, entire or in separate parcels, to make proper deeds, seal, acknowledge and deliver the same to such persons as our attorney may desire; hereby ratifying and confirming all lawful acts done by our said attorney by virtue hereof.

Witness our hands and seals, this ——— day of ———, 18—.

[*Names.*]

——— *of* ———, *County of* ———, *ss.*

On this ——— day of ———, 18—, before me ——— — in and for the county and State aforesaid, appeared ——— personally known to me as the persons whose names are subscribed to the foregoing power of attorney, and acknowledged the execution thereof as their free act and deed, for the purposes therein mentioned.

Given under my hand and ——— seal the day and year above written.

——— ———.

---

* Forms 22, 23, 24, 25, 26, 27, and 28, a e from Carpenter's Mining Code, slightly modified.

FORM 24.

Notice of Right to Water.

The undersigned claims the water running in this ——— stream to the extent of ——— inches for mining purposes, to be conveyed by (ditch or flume) from this point to the ——— placer claim.

Dated ———, 18—.

——— ———,
Locator.

NOTE.—This notice is to be posted near the outlet, and the following form is to be duly recorded in the district or county Recorder's office.

FORM 25.

Pre-emption of Right of Way for Ditch and Location of Water.

To whom these presents may concern, know ye, that I, ———, of the county of ———, in the State of ———, a citizen of the United States, do hereby declare and publish as a legal notice to all the world, that I claim, and have a valid right to the occupation, possession and enjoyment of all and singular, that tract or parcel of land lying and being in the county of ———, in the State of ———, for the exclusive right of way for the purpose of constructing a flume or water ditch from ——— stream to ——— placer claim, more particularly described as follows: Commencing [*here describe the exact route for ditch or flume.*]

I also claim, and have a valid right to the enjoyment and use of ——— inches of water from said stream for mining purposes, to be conveyed through such flume or water ditch to said claim, together with all and singular, the hereditaments and appurtenances thereunto belonging, or in any wise appertaining.

Witness my hand and seal this ——— day of ———, A. D. 18—.

——— ———.
[*Name.*]

Notice posted on the stream ———, 18—.
Ditch commenced at claim or at stream ———, 18—.

——— of ——— County of ———, ss.

On this ——— day of ———, 18—, before me, a ——— in and for the county aforesaid, in the State aforesaid, personally appeared ———, to me personally known to be the person who executed the foregoing written instrument, and acknowledged that he executed the same for the uses and purposes therein set forth.

Witness my hand and official seal. ——— ———.

FORM 26.

Mining Deed.

THIS INDENTURE, made the ——— day of ———, in the year of our Lord one thousand eight hundred and eighty, between ——— ———, of the county of ———, and ——— of ———, party of the first, and ——— ———, of the county of ———, and ——— of ———, party of the second part;

Witnesseth, That the said party of the first part, for and in consideration of the sum of ——— dollars, lawful money of the United States of America, to him in hand paid by the said party of the second part, the receipt whereof is hereby acknowledged, hath granted, bargained, sold, remised, released, and forever quit-claimed, and by these presents does grant, bargain, sell, remise, release, and forever quit-claim, unto the said party of the second part, his heirs and assigns, the ——— lode, as located, surveyed, recorded, and held by said party of the first part, situated in ——— mining district, ———· county, ———, together with all the dips, spurs, and angles, and also all the metals, ores, gold and silver-bearing quartz, rock and earth therein, and all the rights, privileges, and franchises thereto incident, appendant and appurtenant, or therewith usually had and enjoyed; and also, all and singular the tenements, hereditaments and appurtenances thereunto belonging, or in any wise appertaining, and the rents, issues, and profits thereof; and also, all the estate, right, title, interest, property, possession, claim and demand whatsoever, as well in law as in equity, of the said party of the first part, of, in or to the said premises, and every part and parcel thereof, with the appurtenances.

To have and to hold, all and singular, the said premises, together with the appurtenances and privileges thereto incident, unto the said party of the second part, his heirs and assigns forever. In witness whereof the said party of the first part has hereunto set his hand and seal the day and year first above written.

[SEAL] —————— ——————.

—————— of ——————, —————— *County, ss.*

I, Richard Roe, a Notary Public in and for said county, in the State aforesaid, do hereby certify that —————— ——————, personally known to me to be the person whose name is subscribed to the annexed deed, appeared before me this day in person, and acknowledged that he signed, sealed and delivered the said instrument of writing as his free and voluntary act, for the uses and purposes therein set forth.

Given under my hand and official seal, this —————— day of ——————, A. D. 188—.

[SEAL] RICHARD ROE, *Notary Public.*

FORM 27.

Title Bond to Mining Property.

Know all men by these presents, that I, John W. Newton, party of the first part, of the county of Lake, and State of Colorado, am held and firmly bound unto William H. Hunt, party of the second part, of the county of Lake, and State of Colorado, in the penal sum of ten thousand dollars, lawful money of the United States, to the payment of which the party of the first part hereby binds himself, his heirs, executors, and administrators. Witness his hand and seal this 20th day of July, 1880. The conditions of the foregoing obligations are such, that whereas, the above bounden party of the first part, in consideration of the sum of five dollars, in hand paid, has, on the day and year aforesaid, agreed to sell to the party of the second part the following described mining property, viz: An undivided one-eighth interest in and to the Gilt Edge lode claim, as located, surveyed, recorded, and held, situate, lying and being in California Mining District, Lake county, Colorado, together with all and singular, the improvements, hereditaments, and appurtenances thereto belonging, or in any wise appertaining, for the sum of five thousand dollars, to be paid at the times and in the manner following, viz: One thousand dollars on or before August 20, 1880; one thousand dollars on or before September 20, 1880; and three thousand dollars on or before October 20, 1880; which sums of money are to be paid to the party of the first part, in person, or by depositing the same to his credit at the Vermont National Bank of St. Albans, at the times aforesaid, and time shall be of the essence of these conditions. And in case of failure of the party of the second part, or his assigns, to make either of said payments at the times mentioned, such sum or sums as may have been paid hereunder, shall be forfeited to and retained by the party of the first part, as a penalty, and for liquidated damages, and notice of forfeiture is hereby expressly waived, and also all right, demand or claim for the balance or any of said sum of five thousand dollars, is hereby expressly waived by the party of the first part. The party of the first part, his heirs, executors, administrators, and assigns, shall on the 20th day of October, 1880, or at any time before, upon payment of said sums of money hereinbefore mentioned, make, execute, and deliver to the party of the second part, or to such person or persons as he shall designate, good and sufficient deed or deeds of all of the above described property, conveying a clear and perfect title (except the fee-simple title of the United States), free from all incumbrances, with a covenant, that the annual expenditure has been made thereon as required by law. Now, if the party of the second part shall fail to pay the sum or sums of money as hereinbefore provided, and if the party of the first part shall faithfully perform the covenants herein set forth, then this obligation shall be null and void; otherwise, to be and remain in full force and effect.

[SEAL.]   JOHN W. NEWTON.

State of Colorado, Lake County, ss.

Be it known, That on this 20th day of July, 1880, before me, personally came John W. Newton, to me known as the person described in, and who executed the foregoing instrument in writing, and acknowledged the execution thereof to be his free act and deed, for the uses and purposes therein mentioned.

Witness my hand and official seal.

[SEAL.]   ALEX. G. WATSON, *Notary Public.*

FORM 28.

Escrow Agreement.

The inclosed deed of the ———— lode is hereby placed in the ———— Bank of ————, *in escrow*. If A. B. shall place, or cause to be placed to the credit of C. D. and E. F., in said ———— bank of ————, on or before ————, 188–, the full sum of ———— dollars, then and in that case the said bank is hereby authorized to deliver the inclosed deed to A. B., or his order. In case the said A. B. shall not place, or cause to be placed, to the credit of said C. D. and E. F., in said bank, the full sum of ———— dollars, on or before ————, 188–, then the said bank is hereby authorized to deliver the inclosed deed to the said C. D. and E. F., or their joint order.

(Signed)   C. D.
E. F.
A. B.

———— ———— ————, 188–, (Place and date).

NOTE.—When the option for the purchase of a mine is desired by a third party, it is the safest and best plan for the mine owner to put a deed *in escrow*. It saves incumbering of the record, and any questions that might arise concerning the payment of money. The deed should be a warranty, quit-claim, or mining deed, as agreed, fully executed and acknowledged, ready for delivery, put in a sealed envelope, and placed in some bank, or left with some responsible person, with an agreement written upon the envelope, as above.

FORM 29.

Mining Lease.*

THIS INDENTURE, made this ———— day of ————, in the year of our Lord one thousand eight hundred and eighty ————, between ———— lessor and ———— lessee or tenant; *Witnesseth*, That the said lessor for and in consideration of the rents, royalties, covenants and agreements hereinafter reserved, and by the said lessee to be paid, kept and performed, ———— granted, demised and let, and by these presents do grant, demise and let unto the said lessee, all the following described mine and mining property, situated in ———— mining district, county of ————, ———— of ————, to wit: (Here description of property.) Together with the appurtenances ———— to have and to hold unto the said lessee or tenant for the term of ———— from the date hereof, expiring at noon on the ———— day of ————, A. D. 188–, unless sooner forfeited or determined through the violation of any covenant hereinafter against the said tenant ———— reserved.

And in consideration of the said demise, the said lessee does covenant and agree with said lessor as follows, to wit:

To enter upon said mine or premises and work the same mine fashion, in manner necessary to good and economical mining, so as to take out the greatest amount of ore possible, with due regard to the safety, development and preservation of the said premises as a workable mine.

(Here insert special covenants for dead work, etc.)

NOTE.—The covenants of a mining lease are peculiar, and cannot be too particularly stated in the instrument. If for more than one year, it should be in writing, and recorded.

Instead of a lease a license may be granted. The distinctions between a lease and a license are technical, but important.

A license, usually, is not exclusive, and invests no property in the mineral until severed. Work done for lessees cannot subject the ground to a miner's lien.

---

* From Morrison's Mining Rights in Colorado.

To work and mine said premises as aforesaid steadily and continuously from the date of this lease : and that any failure to work said premises with at least ——— persons employed underground for the space of ——— consecutive days may be considered a violation of this covenant.

To well and sufficiently timber said mine at all points where proper, in accordance with good mining ; and to repair all old timbering wherever it may become necessary.

To allow said lessor and ——— agents to enter upon and into all parts of said mine for the purpose of inspection, with use of all passages, ropes, windlass, ladder-ways, and all other means of ingress and egress for such purpose.

To not assign this lease, or any interest thereunder, and to not sublet the said premises or any part thereof, without the written assent of said lessor, and to not allow any person or persons except the said lessee and ——— workmen to take or hold possession of said premises or any part thereof under any pretense whatever.

To occupy and hold all cross or parallel lodes, dips, spurs, feeders, crevices or mineral deposits of any kind, which may be discovered in working under this lease, or in any tunnel run to intersect said ——— lode, or by the said lessee or any person or persons under ———, in any manner at any point within ——— feet of the centre line of said lode, as the property of said lessor ; with privilege to said lessee of working the same as an appurtenance of said demised premises, during the term of this lease ; and to not locate or record the same, or allow the same to be located or recorded, except in the name of said lessor.

To keep at all times the drifts, shafts, tunnels, and other passages and workings of said demised premises thoroughly drained and clear of loose rock and rubbish of all kinds.

To pay and deliver to said lessor as royalty, ——— of all ore to be extracted from said premises during said term, of like assay to that retained by said lessee, delivered at ——— as soon as mined, without offset, deduction, or charge whatever, except lessor's proportion for packing

To deliver up to said lessor the said premises, with the appurtenances and all improvements ——— in good order and condition, with all shafts and tunnels and other passages thoroughly clear of rubbish and drained, and the mine in all points ready for immediate continued working (accidents not arising from negligence alone excusing), without demand or further notice, on said ——— day of ———, A. D. 188-, at noon or at any time previous, upon demand for forfeiture.

And finally, upon the violation by said lessee, or any person under ———, of any covenant or covenants hereinbefore reserved, the term of this lease shall, at the option of said lessor, expire, and the same and said premises with the appurtenances shall become forfeit to said lessor : and said lessor or ——— agent may thereupon, after demand of possession in writing, enter upon said premises and dispossess all persons occupying the same, with or without force, and with or without process of law ; or at the option of said lessor, the said tenant and all persons found in occupation may be proceeded against as trespassers from the beginning of said term both as to realty and the ore served therefrom ; or as guilty of unlawful detainer.

Each and every clause and covenant of this indenture shall extend to the heirs, executors, and administrators of all parties hereto ; and to the assigns of said lessor : and as said lessor may elect, to the assigns of said lessee.

In witness whereof, The said parties, lessor and lessee, have hereunto set their hands and seals.

——— ———.   ——— ———. [SEAL.]
——— ———.   ——— ———. [SEAL.]

IMPORTANT SUGGESTION TO SETTLERS.

In view of the numerous changes in the land service, it is more than probable that the newly appointed officials, while actuated by the best of motives, will make some erroneous rulings. The land system is so complicated that even experienced officials make mistakes occasionally. One of these erroneous rulings may deprive a settler of land that will, in a few years, be worth thousands of dollars. Hence the importance of submitting the question involved to some disinterested land law specialist.

In writing state all the facts; especially give dates. Where the inquiry does not involve the examination of records an opinion will be given without charge. Enclose postage stamps in letters of inquiry.

Address, **HENRY N. COPP, Washington, D. C.**

LAND SCRIP BOUGHT AND SOLD.

Scrip that will Take Unoffered Surveyed Land.

SOLDIERS' ADDITIONAL HOMESTEAD RIGHTS. These Rights are given to Officers, Soldiers, Sailors and Marines (and their heirs) who served honorably for ninety days or more during the Civil war and who made homestead entries prior to June 22, 1874, of less than 16 acres. Thus a soldier homesteaded 135 acres in 1871. He would be entitled to an additional homestead privilege or right of entry for 25 acres (160-135). Rights for 2 and 3 acres and upwards are to be had, but the majority are for 40, 80 and 120 acres. The selling price is now about $6.00 an acre. Certified Soldiers' Rights sell at $20.00 to $30.00 an acre.

This Scrip will take unsurveyed land in Alaska.

This Scrip will take any surveyed unoffered single and double minimum public land which is subject to homestead entry. A Right between 20 and 40 acres will take 40 acres by paying for the difference in cash; the same is true of Rights between 60 and 80 acres, 100 and 120 acres. Certificates for less than 20 acres will take any fractional lot not to exceed double the area named in the Right.

PORTERFIELD SCRIP.—This Scrip is issued in 40-acre pieces under the Act of Congress of April 11, 1860, for the relief of the legal representatives of Robert Porterfield. It is locatable upon surveyed, unoffered, minimum land. Its peculiar features are that according to decisions of the land department it can take land within the limits of an incorporated town or city, and also improved land not otherwise legally appropriated; consequently the price is very high, about $100 an acre. It is assignable, and patent issues in name of the assignee.

PRIVATE ACT SCRIPS.—There are several Scrips on the market under private Acts of Congress, varying in quantity from 40 to 640 acres, which sell for $25.00 to $100.00 an acre.

Scrip that will Take Unsurveyed Land.

VALENTINE SCRIP.—This Scrip was issued under the Act of Congress of April 5, 1872, and the Decrees of Court thereunder, to Thomas B. Valentine. It takes unoccupied, unappropriated, surveyed or unsurveyed, offered or unoffered public land open for settlement. It is in 40-acre pieces and assignable. It is now quoted at $35.00 an acre.

SIOUX HALF-BREED SCRIP.—This Scrip comes in 40, 80 and 160-acre pieces, and is equal in value to Valentine Scrip, except in the matter of transfer of title. Two powers of attorney are necessary, and there is required, in addition, satisfactory evidence of improvements on the land, placed there by the Indian or his agent.

In locating any of the above Scrip, no settlement or residence is required, and there is no limit to the quantity one person may use. The Right attaches at once on filing the Scrip, and transfers of title for Town Sites or other purposes may be made without delay.

Mineral lands, as such, in the mining regions West of the Mississippi, cannot be entered with any of the above Scrip, except in those States where mineral lands may be entered under the laws for the disposal of agricultural lands. Descriptive circular sent free on request.

Address, **HENRY N. COPP, Washington, D. C.**

STATE AND TERRITORIAL MINING LAWS.

ARIZONA.

Chapter XLVII.—Mines and Mining.

3231 (Sec. 1). **Location.**—On the discovery of mineral in place on the public domain of the United States, the same may be located as a mining claim by the discoverer for himself, or for himself and others or for others.

3232 (Sec. 2). **Location—Contents of Location Notice.**—Such location shall be made by erecting at or contiguous to the point of discovery a conspicuous monument of stones not less than three feet in height, or an upright post, securely fixed, projecting at least four feet above the ground, in which monument of stones or on which post there shall be posted a location notice, which shall be signed by the name or names of the locator or locators. The location notice must contain:

1. The name of the claim located.
2. The name or names of the locators.
3. The date of the location.
4. The length and width of the claim in feet, and the distance in feet from the point of discovery to each end of the claim.
5. The general course of the claim.
6. The locality of the claim with reference to some natural object or permanent monument whereby the claim can be identified.

3233 (Sec. 3). **Acquisition of Right.**—Until each and all of the above specified things shall have been done, no right thereto shall have been acquired.

3234 (Sec. 4). **Ninety Days.**—From the time of the location of a mining claim, as above specified, the locator shall be allowed ninety days within which to do or cause to be done the following things:

1. To cause to be recorded in the office of the county recorder of the county in which the claim is situated a copy of the location notice.
2. To sink a discovery shaft in the claim to a depth of at least ten feet from the lowest part of the rim of the shaft at the surface, and deeper, if necessary, until there is disclosed in said shaft mineral in place.
3. To monument the claim on the ground so that its boundaries can be readily traced.

3235 (Sec. 5). **Abandonment.**—The failure to do all things enumerated in this section in the time and place specified shall be construed into an abandonment of the claim, and all right and claim thereto of the discoverer and locator shall be forfeited.

3236 (Sec. 6). **Boundaries—How Marked.**—Such surface boundaries shall be marked by six substantial posts projecting at least four feet above the surface of the ground, or by substantial stone monuments at least three feet high, to wit: One at each corner of said claim and one at the center of each end line thereof.

3237 (Sec. 7). **Discovery Work.**—Any open cut, adit or tunnel which shall be made as above provided for, as a part of the location of a lode mining claim, and which shall be equal in amount of work to a shaft ten feet deep and four feet wide by six feet long, and which shall cut a lode or mineral in place at a depth of ten feet from the surface, shall be equivalent, as a discovery work, to a shaft sunk from the surface.

3238 (Sec. 8). **Amendments.**—Location notices may be amended at any time and the monuments changed to correspond with the amended location: *Provided*, That no change shall be made that will interfere with the rights of others.

3239 (Sec. 9). **Annual Work.**—The amount of assessment or representation work or improvements to be done or made during each year, after the completion of the location, as heretofore provided, and the time for doing the same, shall be as provided by the laws of the United States.

3240 (Sec. 10). **Affidavit of Annual Labor.**—Within three months after the expiration of the period of time fixed for the performance of annual labor or the making of improvements upon any mining claim, the person on whose behalf such work or improvement was made, or some person for him knowing the facts, may make and record in the office of the county recorder of the county wherein such claim is situated an affidavit in substance as follows:

Territory of Arizona, }
    County of ———, } *ss.:*

——— ———, being duly sworn, deposes and says that he is a citizen of the United States and more than twenty-one years of age, resides at ———, in ——— County, Arizona Territory, and is personally acquainted with the mining claim known as ——— mining claim, situated in ——— mining district, Arizona Territory, the location notice of which is recorded in the office of the county recorder of said county, in book ——— of records of mines at page ———; that between the ——— day of ———, A. D. ———, and the ——— day of ——— A. D. ———, at least ——— dollars' worth of work and improvements were done and performed upon said claim, not including the location work of said claim. Such work and improvements were made by and at the expense of ———, owners of said claim, for the purpose of complying with the laws of the United States pertaining to assessments of annual work, and (here name the miners or men who worked upon the claim in doing the work) were the men employed by said owner, and who labored upon said claim, did said work and improvements, the same being as follows, to wit:

(Here describe the work done.)

(Signature.) ———— ————.

Subscribed and sworn to before me this —— day of —— A. D. ——.

My commission as Notary Public expires on the —— day of —— A. D. ——.

(NOTARIAL SEAL.) ———— ————, Notary Public.

3241 (SEC. 11). **Proof of Annual Labor—Relocation.**—Such affidavit, when so recorded, shall be *prima facie* evidence of the performance of such labor or the making of such improvements, and said original affidavit, after it has been recorded, or a certified copy of record of same, or the record of same shall be received as evidence accordingly by the courts of this Territory. The relocation of forfeited or abandoned lode claims shall only be made by sinking a new discovery shaft and fixing the boundary in the same manner and to the same extent as is required in making an original location, or the relocator may sink the original discovery shaft ten feet deeper than it was at the date of the commencement of such location, and shall erect new or make the old monuments the same as originally required. In either case a new location monument shall be erected, and the location notice shall state if the whole or any part of the new location is located as abandoned property, else it shall be void.

3242 (SEC. 12). **Placer Claims.**—The locator of a placer mining claim shall locate his claim in the following manner: By posting a location notice thereon containing the name of the claim, the name of the locator or locators, the date of the location and the number of acres claimed, a description of the claim with reference to some natural object or permanent monument that will identify the claim by marking the boundaries of his claim with a post or monument of stones at each angle of the claim located. When a post is used it must be at least four inches by four feet six inches in length, set one foot in the ground and surrounded by a mound of stone or earth.

3243 (SEC. 13). **Witness Posts.**—Where it is practically impossible on account of a bed of rock or precipitous ground to sink such posts, they may be placed in a pile of stones. And if for any reason it is impossible to erect and maintain a post or monument of stone at any angle of such claim, a witness post or monument may be used, said witness monument to be placed as near the true corner as the nature of the ground will permit. When a mound of stone is used it must be at least three feet in height and four feet in diameter at the base.

3244 (SEC. 14). **Sixty Days.**—The locator of any placer claim shall, within sixty days after the date of location of such claim, have a copy of the location notice claim recorded in the office of the county recorder of the county in which said claim may be situated. Any record of the location of a placer mining claim which shall not contain all the requirements of this section shall be void.

3245 (SEC. 15). **Delinquent Co-owners.**—Whenever a co-owner or co-owners shall give to a delinquent co-owner or co-owners the notice in writing or notice by publication provided for in section twenty-three hundred and twenty-four (2324) of the Revised Statutes of the United States, an affidavit of the person giving such notice, stating the time, place, manner of service, and by whom and upon whom such service was made, shall be attached to a true copy of such notice, and such notice an affidavit must be recorded in the office of the county recorder of the county in which the mining claim is situate within ninety (90) days after giving the notice, or if such notice is given by publication in a newspaper there shall be attached to a printed copy of such notice an affidavit of the editor, publisher or foreman of such paper, stating the date of the first, last and each insertion of such notice therein and when and where the newspaper was published during that time and the name of such newspaper. Such affidavit and notice shall be recorded as aforesaid within one hundred and eighty days after the first publication thereof.

3246 (SEC. 16). **Evidence of Refusal to Contribute.**—The original of such notice and affidavits, or the records thereof, shall be evidence that the delinquent mentioned in section 2324 has failed or refused to contribute his proportion of the expenditure required by that section, and of the services or publication of said notice: *Provided*, The writing or affidavit hereinafter provided for is not of record.

3247 (SEC. 17). **Contribution by Delinquent.**—If such delinquent shall, within the ninety days required by section 2324 aforesaid, contribute to his co-owner or co-owners his proportion of such expenditures, such co-owner or co-owners shall sign and deliver to the delinquent or delinquents, a writing, stating that the delinquent or delinquents, by name, has, within the time required by section 2324 of the Revised Statutes of the United States, contributed his share for the year ―――― upon the ―――― mine, and further stating therein the districts, county and Territory wherein the same is situate, and the book and page where the location notice is recorded. Such writing shall be recorded in the office of the county recorder of said county.

3248 (SEC. 18). **Evidence of Contribution.**—If such co-owner or co-owners shall fail to sign and deliver such writing to the delinquent or delinquents within twenty days after such contribution, the co-owner or co-owners, so failing as aforesaid, shall be liable to a penalty of one hundred dollars, to be recovered by any person for the use of the delinquent or delinquents in any court of competent jurisdiction. If such co-owner or co-owners fail to deliver such writing within twenty days, then the delinquent, with two disinterested persons having personal knowledge of said contribution, may make an affidavit, setting forth in what manner, the amount of, to whom and upon what mine such contribution was made. Such affidavit, or a record thereof, in the office of the county recorder of the county in which said mine is situate, shall be *prima facie* evidence of such contribution.

3249 (SEC. 19). **Description of Claim.**—In all actions, judgments, grants or conveyances it shall be a sufficient description of a mining claim if it can be intelligently learned therefrom the name of the claim, the district, county and territory where it is situate, and the book and page where the location notice thereof is recorded.

3250 (SEC. 20). **County Records.**—The county recorders of the several counties are authorized and required to procure suitable books in which the records of all mines and mineral deposits shall be kept, which said books shall be paid for out of the county treasury.

3251 (SEC. 21). **Prior Locations.**—Nothing in this act shall be so construed as to affect the claims to mines and mineral deposits heretofore located and duly recorded.

3252 (SEC. 22). **Drainage.**—Whenever adjacent or contiguous mines occupied and worked upon the same or upon separate lodes have a common ingress of water, or by reason of subterranean c mmunication of water have a common drainage, it shall be the duty of the owners, lessees or occupants of said mines so related to provide for their proportionate share of such drainage, or to prevent the water in such mine from flowing in or upon neighboring mines, thereby imposing upon them an unjust burden.

3253 (SEC. 23). **Failure to Drain.**—If any owners, lessees or occupants of any such mine shall fail or neglect to provide for the drainage thereof, and by reason of such failure or neglect, the owners, lessees or occupants of any adjacent or contiguous mine are compelled to pump or drain or otherwise provide for the water flowing in from such first mentioned mine, then, and in such event the owners, lessees or occupants of the mine so in default, shall pay, respectively, to those performing the work of drainage their proportion of the actual and necessary cost and expense of pumping, draining or otherwise providing for said water, and if they fail or refuse to make such payment, the same may be recovered by an action in any court of competent jurisdiction.

3254 (SEC. 24). **Common Interest in Draining.**—It shall be lawful for all mining corporations or companies and all individuals engaged in mining having thus a common interest in draining such mines to unite for the purpose of effecting the same under such common name and upon such terms and conditions as may be agreed upon ; and every such association having filed a certificate of incorporation, as provided by law, shall be deemed a corporation, with all the rights, incidents and liabilities of **a body corporate** as far as the same may be applicable.

3255 (Sec. 25). **Failure of Mutual Agreement.**—Failing mutually to agree as indicated in the preceding section for drainage jointly, one or more of said parties may undertake the work of drainage after giving reasonable notice to the other parties interested as aforesaid, and should the remaining parties then fail, neglect or refuse to unite in equitable arrangements for doing or sharing the expense thereof, they shall be subject to an action therefor as already specified, to be enforced in any court of competent jurisdiction.

3256 (Sec. 26). **Inspection of Mines Drained.**—When an action is commenced, as provided herein, to recover the costs and expenses for draining a lode or mine, it shall be lawful for the plaintiff to apply to court or to the judge thereof in vacation, for an order to inspect and examine the lodes or mines claimed to have been drained by the plaintiff, and upon affidavit that such inspection or examination is necessary for a proper preparation of the case for trial, the court or judge shall grant an order for the underground inspection and examination of the lode or mine described in the petition. Such order shall designate the number of persons, not exceeding three, besides the plaintiff or his representative, who may examine and inspect such lode and mines, and take measurements for the purpose of showing the amount of water taken from the lode or mine, or the number of fathoms of ground mined and worked out of the lode or mines claimed to have been drained, the cost of such examination and inspection to be borne by the party applying therefor. The court or judge shall have power to cause the removal of any rock, debris or any other obstacle in any lode or vein when such removal is shown to be necessary to a just determination of the question involved: Provided, that no such order for inspection and examination shall be made except upon notice of at least three days, nor unless it appears that the plaintiff has been refused the privilege of making the examination by the defendant his or their agent.

3257 (Sec. 27). **Undeveloped Mines.**—The provisions hereof shall not apply to unopened or undeveloped mines, but shall apply to all open and developed mines which derive a benefit from being drained.

Assays at University and Recording Notices.

3258 (Sec. 28). **Charge for Assays.**—The Regents of the University of Arizona shall charge for assaying ores taken from deposits and mines within the Territory of Arizona no higher rate than one dollar for each assay producing gold and silver, and two dollars and fifty cents for assaying ores showing more than three metals; that the maximum rate for an assay shall be two dollars and fifty cents and the minimum rate for an assay shall be one dollar.

3259 (Sec. 29). **Fee of County Recorder.**—There shall be a uniform fee of one dollar charged by each county recorder in the

Territory of Arizona for recording each notice of location of a mining claim, including certificate of work done to comply with the law regarding locations, the said one dollar to be in full for filing, recording and indexing said notice and certificate and certifying to the same under seal.

From the Revised Statutes of 1901.

Water and Water Rights.

141 (SEC. 1). That paragraph 3741 [of Revised Code] be amended so as to read as follows:

Appropriation of Water.—Any person or persons, company or corporation shall have the right to appropriate any of the unappropriated waters or the surplus or flood waters in this territory for beneficial use for irrigation, mining, or manufacturing purposes, subject to existing rights, and such person or persons, company or corporation for the purpose of making such appropriation of waters as herein specified shall have the right to construct and maintain reservoirs, dams, canals, ditches, flumes, and any and all other necessary water ways. And the person or persons, company or corporation, first appropriating water for the purposes herein mentioned shall always have the better right to the same.

142 (SEC. 2). That paragraph 3743 be amended so as to read as follows:

Contract to Deliver.—All corporations, associations or individuals, owning, managing or controlling any canals, irrigating ditches, flumes, pipe lines or other means for conveying water from any public stream in this territory, on or to the lands of occupants, for the purpose of irrigating said lands, shall not contract to deliver for such purpose more water than the said canals, ditches, flumes, or pipe lines may be estimated to carry at any one time, whether such contract be made for measured time or acreage quantity.

143 (SEC. 3). That paragraph 3744 be amended to read as follows:

Ditches in Order—Damages.—Such persons, associations or corporations, as provided for in the preceding section shall at all times keep their ditches, canals, flumes or pipe lines in good repair and condition, so as to carry the full amount of water that such persons, association or corporation have contracted to carry and deliver to the persons contracted with, during the time specified in such contract, and a failure to deliver the quantity of water contracted for, when there be sufficent in the stream or head, shall make such persons, corporations or associations liable for all damages that may arise or be sustained by the parties entitled to water from said carriers,

144 (SEC. 4). That paragraph 3774 be amended so as to read as follows:

Natural Channels.—Whenever storage reservoirs shall be constructed in the Territory of Arizona, and water stored therein for subsequent distribution for irrigation or other beneficial use in times of shortage of water, the owners of such reservoirs, or of the right to the use of the waters stored therein, shall have the right to make use of the natural channels of streams in this territory to conduct said waters to the place or places where they shall desire to use said waters, or have them used, and to divert the same from said natural channels at such places as shall be most convenient for said purposes.

Approved March 21, 1901, Session Laws of 1901, page 1483.

Water Storage Reservoirs.

105 (SECTION 1). **County Reservoir—Board of Water Storage Commissioners.**—Any county in the Territory of Arizona having an assessed valuation of eight million dollars or over, may avail itself of the benefits of this Act by complying with the provisions as hereinafter provided. The board of supervisors, upon the petition of fifty qualified electors and freeholders of said county, shall request the district judge (of the district) in which the county is located to appoint a board of water storage commissioners, and the judge shall within ten days thereafter appoint five qualified electors, who shall be resident freeholders of said county, who shall be known and designated as the board of water storage commissioners. Each of said commissioners shall hold office for one year and until his successor is appointed and qualified. Before entering upon the duties of his office he shall give bond in the sum of one thousand dollars payable to the said county for the faithful performance of his duty. Said bond shall be approved by and filed with the board of supervisors of said county. At its first meeting the board shall organize by the election of one of its members as president. It shall also elect a secretary, who may or may not be of its members. The compensation for the members of said board shall be five dollars per day for each day actually employed. They shall also be allowed their actual traveling expenses. The salary of the secretary shall be fixed by the board. The board shall establish and maintain an office at the county seat of said county. It shall be the duty of said water storage commissioners to examine reservoir sites, cause to be made surveys and soundings, determine the capacity and estimate the cost of construction of said proposed reservoir or reservoirs, dam or dams, determine the extent of the water shed and rainfall thereon; to collect such other information as shall show the water available for storage use in said county for irrigating purposes; to provide for the accumulation of such other information as may be required therefor and cause abstracts therefrom to be published in some newspaper published and of general circulation in said county; to employ and fix the compensation of a competent engineer or engineers, to prepare plans, specifications and estimates for said reservoirs and dams, and file a copy of the same with the clerk of the

board of supervisors of said county; to employ and fix the compensation of legal counsel in any matters arising under this act or necessary to authorize the construction of the dam or reservoirs referred to in said act, and to select the most available reservoir site or sites; and to acquire the same, together with any rights of way necessary over public or private property, by purchase or through eminent domain, in the name of said county of Mari Copa, and for the benefit of the people of said county, and to negotiate with and obtain agreements from canal companies in relation to the distribution of water or its delivery to the point of ultimate use, and to co-operate with or contribute towards the expenses of any investigations now being or hereafter to be made by the United States geological survey and to transfer to the National Government any reservoir site or rights therein or thereto or connected therewith, which may have been acquired hereunder in the event that the National Government should undertake the construction of the reservoir.

106 (SEC. 2). **Tax to Defray Expenses—Water Storage Fund.**—For the purpose of defraying the expenses of the board of water storage commissioners, the board of supervisors of any county availing itself of this act, shall, at the time of levying territorial and county taxes, in the year 1901 and in the year 1902, levy an additional tax of one and one-half mills on the dollar on all taxable property within the said county, to be collected as other taxes are collected, and the same shall be denominated and known as a water storage fund. The board of water storage commissioners shall audit and approve all bills for expenses incurred under the provisions of this act, and present the same, together with the claims for their salaries and expenses to the board of supervisors, who shall, if found correct, pay the same out of any money in the water storage fund.

Approved March 20, 1901. Session Laws of 1901, page 1474.

Former Laws.

3221 (SEC. 23). **Fines and Forfeitures.**—All fines and forfeitures, recovered for the use and benefit of any public acequia, shall be applied by the overseers to the improvements, excavations and repairs, which may be necessary on said acequia, and for the construction of bridges where they may be crossed by any public street or road.

3122 (SEC. 24). **Appeal.**—In all cases of conviction under this chapter, an appeal shall be allowed to the probate court, which appeal shall be taken and conducted as all other appeals from the decisions of the justices of the peace.

3223 (SEC. 25). **When Law Enforced.**—The regulations of acequias, which have been worked according to the laws and customs of Sonora and the usages of the people of Arizona, shall remain as they were made and used up to this day, and the provisions of this chapter shall be enforced and observed from the day of its publication.

3224 (SEC. 26). **Plants and Trees.**—All plants and trees of any description growing on the banks of any acequia shall belong to the owners of the land through which said acequia may run.

3225 (SEC. 27). **Spring or Running Stream.**—Any person owning lands which may include a spring or stream of running water, or owning lands upon a river where there is not population sufficient to form a public acequia, may construct a private acequia for his own uses, subject to his own regulations, provided it does not interfere with the rights of others.

3226 (SEC. 28). **Repeal.**—All laws conflicting with the provisions of this chapter are hereby repealed.

Approved, March 10, 1887.

The foregoing chapter is from the Compiled Laws, Chapter LV., p. 538.

An Act Relating to Mines and Mining Claims.

SECTION 1. Any person or persons, who has or may hereafter locate a valid mining claim in this Territory under the laws of the United States, or of the Territory of Arizona, shall be lawfully entitled to the right of way over all adjoining or adjacent mines or mining claims for the purpose of transporting supplies, material or ores, used upon or taken from the claim or claims so entitled to the right of way; and it shall be lawful in the exercise of this right of way to construct such a road, tramway or railway, as may be necessary to transport such supplies, materials or ores; *provided*, that no such right of way shall be exercised in such a manner as to inconvenience or embarrass the owner or owners of such adjoining or adjacent claim or claims; and *provided*, also, that the owner or owners of said adjoining or adjacent claim or claims shall be entitled to remuneration from the person or persons claiming such right of way; the amount of such remuneration, and the manner of ascertaining the same, to be regulated by the rules and regulations as prescribed by an act of the Territorial Legislature, entitled " an act providing for constructing and maintaining toll roads, bridges and ferries in Arizona Territory." Approved February 18, 1871.

Approved March 12, 1881. Session Laws of 1881, p. 167.

An Act to Protect Landmarks.

SECTION 1. That if any person or persons shall wilfully and maliciously deface, remove, pull down, injure or destroy any location stake, side post, corner post, landmark or monument, or any other legal land boundary monument in this Territory, designating or intending to designate the location, boundary or name of any mining claim, lode or vein of mineral, or the name of the discoverer, or date of discovery thereof, the person or persons so offending shall be guilty of a misdemeanor, and on conviction thereof, shall be fined not more than one thousand dollars or imprisoned not more than one year, at the discretion of the court; *provided*, that this act shall not apply to abandoned property.

Approved February 21, 1883. Session Laws of 1883, p. 31.

An Act to Encourage Mining.

SECTION 1. That no lands taken up or held as mining claims under the laws of the United States shall be held or used for agricultural purposes, or irrigated from any stream of water, unless there should be more water in such stream than is required or used for mining purposes; and the use of water for the purpose of irrigating such land for agricultural purposes shall not vest in the person so using the same any right to such water, as against a subsequent appropriation for mining purposes.

Approved March 12, 1881. Session Laws of 1881, p. 162.

An Act Relating to Co-Owners in Mines and Mining Claims.

SECTION 1. **Notice.**—Whenever a co-owner or co-owners shall give to a delinquent co-owner or co-owners the notice in writing or notice by publication provided for in Section 2324 of the Revised Statutes of the United States, an affidavit of the person giving such notice, stating the time, place, manner of service, and by whom and upon whom such service was made, shall be attached to a true copy of such notice, and such notice and affidavit must be recorded in the office of the county recorder of the county in which the mining claim is situate; within ninety (90) days after the giving of such notice, or, if such notice is given by publication in a newspaper, there shall be attached to a printed copy of such notice an affidavit of the editor, publisher or foreman of such paper, an affidavit stating the date of the first, last, and each insertion of such notice therein, and when and where the newspaper was published during that time, and the name of such newspaper. Such affidavit and notice shall be recorded as aforesaid within one hundred and eighty days after the first publication thereof.

SECTION 2. **Evidence.**—The original of such notice and affidavits or the records thereof shall be evidence that the delinquent mentioned in said Section 2324 has failed or refused to contribute his proportion of the expenditure required by that Section, and of the services or publication of said notice, *provided* the writing or affidavit hereinafter provided for is not of record.

SECTION 3. **Payment.**—If such delinquent shall, within the ninety days required by Section 2324 aforesaid, contribute to his co-owner or co-owners his proportion of such expenditures, such co-owner or co-owners shall sign and deliver to the delinquent or delinquents a writing, stating that the delinquent or delinquents by name has within the time required by Section 2324 of the

Revised Statutes of the United States contributed his share for the year ——, upon the —— mine, and further stating therein the district, county and Territory where the same is situate and the book and page where the location notice is recorded; such writing shall be recorded in the office of the County Recorder of said county.

SECTION 4. **Penalty.**—If such co-owner or co-owners shall fail to sign and deliver such writing to the delinquent or delinquents within twenty days after such contribution, the co-owner or co-owners so failing as aforesaid shall be liable to a penalty of one hundred dollars, to be recovered by any person for the use of the delinquent or delinquents in any court of competent jurisdiction. If such co-owner or co-owners fail to deliver such writing within said twenty days, then the delinquent, with two disinterested persons having personal knowledge of such contribution, may make affidavit, setting forth in what manner, the amount of, to whom and upon what mine, such contribution was made. Such affidavit, or a record thereof in the office of the County Recorder of the county in which said mine is situate, shall be *prima facie* evidence of such contribution.

SECTION 5. **Description.**—In all actions, proceedings, judgments, grants, notices, conveyances or writings, it shall be a sufficient description of a mining claim if it can be intelligently learned therefrom the name of the claim, the district, county and Territory where same is situate, and the book and page where the notice thereof is recorded.

[Usual repeal provision and took effect immediately.]

Approved March 19, 1891. Session Laws, 1891, p. 140.

For Taxation Purposes.

SECTION 83. **Land Office Entries.**—The County Clerk of each county shall from time to time and as often at least as once in each year procure from the land office a list of all lands and mineral claims within his county which have been entered in the land office and shall keep a list thereof in his office which shall be a public record. Session Laws, 1902, p. 83.

Approved March 22, 1902.

CALIFORNIA.

Water Rights.

1410. The right to the use of running water flowing in a river or stream, or down a cañon or ravine may be acquired by appropriation.

1411. The appropriation must be for some useful or beneficial purpose, and when the appropriator or his successor in interest ceases to use it for such a purpose, the right ceases.

1412. The person entitled to the use may change the place of diversion, if others are not injured by such change, and may extend the ditch, flume, pipe, or aqueduct by which the diversion is made, to places beyond that where the first use was made.

1413. The water appropriated may be turned into the channel of another stream and mingled with its water, and then reclaimed; but in reclaiming it the water already appropriated by another must not be diminished.

1414. As between appropriators, the one first in time is the first in right.

1415. A person desiring to appropriate water must post a notice, in writing, in a conspicuous place at the point of intended diversion, stating therein:

1. That he claims the water there flowing to the extent of (giving the number) inches, measured under a four-inch pressure;
2. The purposes for which he claims it, and the place of intended use;
3. The means by which he intends to divert it, and the size of the flume, ditch, pipe, or aqueduct in which he intends to divert it.

A copy of the notice must, within ten days after it is posted, be recorded in the office of the Recorder of the county in which it is posted.

1416. Within sixty days after the notice is posted, the claimant must commence the excavation or construction of the works in which he intends to divert the water, and must prosecute the work diligently and uninterruptedly to completion, unless temporarily interrupted by snow or rain.

1417. By "completion" is meant conducting the waters to the place of intended use.

1418. By a compliance with the above rules, the claimant's right to the use of the water relates back to the time the notice was posted.

1419. A failure to comply with such rules deprives the claimant of the right to the use of the water as against a subsequent claimant who complies therewith.

1420. Persons who have heretofore claimed the right to water, and who have not constructed works in which to divert it, and who have not diverted nor appl ed it to some useful purpose, must, after this title takes effect, and within twenty days thereafter, proceed as in this title provided, or their right ceases. Civil Code, Annotated, Title viii., p. 402.

[The above law expresses the usual manner of securing water rights in the mining States and Territories.]

An Act entitled an Act relating to the working, right of way, easement, and drainage of mines in the State of California.

SECTION 1.—**Affidavit of Expenditure.**—Whenever any mine owner, company, or corporation shall have performed the labor and made the improvements required by law for the location and ownership of mining claims or lodes, such owner, company or corporation shall file, or cause to be filed, within thirty days after the time limited for performing such labor or making such improvements, with the County Recorder of Deeds of the county in which the mine or c aim is situated, particularly describing the labor performed and improvements made, and the value thereof, which affidavit shall be *prima facie* evidence of the facts therein stated. Upon the failure of any claimant or mine owner to comply with the conditions of this Act, in the performance of labor, or making of improvements upon any claim, mine or mining ground, the claim or mine upon which such failure occurred shall be opened to re-location in the same manner as if no location of the same had ever been made. But if, previous to re-location, the original locators, their heirs, assigns, or legal representatives, resume work upon such claim, and continue the same with reasonable diligence until the required amount of labor has been performed or improvements made, and the required statement of accounts and affidavit filed with the County Recorder, then the claim shall not be subject to re-location because of previous failure to file accounts. Upon the failure of any one of the several co-owners to contribute his portion of the expenditures required hereby, the co-owners who have performed the labor or made the improvements may, at the expiration of the year, give such delinquent co-owners personal notice, in writing, or by publication in the newspaper published nearest the claim, for at least once a week for ninety days ; and if, at the expiration of ninety days after such notice in writing or publication, such delinquent shall fail or refuse to contribute his portion of the expenditures required by this section, his interest in the claim shall become the property of his co-owners who made the required expenditures. A copy of such notice, together with an affidavit showing personal service or publication, as the case may be, of such notice, when filed or recorded with the Recorder of Deeds of the county in which such mining claim is situated, shall be evidence of the acquisition of title of such co-owners. Where a person or company has or may run a tunnel or cut for the purpose and in good faith for the purpose of developing a lode, lodes, or claims owned by said person, or company, or corporation, the money so expended in running said tunnel shall be taken and considered as expended on said lodes or claims; *provided further*, that said lode, claim or claims shall be distinctly marked on the surface as provided by law.

SEC. 2. **Right of Way.**—All mining locations and mining claims shall be subject to a reservation of the right of way through or over any mining claims, ditches, roads, canals, cuts, tunnels, and other easements, for the purpose of working other mines; *provided*, that any damage occasioned thereby shall be assessed and paid for in the manner provided by law for land taken for public use under the right of eminent domain.

Approved March 31, 1891. Session Laws of 1891, p. 219.

An Act to provide for the Conveyance of Mining Claims.

SECTION 1.—**Bill of Sale—Fraud—Possession.**—Conveyances of mining claims may be evidenced by bills of sale or instruments in writing not under seal, signed by the person from whom the estate or interest is intended to pass, in the presence of one or more attesting witnesses; and also all conveyances of mining claims heretofore made by bills of sale or instruments in writing, not under seal, shall have the same force and effect as *prima facie* evidence of sale, as if such conveyances had been made by deed under seal; *provided*, that nothing in this act shall be construed to interfere with or repeal any lawful local rules, regulations, or customs of the mines in the several mining districts of this State; and, *provided further*, every such bill of sale or instrument in writing shall be deemed and held to be fraudulent and void as against all persons except the parties thereto, unless such bill of sale or instrument in writing be accompanied by an immediate delivery to the purchaser of the possession of the mining claim or claims therein described, and be followed by an actual and continued change of the possession thereof, or unless such bill of sale or instrument in writing shall be acknowledged and recorded as required by law in the case of conveyances of real estate.

SEC. 2. **Gold Claims.**—This act shall apply to gold mining claims only.

Approved April 13, 1860. Session Laws of 1860, p. 175.

SECTION 748 (§ 621). **Local Customs.**—In actions respecting mining claims, proof must be admitted of the customs, usages, or regulations established and in force at the bar or diggings embracing such claim; and such customs, usages, or regulations, when not in conflict with the laws of this State, must govern the decision of the action.

Code of Civil Procedure (Annotated), 1872, p. 667.

SECTION 2515. **Partnership Property.**—The mining ground owned and worked by partners in mining, whether purchased with partnership funds or not, is partnership property.

Civil Code (Annotated), 1872, p. 125.

For statutes relating to sale of deceased persons' estates, which consist in whole or in part of mines or interests in mines, see Code of Civil Procedure, 1872, Secs. 1529, amended in 1880.

Mines within Patented Townsites.

SECTION 1. **Amendment.**—Section fifteen of an Act entitled "An act to authorize and direct the county judges of the several counties of this State to execute certain trusts in relation to the town lands granted to the unincorporated towns in this State by the Act of Congress entitled 'An Act for the relief of the inhabitants of cities and towns upon the public lands,' approved March second, eighteen hundred and sixty-seven," approved March thirtieth, eighteen hundred and sixty-eight, is hereby amended so as to read as follows:

SEC. 15. **Proceeding to Secure Title.**—If within six months after the giving of the public notice that the plat of any townsite has been filed in the Recorder's office, as provided in section twelve of this Act, there shall remain any unoccupied or vacant unclaimed lands, or lands not previously surveyed into town lots under the provisions of this Act, and any person has hitherto or shall hereafter discover gold in any portion thereof in quantities which he may deem sufficient to justify the profitable working thereof (his judgment thereon to be conclusive), and has located and held the same *bona fide* for mining purposes, such mining possession shall constitute him a preferred purchaser thereof, from the Judge of the Superior Court, according to the metes and bounds of his location thereof, within the meaning of this Act; and he may apply to the Judge of the Superior Court for a deed thereto, which application he shall accompany with a deposit to be held by such judge in an amount to be estimated by him sufficient to pay the expenses of a survey and the platting thereof as herein provided for. * * *

Approved March 9, 1897. Session Laws, 1897, p. 93.

Judgments, Records and Work Done.

SECTION 1. **Amendment.**—Section eleven hundred and fifty-nine of an Act entitled an Act to establish a Civil Code, approved March twenty-first, eighteen hundred and seventy-two, is hereby amended to read as follows:

1159. Judgments affecting the title to or possession of real property, authenticated by the certificate of the clerk of the court in which such judgments were rendered (and notices of location of mining claims), may be recorded without acknowledgment, certificate of acknowledgment, or further proof. The record of all notices of location of mining claims heretofore made in the proper office without acknowledgment or certificate of acknowledgment, or other proof, shall have the same force and effect for all purposes as if the same had been duly acknowledged, or proved and certified as required by law. Affidavits showing work or posting of notices upon mining claims may also be recorded in the recorder's office of the county where such mining claims are situated.

Approved March 9, 1897. Session Laws, 1897, p. 97.

COLORADO.

An Act Concerning Mines.

SECTION 1.—**Length.**—The length of any lode claim hereafter located may equal but not exceed fifteen hundred feet along the vein.

SEC. 2.—**Width.**—The width of lode claims hereafter located in Gilpin, Clear Creek, Boulder, and Summit counties shall be seventy-five feet on each side of the center of the vein or crevice; and in all other counties the width of the same shall be one hundred and fifty feet on each side of the center of the vein or crevice: *Provided,* That hereafter any county may, at any general election, determine upon a greater width, not exceeding three hundred feet on each side of the center of the vein or lode, by a majority of the legal votes cast at said election, and any county, by such vote at such election, may determine upon a less width than above specified.

SEC. 3.—**Location Certificate.**—The discoverer of a lode shall, within three months from the date of discovery, record his claim in the office of the recorder of the county in which such lode is situated, by a location certificate, which shall contain: 1st, the name of the lode; 2d, the name of the locator; 3d, the date of location; 4th, the number of feet in length claimed on each side of the center of the discovery shaft; 5th, the general course of the lode as near as may be.

SEC. 4. Any location certificate of a lode claim which shall not contain the name of the lode, the name of the locator, the date of location, the number of lineal feet claimed on each side of the discovery shaft, the general course of the lode, and such description as shall identify the claim with reasonable certainty, shall be void.

SEC. 5.—**Discovery Shaft and Staking.**—Before filing such location certificate, the discoverer shall locate his claim by first sinking a discovery shaft upon the lode, to the depth of at least ten feet from the lowest part of the rim of such shaft at the surface, or deeper, if necessary, to show a well-defined crevice. *Second,* by posting at the point of discovery on the surface a plain sign or notice containing the name of the lode, the name of the locator, and the date of discovery. *Third,* by marking the surface boundaries of the claim.

SEC. 6. Such surface boundaries shall be marked by six substantial posts, hewed or marked on the side or sides which are in toward the claim, and sunk in the ground, to wit: One at each corner and one at the center of each side line. Where it is practically impossible on account of bed-rock or precipitous ground to sink such posts, they may be placed in a pile of stones.

SEC 7.—**Equivalent to a Discovery Shaft.**—Any open cut, cross-cut, or tunnel, which shall cut a lode at the depth of ten feet below the surface, shall hold such lode the same as if a discovery shaft were sunk thereon, or an adit of at least ten feet in along the lode, from the point where the lode may be in any manner discovered, shall be equivalent to a discovery shaft.

SEC. 8.—**Sixty Days.**—The discoverer shall have sixty days from the time of uncovering or disclosing a lode to sink a discovery shaft thereon.

SEC. 9.—**Claim Defined by the Surface Lines.**—The location, or location certificate, of any lode claim shall be construed to include all surface ground within the surface lines thereof, and all lodes and ledges throughout their entire depth, the top or apex of which lies inside of such lines extended downward, vertically, with such par's of all lodes or ledges as continue to dip beyond the side lines of the claim, but shall not include any portion of such lodes or ledges beyond the end lines of the claim or the end lines continued, whether by dip or otherwise, or beyond the side lines in any other manner than by the dip of the lode.

SEC. 10. If the top or apex of a lode in its longitudinal course extends beyond the exterior lines of the claim at any point on the surface, or as extended vertically downward, such lode may not be followed in its longitudinal course beyond the point where it is intersected by the exterior lines.

SEC. 11.—**Right of Way and Right of Surface.**—All mining claims now located, or which may be hereafter located, shall be subject to the right of way of any ditch or flume for mining purposes, or of any tramway or pack trail, whether now in use, or which may be hereafter laid out across any such location. *Provided, always*, That such right of way shall not be exercised against any location duly made and recorded, and not abandoned prior to the establishment of the ditch, flume, tramway, or pack trail, without consent of the owner, except by condemnation, as in case of land taken for public highways. Parol consent to the location of any such easement, accompanied by the completion of the same over the claim, shall be sufficient without writings. *And provided further*, That such ditch or flume shall be so constructed that the water from such ditch or flume shall not injure vested rights by flooding or otherwise.

SEC. 12. When the right to mine is in any case separate from the ownership or right of occupancy to the surface, the owner or rightful occupant of the surface may demand satisfactory security from the miner, and if it be refused, may enjoin such miner from working until such security is given. The order for injunction shall fix the amount of bond.

SEC. 13.—**Re-location by the Owner.**—If at any time the locator of any mining claim heretofore or hereafter located, or his assigns, shall apprehend that his original certificate was defective, erroneous, or that the requirements of the law had not been complied with before filing; or shall be desirous of changing his surface boundaries, or of taking in any part of an overlapping claim which has been abandoned; or in case the original certificate was made prior to the passage of this law, and he shall be desirous of securing the benefits of this Act, such locator or his assigns may file an additional certificate, subject to the provisions of this Act. *Provided*, That such re-location does not interfere with the existing rights of others at the time of such re-location, and no such re-location or the record thereof shall preclude the claimant or claimants from proving any such title or titles as he or they may have held under previous location.

SEC. 14.—**Labor.**—The amount of work done, or improvements made during each year, shall be that prescribed by the laws of the United States.

SEC. 15.—**Proof of Labor.**—Within six months after any set time, or annual period herein allowed for the performance of labor, or making improvements upon any lode claim, the person on whose behalf such outlay was made, or some person for him, shall make and record an affidavit, in substance as follows:

STATE OF COLORADO, }
  County of———. } *ss*:

Before me, the subscriber, personally appeared ———, who, being duly sworn, saith that at least ——— dollars' worth of work or improvements were performed or made upon [here describe claim or part of claim] situate in ——— mining district, County of ———, State of Colorado. Such expenditure was made by or at the expense of———, owners of said claim, for the purpose of said claim.

[Jurat.]   [Signature.]

And such signature shall be *prima facie* evidence of the performance of such labor.

SEC. 16.—**Relocation of Abandoned Claims.**—The re-location of abandoned lode claims shall be by sinking a new discovery shaft and fixing new boundaries in the same manner as if it were the location of a new claim; or the re-locator may sink the original discovery shaft ten feet deeper than it was at the time of abandonment, and erect new, or adopt the old boundaries, renewing the posts, if removed or destroyed. In either case a new location stake shall be erected. In any case, whether the whole or part of an abandoned claim is taken, the location certificate may state that the whole or any part of the new location is located as abandoned property.

SEC. 17.—**One Record for Each Claim.**—No location certificate shall claim more than one location, whether the location be made by one or several locators. And if it purport to claim more than one location, it shall be absolutely void, except as to the first location therein described. And if they are described together, or so that it cannot be told which location is first described, the certificate shall be void as to all.

Approved February 13, 1874. Session Laws, 1874, page 185.

An Act Concerning Mines.

SECTION 1.—**Right of Survey and Inspection.**—In all actions pending in any district court of this Territory, wherein the title or right of possession to any mining claim shall be in dispute, the said court, or the judge thereof, may, upon the application of any of the parties to such suit, enter an order for the underground as well as surface survey of such part of the property in dispute as may be necessary to a just determination of the question involved. Such order shall designate some competent surveyor, not related to any of the parties to such suit, nor in anywise interested in the result of the same; and upon the application of the party adverse to such application, the court may also appoint some competent surveyor, to be selected by such adverse applicant, whose duty it shall be to attend upon such survey, and observe the method of making the same; said second survey to be at the cost of the party asking therefor. It shall also be lawful in such order to specify the names of witnesses named by either party, not exceeding three on each side, to examine such property, who shall thereupon be allowed to enter into such property and examine the same; said court, or the judge thereof, may also cause the removal of any rock, débris, or other obstacle in any of the drifts or shafts of said property, when such removal is shown to be necessary to a just determination of the questions involved: *Provided*, however, that no such order shall be made for survey and inspection, except in open court or in chambers, upon notice of application for such order of at least six days, and not then except by agreement of parties, or upon the affidavit of two or more persons that such survey and inspection is necessary to the just determination of the suit, which affidavits shall state the facts in such case, and wherein the necessity for survey exists; nor shall such order be made unless it appears that the party asking therefor had been refused the privilege of survey and inspection by the adverse party.

SEC. 2.—**Mandatory Writ to Restore Possession.**—The said district courts of this Territory, or any judge thereof, sitting in chancery, shall have, in addition to the power already possessed, power to issue writs of injunction for affirmative relief, having the force and effect of a writ of restitution, restoring any person or persons to the possession of any mining property, from which he or they may have been ousted, by force and violence, or by fraud, or from which they are kept out of possession by threats, or whenever such possession was taken from him or them by entry of the adverse party on Sunday, or a legal holiday, or while the party in possession was temporarily absent therefrom. The granting of such writ to extend only to the right of possession under the facts of the case in respect to the manner in which the possession was obtained, leaving the parties to their legal rights on all other questions as though no such writ had issued.

SEC. 3.—**Unlawful Entry.**—In all cases where two or more persons shall associate themselves together for the purpose of obtaining the possession of any lode, gulch, or placer claim, then in the actual possession of another, by force and violence, or threats of violence, or by stealth, and shall proceed to carry out such purpose by making threats against the party or parties in possession, or who shall enter upon such lode or mining claim for the purpose aforesaid, or who shall enter upon or into any lode, gulch, placer claim, quartz mill, or other mining property, or not being upon such property, but within hearing of the same, shall make any threats, or make use of any language, signs, or gestures, calculated to intimidate any person or persons at work on said property from continuing to work thereon or therein, or to intimidate others from engaging to work thereon or therein, every such person so offending, shall, on conviction thereof, be fined in a sum not to exceed two hundred and fifty dollars, and be imprisoned in the county jail not less than thirty days nor more than six months; such fine to be discharged either by payment or by confinement in said jail until such fine is discharged at the rate of two dollars and fifty cents ($2.50) per day. On trials under this section, proof of a common purpose of two or more persons to obtain possession of property as aforesaid, or to intimidate laborers as above set forth, accompanied or followed by any of the acts above specified by any of them, shall be sufficient evidence to convict any one committing such acts, although the parties may not be associated together at the time of committing the same.

SEC. 4.—**Guilty of Murder.**—If any person or persons shall associate and agree to enter or attempt to enter by force of numbers and the terror such numbers are calculated to inspire; or by force and violence, or by threats of violence against any person or persons in the actual possession of any lode, gulch, or placer claim; and upon such entry or attempted entry, any person or persons shall be killed, said persons, and all and each of them so entering or attempting to enter, shall be deemed guilty of murder in the first degree, and punished accordingly. Upon the trials of such cases, any person or parties cognizant of such entry, or attempted entry, who shall be present, aiding, assisting, or in any wise encouraging such entry, or attempted entry, shall be deemed a principal in the commission of said offense.

Approved, February 13, 1874. Session Laws, 1874, p. 190.

Placer Mining Claims.

SECTION 1.—**Location Certificate.**—The discoverer of a placer claim shall, within thirty days from the date of discovery, record his claim in the office of the recorder of the county in which said claim is situated, by a location certificate, which shall contain: *First*, the name of the claim, designating it as a placer claim. *Second*, the name of the locator. *Third*, the date of location. *Fourth*, the number of acres or feet claimed. And *Fifth*, a description of the claim by such reference to natural objects or permanent monuments as shall identify the claim.

Before filing such location certificate, the discoverer shall locate his claim: *First*, by posting upon such claim a plain sign or notice, containing the name of the claim, the name of the locator, the date of discovery, and the number of acres or feet claimed. *Second*, by marking the surface boundaries with substantial posts, and sunk in the ground, to-wit: One at each angle of the claim.

SEC 2.—**Assessment Work.**—On each placer claim of one hundred and sixty acres or more heretofo e or hereafter located, and until a patent has been issued therefor, not less than one hundred dollars' worth of labor shall be performed or improvements made by the first day of August, 1879, and by the first day of August of each year thereafter. On all placer claims containing less than one hundred and sixty acres, the expenditure during each year shall be such proportion of one hundred dollars as the number of acres bears to one hundred and sixty. On all placer claims containing less than twenty acres, the expenditures during each year shall not be less than twelve dollars; but when two or more claims lie contiguous, and are owned by the same person, the expenditure hereby required for each claim may be made on any one claim; and upon a failure to comply with these conditions, the claim or claims upon which such failure occurred shall be open to relocation in the same manner as if no location of the same had ever been made; *provided*, that the original locators, their heirs, assigns, or legal representatives have not resumed work upon the claim after failure and before such location; *provided*, the aforesaid expenditures may be made in building or repairing ditches to conduct water upon such ground or in making other mining improvements necessary for the working of such claim.

Upon the failure of any one of several co-owners to contribute his proportion of the expenditures required hereby, the co-owners who have performed the labor or made the improvements, may at the expiration of the year, to wit: the fir t of August, 1879, for the locations heretofore made, and one year from the date of locations hereafter made, give such delinquent co-owner personal notice in writing, or if he be a non-resident of the state, a notice by publication in the newspaper published nearest the claim for at least once a week for ninety days, and mailing him a copy of such newspaper if his address be known; and if at the expiration of ninety days after such notice in writing, or after the first publication of such notice, such delinquent should fail or refuse to contribute his proportion of the expenditure required by this action [section], his interest in the claim shall become the property of his co-owners who have made the required expenditures.

[The foregoing was filed in the office of the Secretary of State by the Governor March 12, 1879, without his signature, and became a law under Section 11, Art. IV, Constitution of Colorado.]

MISCELLANEOUS GENERAL LAWS, 1877.

Penal Provisions.

764. SEC. 169.—**False Weights.** If any person shall knowingly have, keep, or use any false or fraudulent scales or weights for weighing gold or gold dust, or any other article or commodity, every such person so offending shall, on conviction, be fined not exceeding five hundred dollars, or imprisoned in the county jail not exceeding six months.

765. SEC. 170.—**Punishment for Certain Mill-Owners.**—The owner, manager, or agent of any species of quartz mill, arastra mill, furnace, or cupel, employed in extracting gold from quartz, pyrites, or other minerals, who shall neglect or refuse to account for or pay over and deliver all the proceeds thereof to the owner of such quartz, pyrites, or other minerals, excepting such portion of said proceeds as he is entitled to in return for his services, shall, on conviction, be fined in a sum not exceeding one thousand dollars, or be imprisoned in the penitentiary not exceeding one year.

776. SEC. 181.—**Salting Ores.**—That every person who shall mingle or cause to be mingled with any sample of gold or silver bearing ore, any valuable metal or substance whatever, that will increase or in any way change the value of said ore, with the intent to deceive, cheat, or defraud any person or persons, shall, on conviction thereof, be punished by a fine of not less than $500 nor more than $1,000, or by confinement in the penitentiary for a term of not less than one nor more than fourteen years, or by bo h such fine and imprisonment.

1603. SEC. 1.—**Destroying Landmarks.**—That if any person or persons shall wilfully and maliciously deface, remove, pull down, injure, or destroy any location stake, side-post, corner-post, landmark, or monument, or any other legal land boundary monument in this state, designating, or intending to designate the location, boundary, or name of any mining claim, lode, or vein of mineral, or the name of the discoverer, or date of discovery thereof; the person or persons so offending shall be guilty of a misdemeanor, and, on conviction thereof, shall be fined not more than one thousand dollars, or imprisoned not more than one year, at the discretion of the court ; *provided*, that this Act shall not apply to abandoned property.

673. SEC. 78.—**Passing Counterfeit Gold Dust.**—Every person who shall mingle or procure to be mingled with any uncoined gold or gold dust now current, or which shall hereafter be current in this state, any counterfeit gold dust, or counterfeit uncoined gold, or any base metal or substance whatever, with intent to utter or pass the same, or to procure the same to be uttered or passed as gold dust or uncoined gold, shall, on conviction thereof, be punished by a fine not to exceed one thousand dol-

lars, or by confinement in the penitentiary for a term not less than one year nor more than fourteen years.

1961. SEC. 5.—**Buying Stolen Ore.**—Any person, association, or corporation, or the agent of any person, association, or corporation, who shall knowingly purchase or contract to purchase, or shall make any payment for or on account of any ore, which shall have been taken from any mine or claim, by persons who have taken or may be holding possession of any such mine or claim, contrary to any penal law now in force, or which may be hereafter enacted, shall be considered as an accessory after the fact to the unlawful holding or taking of such mine or claim, and upon conviction shall be subjected to the same punishment to which the principals may be liable.

1962. SEC. 6.—**False Mill Weights.**—Any person, association, or corporation, or the agent of any person, association or corporation engaged in the business of milling, sampling, concentrating, reducing, shipping, or purchasing ores as aforesaid, who shall keep or use any false or fraudulent scales or weights for weighing ore, or who shall keep or use any false or fraudulent assay scales or weights for ascertaining the assay value of ore, knowing them to be false, every person so offending shall be deemed guilty of a misdemeanor, and on conviction thereof, shall be fined in a sum not exceding one thousand (1,000) dollars, nor less than one hundred (100) dollars, or imprisonment not more than one year, or both, at the discretion of the court.

1963. SEC. 7.—**False Mill Returns.**—Any person, corporation, or association, or the agent of any person, corporation, or association, engaged in the milling, sampling, concentrating, reducing, shipping, or purchasing of ores in this state, who shall, in any manner, knowingly alter or change the true value or any ores delivered to him or them, so as to deprive the seller of the result of the correct value of the same, or who shall substitute other ores for that delivered to him or them, or who shall issue any bill of sale or certificate of purchase that does not exactly and truthfully state the actual weight, assay value, and total amount paid for any lot or lots of ore purchased, or who, by any secret understanding or agreement with another, shall issue a bill of sale or certificate of purchase that does not truthfully and correctly set forth the weight assay value, and total amount paid for any lot or lots of ore purchased by him or them, shall be deemed guilty of a misdemeanor, and on conviction thereof shall be fined in a sum not exceeding one thousand (1,000) dollars, nor less than one hundred (100) dollars, or imprisonment not more than one year, or both, at the discretion of the court.

1964. SEC. 8.—**Larceny of Ores.**—If any person, lessee, licensee, or employee in or about any mine in this State, shall break and sever, with intent to steal the ore or mineral from any mine, lode, ledge, or deposit in this State, or shall take, remove, or conceal the ore or mineral from any mine, lode, ledge, or deposit, with intent to defraud the owner or owners, lessee, or licensee of any such mine, lode, ledge, or deposit, such offender shall be deemed guilty of felony, and on conviction, shall be punished as for grand larceny.

Drainage of Mines.

1830. SECTION 1.—**Proportionate Share.**—Whenever contiguous and adjacent mines upon the same or upon separate lodes have a common ingress of water, or from subterraneous communication of the water have a common drainage, it shall be the duty of the owners, lessees, or occupants of each mine so related to provide for their proportionate share of the drainage thereof.

1831. SEC. 2.—**Failure to Drain.**—Any parties so related, failing to provide as aforesaid, for the drainage of the mines owned or occupied by them, thereby imposing an unjust burden upon neighboring mines whether owned or occupied by them, shall pay respectively to those performing the work of drainage, their proportion of the actual and necessary cost and expense of doing such drainage, to be recovered by an action in any court of competent jurisdiction.

1832. SEC. 3.—**Draining Corporation.**—It shall be lawful for all mining corporations or companies, and all individuals engaged in mining, having thus a common interest in draining such mines, to unite for the purpose of effecting the same, under such common name and upon such terms and conditions as may be agreed upon ; and every such association, having filed a certificate of incorporation, as provided by law, shall be deemed a corporation, with all the rights, incidents, and liabilities of a body corporate, so far as the same may be applicable.

1833. SEC. 4.—**Failure to Mutually Agree.**—Failing to mutually agree, as indicated in the preceding section, for drainage jointly, one or more of the said parties may undertake the work of drainage, after giving reasonable notice ; and should the remaining parties then fail, neglect or refuse to unite in equitable arrangements for doing the work, or sharing the expense thereof, they shall be subject to an action therefor as already specified, to be enforced in any court of competent jurisdiction.

1834. SEC. 5.—**Court Proceedings.**—When action is commenced to recover the cost and expenses for draining a lode or mine, it shall be lawful for the plaintiff to apply to the court, if in session, or to the judge thereof in vacation, for an order to inspect or examine the lodes or mines claimed to have been drained by the plaintiff; or some one for him, shall make affidavit that such inspection or examination is necessary for a preparation of the case for trial. The court or judge shall grant an order for the underground inspection and examination of the lode or mines described in the petition. Such order shall designate the number of persons, not exceeding three besides the plaintiff or his representative, to examine and inspect such lode and mines, and take the measurement thereof, relating the amount of water drained from the lode or mine, or the number of fathoms of ground mined and worked out of the lode or mines claimed to have been drained, the cost of such examination and inspection to be borne by the party applying therefor. The court or judge shall have power to cause the removal of any rock, débris, or other obstacles in any lode or vein, when such removal is shown to be necessary to a just determination of the question involved; *provided*, that no such order for inspection and examination shall be made except in open court, or at chambers, upon notice of application for such order of at least three days, and not then except by agreement of parties, nor unless it appears that the plaintiff has been refused the privilege of making the inspection and examination by the defendant, his or their agent.

1835. SEC. 6.—**Water Beyond Control.**—That hereafter, when any person or persons, or corporation, shall be engaged in mining or milling, and in the prosecution of such business shall hoist or raise water from the mines or natural channels, and the same shall flow away from the premises of such persons, or corporations, to any natural channel or gulch, the same shall be considered beyond the control of the party so hoisting or raising the same, and may be taken and used by other parties the same as that of natural water courses.

1836. SEC. 7.—**Liable for Injury.**—After any such water shall have been so raised, and the same shall have flown into any such natural channel, gulch, or draw, the party so hoisting or raising the same shall only be liable for injury caused thereby, in the same manner as riparian owners along natural water courses.

1837. SEC. 8.—**Undeveloped Mines.**—The provisions of this Act shall not be construed to apply to incipient or undeveloped mines, but to those only which shall have been opened, and shall clearly derive a benefit from being drained.

1838. SEC. 9.—**Admissible Evidence.**—In trial of cases arising under this Act, the court shall admit evidence of the normal stand, or position of the water while at rest in an idle mine, also the observed prevalence of a common water level, or a standing water line in the same, or separate lodes; also, the effect (if any) the elevating or depressing the water by natural or mechanical means in any given lode, has upon elevating or depressing the water in the same, contiguous, or separate lodes or mines; also, the effect which draining or ceasing to drain any given lode or mine had upon the water in the same or contiguous or separate lodes or mines, and all other evidence which tends to prove the common ingress or subterraneous communication of water into the same lode or mine, or contiguous or separate lodes or mines.

Ore.

1957. SECTION 1.—**Contents of Record.**—That every person, association, or corporation that shall be engaged in the business of milling, sampling, concentrating, reducing, shipping, or purchasing ores in the State of Colorado, shall keep and preserve a book in which shall be entered at the time of the delivery of each lot of ore:

First—The name of the party on whose behalf such ore is delivered, as stated.

Second—The name of the teamster, packer, or other persons actually delivering such ore, and the name of the owner of the team or pack train delivering such ore.

Third—The weight or amount of every such lot of ore.

Fourth—The name and location of the mine or claim from which it shall be stated that the same has been mined or procured.

Fifth—The date of delivery of any and all lots or parcels of ore.

1958. SEC. 2.—**Proceedings when Ore is Stolen.**—Whenever affidavit shall have been made before any police magistrate of any town in this State, or any justice of the peace of any county, by any person, that ore has been stolen from him, stating as near as may be the amount and value of the ore stolen, such person upon presentation of a certified copy of such affidavit, shall have access to such book, and may examine the entries which may have been made therein during a period of fifteen days next preceding the filing of such affidavit; *provided*, that the person making such affidavit shall, at the time of making the same, have a present interest in the product of the mine or claim from which said ore has been stolen, or in the ore alleged to have been stolen.

1959. SEC. 3.—**Failure to Keep Required Books.**—Every person, association, or corporation that shall fail or refuse to keep the book required by the terms of the first section of this Act, or shall fail or refuse to make any proper entry therein, or who shall make any false entry therein, or who shall refuse to any person who may be entitled to the same, as provided by section two (2) of this Act, the right of inspection thereof, shall forfeit and pay for each and every violation of the provisions of said section a penalty of not less than fifty (50) nor more than three hundred (300) dollars, to be collected by action of debt at the suit of any person who may sue for the same. In addition to such penalty, any person, association, or corporation violating the provisions of said first section, shall be liable at the suit of the party or persons aggrieved, in the proper form of action, for all damages which may accrue to any party or person by reason of such violation. And in all actions the fact that a false entry has been made shall be *prima facie* evidence that the same was made wilfully or knowingly.

1960. SEC. 4.—**Failure to Make Inquiries.**—If any person, association, or corporation shall fail or neglect to make inquiries necessary to the making of the proper entries in said book, as provided in section one (1) of this Act, or shall so negligently make entries therein that any lot of ore cannot be particularly identified, or so negligently that it cannot be perceived therefrom what person delivered any lot of ore or received the proceeds of the same when purchased, or shall fail to keep such book, or shall wilfully suffer the same to be lost, or mislaid, so that the same cannot be produced for inspection, such failure or neglect shall not excuse any party defendant in any suit brought under the preceding section from judgment for any penalty prescribed by said section.

Water Rights.

1798. SEC. 2.—**Right of Way.**—Whenever any person or persons are engaged in bringing water into any portions of the mines, they shall have the right of way secured to them, and may pass over any claim, road, ditch, or other structure; *provided*, the water be guarded so as not to interfere with prior rights.

1821. SEC. 11. All mining claims now located, or which may be hereafter located, shall be suject to the right of way of any ditch or flume for mining purposes, or of any tramway or pack-trail, whether now in use, or which may be hereafter laid out across any such location; *provided, always*, that such right of way shall not be exercised against any location duly made and recorded, and not abandoned prior to the establishment of the ditch, flume, tramway, or pack-trail, without consent of the owner, except by condemnation, as in case of land taken for public highways. Parol consent to the location of any such easement, accompanied by the completion of the same over the claim, shall be sufficient without writings; *and provided further*, that such ditch or flume shall be so constructed that the water from such ditch or flume shall not injure vested rights by flooding or otherwise.

2779. SEC. 3.—**Miners' Inch.**— * * * And water sold by the inch by any individual or corporation, shall be measured as follows, to wit: Every inch shall be considered equal to an inch square orifice under a five-inch pressure, and a five-inch pressure shall be from the top of the orifice of the box put into the banks of the ditch, to the surface of water; said boxes, or any dot or aperture through which such water may be measured, shall in all cases be six inches perpendicular inside measurement, except boxes delivering less than twelve inches, which may be square, with or without slides; all slides for the same shall move horizontally and not otherwise; and said box put into the banks of ditch shall have a descending grade from the water in ditch of not less than one-eighth of an inch to the foot.

Tailings.

1804. SEC. 8.—**Miners Responsible.**—In no case shall any person or persons be allowed to flood the property of another person with water, or wash down the tailings of his or their sluice upon the claim or property of other persons, but it shall be the duty of every miner to take care of his own tailings, upon his own property, or become responsible for all damages that may arise therefrom.

Hauling Quartz.

1805. SEC. 9.—**Right of Way.**—Every miner shall have the right of way across any and all claims for the purpose of hauling quartz from his claim.

Mining Claims, Real Estate, Actions.

185. SEC. 26.—**Definitions.**—The terms "land" and "real estate," as used in this chapter, shall be construed as co-extensive in meaning with the terms "lands, tenements, hereditaments," and as embracing mining claims and other claims, and chattels real. The term "deed" includes mortgages, leases, releases, and every conveyance or incumbrance under seal.

2126. SEC. 3.—**Transferable Interest.**—The owner of every claim or improvement, on every tract or parcel of land, has a transferable interest therein, which may be sold in execution or otherwise; and any sale of such improvement is a sufficient consideration to sustain a promise.

2131. SEC. 8.—**Claimant May Maintain Action.**—Any person settled upon any of the public lands belonging to the United States may maintain trespass *quare clausum fregit*, trespass, ejectment, forcible entry and detainer, unlawful detainer, and forcible detainer, for injuries done to the possession thereof.

2135. SEC. 12.—**City and Village Lots.**—Any person who may have a title to occupy any lot or lots within any city or village plot, or any lots or mining claim within any mining district in this State, in virtue of a certificate, deed of gift or purchase from the original claimant or claimants, or their assigns, as well as all purchasers, under any decree or execution of any of the so-called provisional government courts, people's or miners' courts, of the lands situate within any city or village plot, or any lots, land, or mining claims situate within any mining district, together with the original claimant or claimants of said lots, land, or mining claims, shall be entitled to maintain the actions authorized by the eighth section of this chapter, against any and all persons who shall enter upon and occupy said lots, lands, or mining claims, or any of them; *provided*, it shall be lawful for the citizens of any mining district to declare an abandonment of any creek, river, gulch, bank, or mining claim a forfeiture of the rights of the claimants thereto; in which case the parties claimant shall not be enabled to maintain either of the actions mentioned in section eight of this chapter.

2136. SEC. 13.—**United States Title.**—Nothing in this chapter contained shall be construed to deny the right of the United States to dispose of any lands in this State; nor shall the fact that the title to any lot, lands, lodes, or mining claims hath not passed from the United States, be any bar to the recovery of the plaintiff in either of the actions specified in section eight of this chapter. As against the United States, and all persons holding any of said lands under the United States, or the laws thereof, this chapter shall be of non-effect and void.

For laws as to liens of miners and mechanics, see Session Laws of 1881, p. 168; Laws of 1883, p. 225; Laws of 1893, p. 315; Laws of 1895, p. 202.

Annual Assessment.

SECTION. 1. **Affidavit of Expenditure.**—That section one of an act entitled "An Act to amend section twenty-four hundred and ten of the General Statutes, being section twenty six of Chapter LXXIV thereof, entitled 'Mines,'" approved March 31, 1887, be, and the same is hereby, amended to read as follows: Sec. 1. That section twenty-four hundred and ten of the General Statutes, being section twenty-six of Chapter LXXIV thereof, entitled "Mines," be, and the same is hereby, amended so as to read as follows: 2410. Sec. 26. Within six months after any set time or annual period allowed for the performance of labor or making improvements upon any lode claim or placer claim, the person on whose behalf such outlay was made, or some person for him, may make and record in the office of the Recorder of the county wherein such claim is situate an affidavit in substance as follows:

STATE OF COLORADO, } ss.:
—— County.

Before me, the subscriber, personally appeared ——, who, being duly sworn, saith that at least —— dollars' worth of work or improvements were performed or made upon (here describe claim or part of claim), situate in —— mining district, County of ——, State of Colorado, between the —— day of ——, A. D. ——, and the —— day of ——, A. D. ——. Such expenditure was made by or at the expense of ——, owners of said claim, for the purpose of complying with the law and holding said claim.

[Jurat.]   [Signature.]

And such affidavit, when so recorded, shall be *prima facie* evidence of the performance of such labor, or the making of such improvements: *Provided*, That all affidavits of labor or improvements upon placer claims heretofore filed and recorded within the period prescribed in this section, or within the period prescribed in section twenty-four hundred and ten of the General Statutes, which shall contain in substance the requirements of the affidavit prescribed by this section, or said section twenty-four hundred and ten, shall be *prima facie* evidence of the performance of such labor or the making of such improvements; and the original thereof, or a certified copy of the record of the same, shall be received as evidence accordingly by the courts of this State, and this class of evidence shall be receivable, where relevant or material, in all cases, whether now pending or hereafter brought.

Approved April 20, 1889. Session Laws of 1889, p. 261.

Liens on Mines.

An Act to amend Sec. 8 of an Act entitled "An Act to secure liens to mechanics and others, and to repeal all laws in conflict therewith." Approved April 3d, 1893:

SEC. 8. **Workmen and Materials.**—The provisions of this Act shall apply to all persons who shall do work, or shall furnish material for the working, preservation or development of any mine, lode or mining claim or deposit, yielding metals or minerals of any kind, or for the working, preservation or development of any such mine, lode or deposit, in search of such metals or minerals; and to all persons who shall do work or furnish materials upon any shaft, tunnel, incline, adit, drift or draining of any such mine, lode or deposit: *Provided*, That when two or more lodes, mines or deposits, owned or claimed by the same person or persons, shall be worked through a common shaft, tunnel, incline, adit, drift or other excavation, then all the mines, lodes or deposits so worked shall, for the purpose of this Act, be deemed one mine: and *Provided further*, That this section shall not be deemed to apply to the owner or owners of any mine, lode, deposit, shaft, tunnel, incline, adit, drift or other excavation, who shall lease the same in small blocks of ground to one or more sets of lessees. [Immediate.]

Approved April 13, 1895. Session Laws of 1895, p. 202.

Mining Tunnels.

SECTION 1. **Rights of Tunnel Owners.**—Any person or company who has or hereafter may have a tunnel or cross-cut, the mouth of which is located upon his own ground or upon ground in his lawful occupation, shall have the right to drive and continue the same through and across any located or patented claim in front of the mouth of such tunnel, but not to follow or drive upon any vein belonging to the owner of such claim.

SEC. 2. **Rights of Owners of Intersecting Claims.**—Such tunnel or cross-cut may be driven and worked for the purpose of drainage and for the purpose of reaching and working mining ground of the tunnel owner beyond the intersected claim. The owner or owners of any vein or any claim or claims so intersected, or his duly authorized agent, shall have the right to enter such tunnel upon application to the owner or owners of said tunnel without resorting to any process of law for the purpose of making a survey and inspecting such vein or veins as may be crossed within the boundary lines of such intersected claim, and if the owner or owners of such tunnel shall, by bulk heading, damming back or in any manner prevent the inspection or survey herein provided for, or if such owner or owners shall in any manner prevent the natural drainage of water from such intersected claim or claims without the consent of the owner or owners thereof, it shall work a forfeiture of all rights granted under section one of this Act.

Sec. 3. **Owner of Ore—Damages.**—If any ore, the property of the owner of the claim intersected or crossed, be extracted in driving such tunnel, it shall be the property of the owner of the vein from which it was taken, and the owner of the tunnel shall be liable for all actual damages or injury done to the owner of the claim crossed by his tunnel.

Sec. 4. **Burden of Proof.**—In all actions between the tunnel owner and others involving the right to any vein discovered in such tunnel, the burden of proving that the vein so discovered is not the property of the adverse claimant in such action shall be on the tunnel owner.

Approved April 17, 1897. Session Laws, 1897, p. 181.

IDAHO.

Miners' Lien.

SECTION 12. Quartz Mine or Material.—Every sub-contractor, journeyman, laborer, or other person, performing labor or furnishing materials for any contractor, in or upon any quartz claim, ledge, or mine, in working in the same or in the improvement or development thereof in the completion or performance of any contract entered into by any person in this Territory, every such person or persons so performing such labor or furnishing such material shall have a lien upon all the interest in such quartz claim, ledge, or mine, of the person or persons employing him or them, or purchasing such materials with the improvements thereon and appurtenances thereto belonging, and also upon all the interest of the person or persons for whom such person or persons acts as agent, or the owner or owners, for the value of such work, or labor or materials furnished, and all the provisions of this act shall apply in respect to recording, recovering, and enforcing such liens provided for in this section : *Provided*, the person or persons claiming such lien shall within thirty days after the performance of such labor or furnishing such materials, give notice in writing to any person or persons, agent or agents, owner or owners, and shall within forty days file their lien in other respects as provided by this act.

SEC. 13. Quartz Mine or Ore.—When any person or persons shall do or perform any work or labor in or upon or for any quartz claim, mine, or ledge, in working the same or in the improvement or development thereof; or in the preparation of the ores thereof for reduction; or in the hauling of the ores thereof; or shall perform labor or service as superintendent, manager or foreman of any mine or ledge, or shall perform labor as a mechanic or artisan therefor; such person or persons shall have a lien upon all the interest in such quartz claim, ledge or mine of the person or persons employing him or them, or purchasing such materials, together with the improvements thereon and appurtenances for the value of such work, labor, or services, or materials furnished, and all the provisions of this act respecting the filing, recording and recovering and enforcing mechanics' liens are made applicable to this section : *Provided*, the person or persons claiming such liens shall, within sixty days after the completion of such work or labor, or rendering said services or furnishing said materials, file their lien in other respects as provided by this Act.

SEC. 14. What is Included.—This Act shall be so construed as to include in its provisions bridges, ditches, flumes, aqueducts to create hydraulic power for mining purposes, and all improvements on mining claims.

Extract from an Act approved Jan. 11, 1875. Session Laws of 1874-5, p. 615. See Act approved February 27, 1893. Session Laws of 1893, p. 49.

General Law of February 14, 1899.

SECTION. 1. **Width of Lode Claims.**—That Section 3100 of the Revised Statutes of Idaho be amended to read as follows:

Section 3100. Mining claims hereafter located upon veins or lodes of quartz, or other rock in place bearing any of the metals or other valuable deposits mentioned in section 2320 of the Revised Statutes of the United States, may extend to three hundred feet on each side of the middle of the vein or lode:

Provided, That when the locators have set stakes, posts or monuments described in section 2 hereof, to indicate the line of the vein, ledge or lode, such stakes, posts or monuments must be taken for the purpose of such location, to mark correctly the line thereof, and such line must not afterwards be changed so as to affect rights acquired or interfere with any locations made subsequent thereto.

SEC. 2. Section 3101 of the Revised Statutes of Idaho be amended to read as follows:

Section 3101. **Monument and Location Notice.**—The locator, at the time of making the discovery of such vein or lode, must erect a monument at such place of discovery, upon which he must place his name, the name of the claim, the date of discovery and distance claimed along the vein each way from such monument. Within ten days from the date of discovery, he must mark the boundaries of his claim by establishing at each corner thereof and at any angle in the side lines, a monument, marked with the name of the claim and the corner or angle it represents; also at the time of so marking his boundaries, he must post at his discovery monument his notice of location in which must be stated: First, the name of the locator; second, the name of the claim; third, the date of discovery; fourth, the direction and distance claimed along the ledge from the discovery; fifth, the distance claimed on each side of the middle of the ledge; sixth, the distance and direction from the discovery monument to such natural object or permanent monument, if any such there be, as will fix and describe in the notice itself the location of the claim; and seventh, the name of the mining district, county and State. When, from any cause, a monument cannot be safely planted at the true corner or angle, it may be placed as near thereto as practicable, and so marked as to indicate the place of such corner or angle. Monuments may be made of any such material or form as will readily give notice, and when of posts or trees, they must be hewn and marked upon the side facing towards the discovery, and must be at least four inches square or in diameter. Monuments must be at least four feet high above the ground, and trees must be so hewn as to readily attract attention. At the time the locator so marks the boundaries of his claim, he may do so in any direction that will not interfere with rights or claims which existed prior to his discovery.

SEC. 3. **Assessment Work.**—Within sixty days after such location, the locator or his assigns must sink a shaft upon the lode to the depth of at least ten feet from the lowest part of the rim of such shaft at the surface, and of not less than sixteen square feet area. Any excavation which shall cut such vein ten feet from the lowest part of the rim of such shaft and which shall measure one hundred and sixty cubic feet in extent shall be considered a compliance with this provision. Any located claim upon which work has been done in compliance with the above requirements is not, unless abandoned, subject to relocation for a period of ninety days from and after the date of location.

SEC. 4. **Recording Notice.**—Within ninety days after the location of the claim the locator or his assigns must file for record in the office of the county recorder of the county or of the deputy recorder of the mining district in which the claim is situated a substantial copy of his notice of location.

SEC. 5. **Relocation.**—If at any time the locator of any mining claim heretofore or hereafter located, or his assigns, shall apprehend that his original certificate was defective, erroneous, or that the requirements of the law had not been complied with before filing, or shall be desirous of changing the surface boundaries, or of taking any part of an overlapping claim which has been abandoned, or in case the original certificate was made prior to the passage of this law, and he shall be desirous of securing the benefits of this Act, such locator or his assigns, may file an additional certificate subject to the conditions of this Act and to contain all that this Act required an original certificate to contain: *Provided*, That such amended location does not interfere with the existing rights of others at the time when such amendment is made.

SEC. 6. **Labor Affidavit.**—Within sixty days after any time set or period allowed for the performance of labor, or making improvements upon any lode, or placer claim, the person in whose behalf such work or improvement is performed, or some person for him, must make and record an affidavit in substance as follows:

STATE OF IDAHO, }
County of ———, } ss:

Before me the subscriber, personally appeared ——— ———, who, being first duly sworn, says that at least ——— dollars' worth of work or improvements were performed or made upon ——— claim, situate in ——— mining district, County of ———, State of Idaho: that such expenditure was made by, for, or at the expense of ——— ———, owner of said claim, and all stakes, monuments or trees marking boundaries of said claim are in proper places and positions.

Signature. ——— ———.

Subscribed and sworn to before me this ——— day of ———, 189-.
——— ———.

The fee for administering the oath and recording the foregoing affidavit, when taken before the county recorder or deputy mining recorder, shall be fifty cents; the fee for recording the same when the oath is taken before any other officer authorized to administer oaths shall be fifty cents.

Such affidavit, or a certified copy thereof in case the original is lost, shall be *prima facie* evidence of the performance of such labor. The failure to file such affidavit shall be considered *prima facie* evidence that such labor has not been done.

SEC. 7. **Location of Abandoned Claims.**—The location of abandoned claims shall be done in the same manner as if the location were of a new claim; but the locator may, instead of sinking a new discovery shaft, sink the original discovery shaft ten feet deeper than it was at the time of his location, or he may drive the open cut, or tunnel, ten feet further along the course of the lead, lode or vein, and must erect new posts or monuments.

SEC. 8. **Void Location.**—No location notice shall claim more than one location, whether the location is made by one or several locators, and if it purport to claim more than one location, it is absolutely void.

SEC. 9. **County Records—Deputy Recorder.**—That section 3103 of the Revised Statutes of Idaho is hereby amended to read as follows:

Section 3103. For the convenience of prospectors and locators, the county recorders of the several counties must appoint a deputy at any place where he may deem it necessary, and at all places more than twenty miles distant from an existing office whenever ten or more mining locators interested, petition for the appointment of a deputy. Upon failure of any recorder to appoint a deputy for ten days after the petition in writing has been presented to him, the resident miners in such district may appoint temporarily, one of their number to act as the recorder for the district, whose record shall be as valid as if made by the deputy, and must be entered by the recorder as hereinafter required: *Provided*, That whenever at any time afterwards, the recorder has appointed a deputy for such district or place, the authority of the person elected by the resident miners ceases.

SEC. 10. **Surface Ground.**—When the right to mine is in any case separate from the ownership or right of occupancy of the surface ground, the owners or rightful occupants of the surface ground may demand satisfactory security from the miners, and if it be refused or not given, may enjoin such miners from working such ground until such security is given. The court granting the writ of injunction shall fix the amount and nature of the security.

SEC. 11. **Placer Locations.**—Placer claims, as mentioned in section 2329 of the Revised Statutes of the United States, may be located for the purpose of mining deposits and precious stones after the discovery of such deposits.

SEC. 12. **Placer Records.**—The locator of any placer mining claim located for the purpose of mining placer deposits or precious stones must, at the time of making the location, place a substantial post or monument as is required in the location of quartz claims at each corner of the location and must also post on one of the same a notice of location, containing the date of the location, the name of the locator, the name and dimensions of the claim, the mining district (if any) and county in which the same is situated; and must also give the distance and direction from said post or monument to such natural object or permanent monument, if any such there be, as will fix and describe in the notice itself the location of the claim. Within fifteen days after making the location, the locator must make an excavation upon the claim of not less than one hundred cubic feet, for the purpose of prospecting the same. Within thirty days after the location, the locator must file for record in the office of the county recorder of the county, or of the deputy recorder of the mining district in which the claim is situated, a substantial copy of his copy of notice of location, to which must be attached an affidavit such as is required in the case of quartz claims.

SEC. 13. **Locator's Affidavit.**—That section 3104 of the Revised Statutes of Idaho be amended to read as follows:

SECTION 3104. At or before the time of presenting a location notice for record, whether it be for a quartz or placer claim, one of the locators named in the same must make and subscribe an affidavit, in writing, on or attached to the notice, substantially in the following form, to wit:

STATE OF IDAHO, } ss:
County of ———, }

I, ——— ———, do solemnly swear that I am a citizen of the United States of America (or have declared my intention to become such) and that I am acquainted with the mining ground described in this notice of location, and herewith called the ——— ledge, lode or claim; that the ground and claim therein described or any part thereof has not, to the best of my knowledge and belief, been located according to the laws of the United States and of this State, or if so located, that the same has been abandoned or forfeited by reason of the failure of such former locators to comply in respect thereto with the requirements of said laws, and (in the case of quartz claims) that I have opened new ground to the extent or depth of ten feet as required by the laws of Idaho.

Signature ——— ———.

Subscribed and sworn to before me this ——— day of ———, A. D. 189—.

Signature ——— ———.

SEC. 14. **Record Book—Fee.**—That Section 3105 of the Revised Statutes of Idaho is amended so as to read as follows, to wit:

Section 3105. The location notice herein required to be recorded must be recorded by the deputy appointed for the district, or the person appointed for that purpose as above provided (when the legal fee therefor is tendered) in a book to be kept for that purpose. Said book must be indexed, with the names of all the locators arranged in alphabetical order, according to the family or surname of each. The fee to be tendered for making such record, administering the oath to the locator and certifying the same, for indexing the names appearing on the notice, and to include recording the notice by the recorder as hereinafter required, and the indexing by said recorder, is two dollars, which fee must be equally divided between the recorder and the deputy or the person acting under an election as hereinbefore provided, and no other additional sum of money must be demanded or received by either of them for any services connected with the recording of any location notice made pursuant to the requirements of this chapter.

Sec. 15. Section 3102 of chapter 1, title 8, and sections 3120, 3121 and 3122, chapter 2, title 8, of the Revised Statutes of the State of Idaho are hereby repealed. [Took effect immediately.]

Approved February 14, 1899, as amended March 13, 1899. Session Laws, 1899, pp. 237 and 440.

An Act Concerning Mining Tunnels.

Section 1. **Tunnel Rights.**—Any person or company who has or may hereafter have a tunnel or cross-cut, the mouth of which is located upon his own ground or upon ground in his lawful occupation, shall have the right to drive and continue the same through and across any located or patented claim in front of the mouth of such tunnel, but not to follow or drive upon any vein belonging to the owner of such claim.

Sec. 2. **Drainage Inspection.**—Each tunnel or cross-cut may be driven and worked for the purpose of drainage and for the purpose of reaching and working mining ground of the tunnel owner beyond the intersected claim. The owner or owners of any vein or any claim or claims so intersected or his duly authorized agent shall have the right to enter such tunnel upon application to the owner or owners or person in charge of said tunnel without resorting to any process of law for the purpose of making a survey and inspecting such vein or veins as may be crossed within the boundary lines of such intersected claim, and if the owner or owners of such tunnel shall, by bulk-heading, damming back or in any manner prevent the inspection or survey herein provided for, or if such owner or owners shall in any manner prevent the natural drainage of water from such intersected claim or claims without the consent of the owner or owners thereof, it shall work a forfeiture of all rights granted under section one of this Act.

Sec. 3. **Damage.**—If any ore, the property of the owner of the claim intersected or crossed, be extracted in driving such tunnel, it shall be the property of the owner of the vein from which it was taken and the owner of the tunnel shall be liable for all actual damages or injury done to the owner of the claim crossed by his tunnel.

Sec. 4. **Burden of Proof.**—In all actions between the tunnel owner and others involving the right to any vein discovered in such tunnel, the burden of proving that the vein so discovered is not the property of the adverse claimant in such action shall be on the tunnel owner.

[Repeal provision and immediate effect.]

Approved March 15, 1899. Session Laws, 1899, p. 442.

Rights of Way and Easements.

Section 3132. **Right of Way.**—When the owner, claimant, or occupant of any mine or mining claim desires to work the same, and it is necessary to enable him to do so successfully and conveniently, that he have a right of way for any of the purposes mentioned in the foregoing sections, if such right of way cannot be acquired by agreement with the claimant or owner of the lands or claims over, under, through, across or upon which he seeks to acquire such right of way, he may commence an action in the district court in and for the county in which such right of way, or some part thereof, is situated, by filing a verified complaint containing a particular description of the character and extent of the right sought, a description of the mine or claim of the plaintiff, and of the mine or claim and lands to be affected by such right of way or privilege, with the name of the occupant or owner thereof. He may also set forth any tender of compensation that he may have made, and demand the relief sought.

Sec. 3133.—**Summons.**—Upon the filing of such complaint the clerk must issue a summons as provided in other civil actions, and the same must be served in the manner prescribed by law for service in ordinary actions.

Sec. 3134. **Appointment of Commissioners.**—At any time after the service of the summons the plaintiff may upon ten days' notice to the defendant apply to the district court or the judge thereof for the appointment of commissioners, to assess the damages resulting from the grant of such right of way. If upon the hearing of such motion, and the affidavit and proofs offered by the respective parties, the judge shall be of the opinion that the plaintiff has made a *prima facie* case entitling him to the relief demanded in the complaint, or any part thereof, he shall appoint three commissioners, who must be disinterested persons, residents of the county, to assess the damages resulting to the claims, mines, or lands of defendant. But if such commissioners are not applied for and appointed, or their award is not approved by the judge or court, or if an appeal is taken from their award as hereinafter provided, the action shall be tried and determined by the court, and the provisions of the Code of Civil Procedure applicable thereto shall govern the proceedings therein as in other civil actions; either party shall be entitled to a jury trial and may move for a new trial and appeal as in other cases.

SEC. 3140. **Effect of Appeal.**—The prosecution of an appeal from the award of the commissioners or from the judgment of the district court does not hinder, delay or prevent the plaintiff from exercising all the rights and privileges granted by the award or judgment, if he deposit with the clerk of the district court the full amount of the damages awarded or adjudged the defendant and execute and deliver to the clerk a bond with sufficient sureties to be approved by the clerk, in an amount to be fixed by the judge of the district court, conditioned to pay to the defendant any additional amount, over and above the amount so deposited that defendant may recover, and all costs to which he may be entitled under the provisions of this chapter. At any time after such deposit and before the final determination of the action the defendant may, upon demand, receive from the clerk the amount so deposited, but his acceptance of the same, or any part thereof, shall bar any further prosecution of the appeal and shall be deemed an acquiescence and consent to the award and judgment, and the defendant shall not be entitled to any costs subsequent to the deposit.

SEC. 3141. **Costs of Appeal**—If the defendant recover judgment against the necessity of the easement, or for fifty dollars more damages than the plaintiff has tendered him, as provided in the next section, or for fifty dollars more damages than the commissioners or judgment of the district court awarded him, he shall recover the costs of the appeal, otherwise he must pay all such costs.

Filed March 9, 1899. Session Laws, 1899, p. 350.

Recording Location Notices with Deputy Mining Recorder.

SECTION 1.—It shall be the duty of the county recorder of the several counties of this state, within fourteen days after receiving them, to transmit to the deputy mining recorder of the district wherein the claims located are situated, all location notices, both quartz and placer which shall not have been already recorded in the office of the deputy mining recorder.

It shall be the duty of such deputy mining recorder to record in his records all such notices received by him and he shall receive as compensation therefor from the clerk sending them one-half the fee authorized by law to be charged for the recording of mining claims. After recording such notices, the deputy mining recorder shall return the same to the county recorder. Session Laws, 1903, p. 290.

Approved March 11, 1903.

Mining Partnership.

SECTION 3300.—A mining partnership exists when two or more persons who own or acquire a mining claim for the purpose of working it and extracting the mineral therefrom, actually engage in working the same.

SEC. 3301.—An express agreement to become partners or to share the profits and losses of mining is not necessary to the formation or existence of a mining partnership. The relation arises from the ownership of shares or interests in the mine and working the same for the purpose of extracting the minerals therefrom.

SEC. 3302.—A member of a mining partnership shares in the profits and losses thereof in the proportion which the interest or share he owns in the mine bears to the whole partnership capital or whole number of shares.

SEC. 3303.—Each member of a mining partnership has a lien on the partnership property for the debts due the creditors thereof, and for money advanced by him for its use. A lien exists in favor of the creditors notwithstanding there is an agreement among the partners that it must not.

SEC. 3304.—The mining ground owned and worked by partners in mining, whether purchased with partnership funds or not, is partnership property.

SEC. 3305. One of the partners in a mining partnership may convey his interest in the mine and business without dissolving the partnership. The purchaser, from the date of his purchase, becomes a member of the partnership.

SEC. 3306.—A purchaser of an interest in the mining ground of a mining partnership takes it subject to the liens existing in favor of the partners for debts due all creditors thereof, or advances made for the benefit of his partnership unless he purchased in good faith, for a valuable consideration, without notice of such lien.

SEC. 3307.—A purchaser of the interest of a partner in a mine when the partnership is engaged in working it, takes with notice of all liens resulting from the relation of the partners to each other and to the creditors of the partnership.

SEC. 3308.—No member of a mining partnership or other agent or manager thereof can, by a contract in writing, bind the partnership except by express authority derived from the members thereof.

SEC. 3309.—The decision of the members owning a majority of the shares or interests in a mining partnership binds it in the conduct of its business.

From the Civil Code.

Recording, Prospecting and Mining Contracts.

SECTION 1. **County Records.**—Written contracts relating to prospecting or mining, or to the formation of co-partnership for that purpose, when signed by the parties thereto and endorsed by at least one witness, may be recorded in the office of the county recorder of the county wherein it is proposed to prosecute the business of said co-partnership, or where the property affected by such contract is situated.

SEC. 2. **Notice.**—Such record shall be constructive notice to all persons of the matters contained in such contract or co-partnership agreement. (Repeal provision.)

Approved March 7, 1899. Session Laws, 1899, p. 366.

An Act to Authorize Aliens to Hold Mining Property.

SECTION 1. **Aliens Except Chinese.**—That any person, whether citizen or alien (except as hereinafter provided), natural or artificial, may take, hold and dispose of mining claims and mining property, real or personal, tunnel rights, mill sites, quartz mills and reduction works used or necessary or proper for the reduction of ores, and water rights used for mining or milling purposes, and any other lands or property necessary for the working of mines or the reduction of the products thereof; *Provided*, That Chinese, or persons of Mongolian descent not born in the United States, are not permitted to acquire title to land or any real property under the provisions of this act. [Took effect immediately.]

Approved March 2, 1891. Session Laws, 1891, p. 118.

MONTANA.

Extracts from Code of 1895.

Section 3610. **Mineral Claim—Location—Notice.**—Any person, a citizen of the United States, or one who has declared his intentions to become such, who discovers a vein or lode bearing gold, silver, cinnabar, lead, tin, copper or other valuable deposits, or who discovers or locates a placer deposit of gold or other deposits of minerals, including building stone, limestone, marble, clay, sand or other mineral substances having a commercial value, may locate a claim upon such vein, lode or deposit, by defining the boundaries of a claim in the manner hereinafter described, and by posting a notice of such location at the point of discovery, which notice must contain: 1. The name of the lode or claim. 2. The name of the locator or locators. 3. The date of the location. 4. If a lode claim, the number of lineal feet claimed in length along the course of the vein, each way from the point of discovery, with the width on each side of the centre of the vein, and the general course of the vein or lode as near as may be. 5. If a placer or mill-site claim, the number of acres or superficial feet claimed.

Sec. 3611. **Discovery Shaft—Defining Boundaries.**—Before the expiration of sixty days from the date of posting such notice upon the claim, the locator or locators must sink a discovery shaft upon the lode or claim (mill-site claims excepted) to the depth of at least ten feet from the lowest part of the rim of such shaft at the surface, or deeper if necessary, to show a well defined crevice or valuable deposit. Its equivalent in work must be done upon placer claims. A cut, cross-cut or tunnel which cuts a lode at the depth of ten feet below the surface, or an open cut of at least ten feet in length along the lode from the point where the lode may be in any manner discovered, is equivalent to a discovery shaft. The locator or locators must, within thirty days after posting of notice of location aforesaid, define the boundaries of his or their claim by marking a tree or rock in place, or by setting a post or stone at each corner or angle of the claim. When a post is used it must be at least four inches square by four feet six inches in length, and set one foot in the ground, with a mound of earth or stone at least four feet in diameter by two feet in height around the post. When a stone is used, not a rock in place, it must be at least six inches square and eighteen inches in length, set two-thirds of its length in the ground, which trees, stakes or monuments must be so marked as to designate the corners.

Sec. 3612. **Declaratory Statement—County Clerk's Office.**—Within sixty days of the date of posting the location notice upon the claim, there shall be filed in the office of the county clerk of the county in which the lode or claim is situated, a declaratory statement which shall contain :

1. The name of the lode or claim.
2. The name of the locator or locators.
3. The date of location and such description of the location of said claim with reference to some natural object or permanent monument as will identify the claim.
4. If a lode claim, the number of lineal feet claimed in length along the course of the vein each way from the point of discovery, with the width on each side of the centre of the vein, and the general course of the lode or vein as near as may be.
5. If a placer or mill-site claim, the number of acres or superficial feet claimed.
6. The dimensions and location of the discovery shaft, cut, or tunnel, or its equivalent, sunk upon lode or placer claims.

Such declaratory statement must be verified by the oath of the locator or one of the locators, and in case of a corporation, by an officer thereof duly authorized to act.

SEC. 3613.—**Prior Records.**—All placer mining locations or locations of valuable mineral deposits, which have heretofore been recorded in the office of the county clerk or recorder, have the same force and effect as though such records had been authorized by law, except in cases where the rights of third persons had been acquired before the passage of this Code; and such record is entitled to be admitted in evidence in any court.

SEC. 3614. **Affidavit—Annual Assessment—County Clerk.**—The owner of a lode or placer claim who performs or causes to be performed the annual work or makes the improvements required by the laws of the United States in order to prevent the forfeiture of the claim, may, within twenty days after the annual work, file in the office of the county clerk of the county in which such claim is situated an affidavit of his own, or an affidavit of the person who performs such work or made the improvements, showing: 1. The name of the mining claim and where situated. 2. The number of days' work done, and the character and value of the improvements placed thereon. 3. The date of performing such work, and of making the improvements. 4. At whose instance the work was done or the improvements made. 5. The actual amount paid for work and improvements, by whom paid when the same was not done by the owner. Such affidavits, or a certified copy thereof, are *prima facie* evidence of the facts therein stated.

SEC. 3615. **Relocation of Abandoned Mines.**—The relocation of an abandoned lode or placer claim must be made by sinking a new discovery shaft, and fixing new boundaries in the same manner as if it were an original location made under this Chapter; or the relocator may sink the original discovery shaft ten feet deeper, in which case the declaratory statement must give the depth and dimension of the original discovery shaft at the date of such relocation. In any case, whether the whole or part of an abandoned claim is taken, the declaratory statement may state that the whole or any part of the new location is located as abandoned property. If it is not known to the locator that his location is on an abandoned claim, then the provisions of this section do not apply.

SEC. 3616. **Declaratory Statement—Official Survey.**—Where a locator or owner of a mining claim has the boundaries and corners of his claim established by a United States deputy mineral surveyor, and his claim connected with a corner of the public or minor surveys or an established initial point, and incorporates into the declaratory statement the field-notes of such survey, and attaches to and files with such declaratory statement a certificate by the surveyor setting forth: 1. That said survey was actually made by him, giving the date thereof. 2. The name of the claim surveyed and the locators thereof. 3. That the description incorporated in the declaratory statement is sufficient to identify the claim. Such survey and certificate become a part of the declaratory statement, and such declaratory statement is *prima facie* evidence of the facts therein contained.

Political Code, 1895, p. 304. Amended March 15, 1901.

SECTION 3630. **Miners' Right of Way.**—The owner of a mining claim held under the laws of the United States by patent or otherwise, or under the local laws and customs of the State, has a right of way over and across the land or mining claim, patented or otherwise, of another, as prescribed in this chapter.

SEC. 3631. **Road—Ditch—Cut—Flume—Shaft—Tunnel.**—Whenever a mine or mining claim is so situated that it cannot be conveniently worked without a road thereto, or a ditch to convey water thereto, or a ditch or a cut to convey the water therefrom, or without a flume to carry water and tailings therefrom, or without a shaft or tunnel thereto, which road, ditch, cut, flume, shaft, or tunnel must necessarily pass over, under, through, or across any lands or mining claims owned or occupied by another, such owner is entitled to a right of way for said road, ditch, cut, flume, shaft or tunnel over, under, through and across the lands or mining claims belonging to another, upon compliance with the provisions of this Chapter.

For proceedings in court to secure right of way, see sections 3632 to 3641, Political Code, 1895, p. 307.

SEC. 494. **Statute of Limitations.**—No action for the recovery of mining claims (lode claims excepted), or for the recovery of possession thereof, shall be maintained, unless it appears that the plaintiff or his assigns was seized or possessed of such mining claims within one year before the commencement of such action. [Code of Civil Procedure, 1895, p. 785.]

SEC. 1321. **Customs as Proof.**—In actions respecting mining claims, proof must be admitted of the customs, usages, or regulations established and in force at the bar or diggings embracing such claim, and such customs, usages, or regulations, when not in conflict with the laws of this State or the United States, must govern the decision of the action.

SEC. 1322. **Patent Application—Possession.**—In an action brought to determine the respective rights of claimants to the possession of a mining claim or quartz lode, under the provisions of the Acts of Congress of the United States, it is immaterial which party is in possession, and it is sufficient to confer jurisdiction upon the court if it appears from the pleadings that the application for a patent has been made, and an adverse claim thereto filed and allowed in the proper land office; and the verdict or decision must find which party is entitled to the possession of the premises in dispute.

Code of Civil Procedure, 1895, p. 853.

See Code of 1895, Index, p. 2068, for references to "mines," and "mines and mining," and "mining claims."

For statutes relating to Easements, see Civil Code, 1895, Sections 1250 to 1260, pp. 594 and 595.

Standard of Measurement for Water.

SEC. 1. **Water Measure.**—Hereafter a cubic foot of water (7.48 gallons) per second of time shall be the legal standard for the measurement of water in this State.

SEC. 2. **Water Rights.**—Where water rights expressed in miners' inches shall be considered equivalent to a flow of two and one-half cubic feet (18.7 gallons) per second; two hundred miners' inches shall be considered equivalent to a flow of five cubic feet (37.4 gallons) per second, and this proportion shall be observed in determining the equivalent flow represented by any number of miners' inches.

SEC. 3. **Prior Decree.**—Provided, that the provisions of this bill shall not affect or change the measurement of water heretofore decreed by a court, but such decreed waters shall be measured according to the law in force at the time such decree was made and entered.

SEC. 4. **Repeal.**—Section 1893, Title VIII, Part IV, Division II, of the Civil Code of the State of Montana and any laws in conflict with this Act, are hereby repealed.

Approved March 3, 1899. Session Laws, 1899, p. 117.

NEVADA.

State General Laws.

SECTION 1. **Lode Claims—How Located.**—Any person, a citizen of the United States, or one who has declared his intention to become such, who discovers a vein or lode may locate a claim upon such vein or lode by defining the boundaries of the claim in the manner hereinafter described, and by posting a notice of such location at the point of discovery, which notice must contain:

First—The name of the lode or claim.
Second—The name of the locator or locators.
Third—The date of the location.
Fourth—The number of linear feet claimed in length along the course of the vein, each way from the point of discovery, with the width on each side of the center of the vein, and the general course of the vein or lode as near as may be.

SEC. 2. **Locations—How Evidenced.**—Before the expiration of one hundred and twenty days from the posting of the notice of location, the locator shall sink a discovery shaft upon the claim to a depth of at least ten feet from the lowest part of the rim of such shaft at the surface, or deeper if necessary to show by such work a lode or deposit of mineral in place. A cut or crosscut, or tunnel, which cuts the lode at a depth of ten feet or more, or an open cut of at least ten feet in length along the lode from the point where the lode may be in any manner discovered, shall be equivalent to a discovery shaft. At the location point, and at each corner and angle of the claim, he shall distinctly mark a tree or rock in place, or shall set a stone, which shall be at least six inches wide and eighteen inches long, firmly in a mound or in the earth, so that at least six inches in height of said stone shall be plainly visible from all sides, or shall substantially build a monument which shall rise at least three feet above the surface, or shall erect a post at least four inches square or four inches in diameter, which must be firmly set in the ground or in a mound of earth or rock, and must rise at least three feet above the surface. The tree, rock, stone, post or monument at each corner shall be so marked by letters, figures or otherwise, as to indicate its purpose. The posting of location notice and descriptive memoranda of corners (if that method of marking be used) shall be by conspicuously displaying the same, where practicable, and in other cases by such posting as is in accord with the usage and custom of miners. Where it is impracticable or dangerous to life or limb to mark a tree or rock, or set a stone, or erect a post or monument precisely upon a corner or angle, then the marking of that corner or angle by means of tree, or rock, or stone, or post, or monument, may be done at the nearest practicable point, in such manner as to indicate the right place.

Sec. 3. **Record of Location.**—Within ninety days of the date of posting the location notice upon the claim, the locator shall record his claim with the mining district recorder and the county recorder of the mining district or county in which such claim is situated by a location certificate, which must contain: 1st, the name of the lode or vein; 2d, the name of the locator or locators, 3d, the date of the location, and such description of the location of said claim, with reference to some natural object or permanent monument, as will identify the claim; 4th, the number of linear feet claimed in length along the course of the vein each way from the point of discovery, with a width on each side of the center of the vein, and the general course of the lode or vein as near as may be; 5th, the dimensions and location of the discovery shaft, or its equivalent, sunk upon the claim; 6th, the location and description of each corner, with the markings thereon. Any record of the location of a lode mining claim which shall not contain all the requirements named in this section shall be void. All records of lode or placer mining claims, mill sites or tunnel rights heretofore made by any recorder of any mining district, or any county recorder, are hereby declared to be valid, and to have the same force and effect as records made in pursuance of the provisions of this Act. And any such record, or copy thereof, duly verified by a mining recorder, or duly certified by a county recorder, shall be *prima facie* evidence of the facts therein stated.

Sec. 4. **Extent of Claim.**—The location or record of any vein or lode claim shall be construed to include all surface ground within the surface lines thereof, and all lodes and ledges throughout their entire depth, the top or apex of which lies inside of such lines extended downward, vertically with all parts of such lodes or veins as continue to dip beyond the side lines of the claim, but shall not include any portion of such lodes, veins, or ledges beyond the end lines of the claim, or the end lines continued, whether by dip or otherwise, or beyond the side lines in any other manner than by the dip of the lode.

Sec. 5. **Vein, How Followed.**—If the top or apex of the lode in its longitudinal course extends beyond the exterior lines of the claim at any point on the surface, or as extended vertically downward, such lode may not be followed in its longitudinal course where it is intersected by the exterior lines.

Sec. 6. **Relocations, How Made.**—If at any time the locator of any mining claim heretofore or hereafter located, or his assigns, shall apprehend that his original certificate was defective, erroneous, or that the requirements of the law had not been complied with before filing; or shall be desirous of changing his surface boundaries, or of taking in any part of an overlapping claim which has been abandoned; or in case the original certificate was made prior to the passage of this law, and he shall be desirous of securing the benefits of this Act, such locator or his assigns may file an additional certificate, subject to the provisions of this Act;

provided, that such relocation does not interfere with the existing rights of others at the time of such relocation, and no such relocation or the record thereof shall preclude the claimant or claimants from proving any such titles as he or they may have held under previous location.

SEC. 7. **Relocations of Abandoned Lode Claims.**—The relocation of abandoned lode claims shall be by sinking a new discovery shaft, and fixing new boundaries, in the same manner as if it were the location of a new claim; or the relocator may sink the original discovery shaft ten feet deeper than it was at the time of abandonment, in which case the record must give the depth and dimensions of the original discovery shaft at the date of such relocation, and erect new or adopt the old boundaries, renewing the posts or monuments if removed or destroyed. In either case a new location stake shall be erected. In any case whether the whole or part of an abandoned claim is taken, the record may state that the whole or any part of the new location is located as abandoned property. If it is not known to the relocator that his location is on an abandoned claim, then the provisions of this section do not apply.

SEC. 8. **Survey of Claim.**—Where a locator, or his assigns, has the boundaries and corners of his claim established by a United States deputy mineral surveyor, or a licensed surveyor of this State, and his claim connected with a corner of the public or minor surveys of an established initial point, and incorporates into the record of the claim the field-notes of such survey, and attaches to and files with such location certificate a certificate of the surveyor, setting forth: First, that said survey was actually made by him, giving the date thereof; second, the name of the claim surveyed and the location thereof; third, that the description incorporated in the declaratory statement is sufficient to identify. Such survey and certificate becomes a part of the record, and such record is *prima facie* evidence of the facts therein contained.

SEC. 9. **Annual Assessment.**—The amount of work done or improvements made during each year to hold possession of a mining claim shall be that prescribed by the laws of the United States, to wit: One hundred dollars annually. In estimating the worth of labor required to be performed upon any mining claim, to hold the same under the laws of the United States, the value of a day's labor is hereby fixed at the sum of four dollars; provided however that in the sense of this statute eight hours of labor actually performed upon the mining claim shall constitute a day's labor.

SEC. 10. **Affidavit of Work Done.**—Within sixty days after the performance of labor or making of improvements, required by law to be annually performed or made upon any mining claim, the person in whose behalf such labor was performed, or improvements made, or some one in his behalf, shall make and have recorded by the mining district recorder or the county recorder in books kept for that purpose in the mining district or county in which such mining claim is situated, an affidavit setting forth the amount of money expended, or value of labor or improvements made, or both, the character of expenditures or labor or improvements, a description of the claim or part of the claim affected by such expenditures, or labor or improvements, for what year, and the name of the owner or claimant of said claim, at whose expense the same was made or performed. Such affidavit, or a copy thereof, duly certified by the county recorder, shall be *prima facie* evidence of the performance of such labor or the making of such improvements, or both.

SEC. 11. **Rights of Co-owners.**—Whenever a co-owner or co-owners shall give to a delinquent co-owner or co-owners the notice in writing or notice by publication provided for in Section 2324, Revised Statutes of the United States, an affidavit of the person giving such notice, stating the time, place, manner of service, and by whom and upon whom such service was made, shall be attached to a true copy of such notice, and such notice and affidavit must be recorded by the mining district recorder or county recorder, in books kept for that purpose, in the mining district or county in which the mining claim is situated; within ninety days after the giving of such notice, or if such notice is given by publication in a newspaper, there shall be attached to a printed copy of such notice an affidavit of the printer or his foreman or principal clerk of such paper, stating the date of the first, last, and each insertion of such notice therein, and when and where the newspaper was published during that time, and the name of such newspaper. Such affidavit and notice shall be recorded as aforesaid within one hundred and eighty days after the first publication thereof. The original of such notice and affidavits, or a duly certified copy of the record thereof sha'l be evidence that the delinquent mentioned in section 2324 has failed or refused to contribute his proportion of the expenditure required by that section and of the service or publication of said notice; provided, the writing or affidavit hereinafter provided for is not of record. If such delinquent shall, within the ninety days required by section 2324 aforesaid, contribute to his co-owner or co-owners his proportion of such expenditures, such co-owner or co-owners shall sign and deliver to the delinquent or delinquents a writing, stating that the delinquent or delinquents by name has within the time required by Section 2324 of the Revised Statutes of the United States contributed his share for the year ———, upon the ——— mine, and further stating therein the district, county and State where the same is situate, and the book and page where the location notice is recorded; such writing shall be recorded in the office of the county recorder of said county. If such co-owner or co-owners shall fail to sign and deliver such writing to the delinquent or delinquents within twenty days after such contribution, the co-owner or co-owners so failing as aforesaid shall be liable to a penalty of one hundred dollars, to be recovered by any person for the use of the delinquent or delinquents in any court of competent jurisdiction. If such co-owner or co-owners fail to deliver such writing within said twenty days, then the delinquent, with two disinterested persons having personal knowledge of such contribution, may make affidavit setting forth in what manner, the amount of, to whom and upon what mine, such contribution was made. Such affidavit, or record thereof in the office of the county recorder of the county in which said mine is situate, shall be *prima facie* evidence of such contribution.

SEC. 12. **One Claim—Void Location.**—No notice of location of a lode claim shall claim more than one location, whether the location be made by one or several persons. And if such notice purport to claim more than one location, it shall be absolutely void, except as to the first location therein described. And if they are described together, or so that it cannot be told which location is first described, the notice of location shall be void as to all.

SEC. 13. **Placer Claims—How Located.**—The location of a placer claim shall be made in the following manner: By posting thereon, upon a tree, rock in place, stone, post, or monument, a notice of location, containing the name of the claim, name of locator or locators, date of location, and number of feet or acres claimed, and by marking the boundaries and the location point in the same manner and by the same means as required by the laws of this State for marking the boundaries of lode claim locations; *provided* that where the United States survey has been extended over the land embraced in the location, the claim may be taken by legal subdivisions, and, except the marking of the location point as hereinbefore prescribed, no other markings than those of said survey shall be required.

SEC. 14. **Labor—Certificate.**—Within ninety days after the posting of the notice of location of a placer claim, the locator shall perform not less than twenty dollars' worth of labor upon the claim for the development thereof and shall have recorded by the mining district recorder and the county recorder of the district and county in which the claim is situated, a certificate which shall state the name of the claim, designating it as a placer claim, name of locator or locators, date of location, number of feet or acres claimed, a description of the claim with regard to some natural object or permanent monument, so as to identify the claim, and the kind and amount of work done by him as herein required, and the place on the claim where said work was done. This certificate, or the record thereof, or a duly certified copy of said record, shall be *prima facie* evidence of the recitals therein. But if such certificate do not state all the facts herein required to be stated, it shall be void.

SEC. 15. **Area of Mill Sites.**—The proprietor of a vein or lode claim or mine, or the owner of a quartz mill or reduction works, may locate five acres of non-mineral land as a mill site.

SEC. 16. **Mill Sites, How Located.**—The locator of a mill site shall locate his claim by posting a notice of location thereon, which must contain : 1st, the name of the locator or locators ; 2d, the name of the vein or lode claim, or mine, of which he is the proprietor, or the name of the quartz mill or reduction works of which he is the owner ; 3d, the date of the location ; 4th, the number of feet or acres claimed ; 5th, a description of the claim by such reference to a natural object or permanent monument as shall identify the claim or mill site. And by marking the boundaries of his claim in the same manner as provided in this Act for the marking of the boundaries of a placer mining claim, so far as the same may be applicable thereto.

SEC. 17. **Record of Mill Sites.**—The locator of a mill-site claim or location shall within thirty days from the date of his location, record his location with the mining district recorder and the county recorder of the district or county in which such location is situated by a location certificate, which must be similar in all respects to the one posted on the location.

SEC. 18. **Mill Sites—Void Locations.**—Any record of a mill-site location which shall not contain the name of the locator or locators, the name of the vein or lode claim or mine of which the locator is the proprietor, or the name of the quartz mill or reduction works of which the locator is the owner, the number of feet or acres claimed, and such description as shall identify the claim with reasonable certainty, shall be void.

SEC. 19. **Tunnel Locations—How Made.**—The locator of a tunnel right or location shall locate his tunnel right or location by posting a notice of location at the face or point of commencement of the tunnel which must contain : 1st, the name of the locator or locators; 2d, the date of the location ; 3d, the proposed course or direction of the tunnel ; 4th, the height and width thereof; 5th, the position and character of the boundary monuments ; 6th, a description of the tunnel by such reference to a natural object or permanent monument as shall identify the claim or tunnel right.

SEC. 20. **Tunnel Lines, How Established.**—The boundary lines of the tunnel shall be established by stakes or monuments placed along such lines at an interval of not more than three hundred feet from the face or point of commencement of the tunnel to the terminus of three thousand feet therefrom. The stakes or monuments shall be of the same size and character as those provided for lode or placer claims in this act.

SEC. 21. **Record of Tunnel Locations.**—The locator of a tunnel right or location shall within sixty days from the date of the location record his location with the mining district recorder and the county recorder of the county or district in which such location is situated, which must be similar in all respects to the one posted on the location. Any record of a tunnel right or location which shall not contain all the requirements named in this section, shall be void.

Sec. 22. **Blind Lodes, How Located.**—All blind lodes, or veins or lodes not previously known to exist, discovered in a tunnel run for the development of a vein or lode, or for the discovery of mines, and within three thousand feet from the face of such tunnel, shall be located upon the surface and held in like manner as other lode claims under the provisions of this Act.

Sec. 23. **Application of Provisions of Act.**—The provisions of this Act shall be construed as equally applicable to all classes of locations, except where the requirement as to any one class is manifestly inapplicable to any other class or classes.

Sec. 24. **Certificates.**—Certificates of location and of labor and improvements necessary to hold claims need not be sworn to, and are not required to be in any specified form, nor to state facts in any specific order; but must truly state the required facts.

Sec. 25. **Records.**—Where there is no mining district, or where a district having once existed, the residence of the officers within the district and their places of business within the district where the books are kept are not publicly known, district recording shall not be required of the locator or claim owner. But recording shall be required in the office of the county recorder in all cases; as well where there is a district recorder as where there is none.

Approved March 14, 1899. Session Laws of 1899, p. 93.
Approved March 16, 1897. Session Laws 1897, p. 103.

Preservation of the Mining Records.

Section 1. **Duplicate Copy.**—It shall be the duty of each and every mining recorder of the several mining districts of the State to require all persons locating and recording a mining claim to make a duplicate copy of each and every mining notice, which copy the said mining recorder shall carefully compare with the original, and mark "Duplicate," on its face or margin, and he shall immediately deposit with or transmit the same to the county recorders of the respective counties in which said mining district may be located.

Sec. 2. **District Recorder's Fee.**—The said district mining recorders, at the time of comparing said duplicate notices with the original, shall collect from the locators of said mining claims the sum of one dollar for each and every notice compared, which sum he shall transmit, together with the said duplicate notices, to the county recorders of the respective counties in which said mining claims shall be located.

Sec. 3. **Forwarding Copies.**—Whenever, owing to the distance of the mining district from the county seat, it becomes inconvenient for the district mining recorder to personally deposit the duplicate copy with the county recorder, then in that case he may forward the same by mail or express, or such other manner as will insure safe transit and delivery to the county recorder.

Sec. 4. **County Recorder's Fee.**—The county recorders of the several counties shall receive for their services for recording each of said duplicate notices mentioned in section two of this Act, the sum of one dollar; *provided*, that in case the location is made outside of any organized mining district, or in the absence of a mining recorder in any organized district, then the person or persons making such location shall within ninety days after making such location transmit a duplicate copy of such notice to the recorder of the county in which the location is made, and the recorder shall record the same for a fee of one dollar.

Sec. 5. **Evidence.**—The record of any original or duplicate notice of the location of a mining claim in the office of the county recorder, as herein provided, shall be received in evidence, and have the same force and effect in the courts of the State as the original mining district records.

Sec. 6. **Fine for Misdemeanor.**—Any person neglecting or refusing to comply with the provisions of this Act shall be deemed guilty of a misdemeanor, and upon conviction thereof shall be punished by a fine not exceeding five hundred dollars, or by imprisonment in the county jail not exceeding six months, or by such fine and imprisonment.

Approved February 14, 1885. Session Laws, 1885, p. 27.
Amended March 10, 1897. Session Laws, 1897, p. 77.

An Act to Encourage Mining.

Section 1.—**Mineral Lands.**—The several grants made by the United States to the State of Nevada reserved the mineral lands. Sales of such lands made by the State were made subject to such reservation. Any citizen of the United States, or person having declared his intention to become such, may enter upon any mineral land in this State, notwithstanding the State's selection, and explore for gold, silver, copper, lead, cinnabar, or other valuable minerals, and upon the discovery of such valuable mineral, may work and mine the same in pursuance of the local rules and regulations of the miners, and the laws of the United States; *provided*, that after a person who has purchased land from the State has made valuable improvements thereon, such improvements shall not be taken or injured without full compensation. But such improvement may be condemned for the uses and purposes of mining in like manner as private property is by law condemned and taken for public use. Mining for gold, silver, copper, lead, cinnabar, and other valuable mineral, is the paramount interest of this State, and is hereby declared to be a public use.

Sec. 2. **Minerals Excluded.**—Every contract, patent or deed hereafter made by this State, or the authorized agents thereof, shall contain a provision expressly reserving all mines of gold, silver, copper, lead, cinnabar, and other valuable minerals that may exist in such land, and the State, for itself and its grantees, hereby disclaims any interest in mineral lands heretofore or hereafter selected by the State on account of any grant from the United States. All persons desiring titles to mines upon lands which have been selected by the State must obtain such title from the United States under the laws of Congress, notwithstanding such selection.

Approved March 3, 1887. Session Laws of 1887, p. 102.
Amended March 5, 1897. Session Laws, 1897, p. 36.

Better Preservation of Titles to Mining Claims.

SECTION 1.—Co-owners.—Upon the failure of any one of the several co-owners of a mining claim to contribute his portion of the expenditures required by law, the co-owners who have performed the labor or made the improvements, and who have given such delinquent co-owner the requisite notice, either personally, in writing, or by publication in a newspaper, shall within thirty days after the expiration of the period required by law to vest the interest of such delinquent co-owner in the co-owners who have made the required expenditures, have recorded in the office of the county recorder of the county wherein such mining claim is situated a copy of the notice in writing, if the same shall have been personally served, with an affidavit of such service, or, if the same shall have been given by publication, then a copy of the printed notice, with the affidavit of the newspaper publisher or his clerk, that the same was published ninety days, together with the affidavit of the party signing the notice, to the effect that one or more of the co-owners named in said notice have neither paid their share of the expenditures, nor made or performed their share of the improvements or labor. And such record, or a copy thereof, duly certified by the recorder, shall be *prima facie* evidence of the facts therein stated.

SEC. 2.—Affidavit.—Within thirty days after the performance of labor or making of improvements, required by law to be annually performed or made, upon any lode or mining claim, the person in whose behalf such labor was performed, or improvements made, or some one in his behalf, shall make before and record with the mining recorder of the district wherein such claim is situated, an affidavit setting forth the amount of money expended, or value of labor or improvements made, or both, the character of expenditures, or labor or improvements, a description of the claim, or part of claim affected by such expenditures, or labor or improvements, for what year, and the names of the owners or claimants of said claim at whose expense the same was made or performed. Such affidavit, or a copy thereof, duly certified by the recorder, shall be *prima facie* evidence of the performance of such labor, or the making of such improvements, or both. For taking and recording the affidavit herein required, the mining recorder shall receive a fee of one dollar.

SEC. 3.—**Notice.**—The instruments and records mentioned in sections one and two shall be deemed to impart to subsequent purchasers and incumbrancers, and to all other persons whomsoever, notice of the contents thereof.

Approved March 5, 1887. Session Laws of 1887, p. 136.

NEW MEXICO.

General Territorial Mining Law.

SECTION 2286. **Requirements of a Location.**—Any person or persons desiring to locate a mining claim upon a vein or lode of quartz or other rock in place bearing gold, silver, cinnabar, lead, tin, copper or other valuable deposit, must distinctly mark the location on the ground so that its boundaries may be readily traced, and post in some conspicuous place on such location a notice in writing stating thereon the name or names of the locator or locators, his or their intention to locate the mining claim, giving a description thereof by reference to some natural object or permanent monument as will identify the claims ; and also within three months after posting such notice, cause to be recorded a copy thereof in the office of the recorder of the county in which the notice is posted : *and provided*, no other record of such notice snall be necessary.

SEC. 2287. **Recording Location Certificates.**—In order to carry out the intent of the preceding section, it is hereby made the duty of the probate clerk of the several counties of this Territory, and they are hereby required to provide at the expense of their respective counties such book or books as may be necessary and suitable in which to enter the record hereinbefore provided for. The fees for recording such notices shall be ten cents for every one hundred words.

SEC. 2289. **Ejectment.**—An action of ejectment will lie for the recovery of the possession of the mining claim, as well also of any real estate, where the party suing has been wrongfully ousted from the possession thereof, and the possession wrongfully detained.

SEC. 2290. **Suit by Contestant.**—That when an application is made for a patent to a mine or mining claim under the laws of the United States by any person, persons, company or corporation claiming to own or have an interest therein, and such application is contested by any other person, persons, company or corporation in the land office of the United States, such person, persons, company or corporation so contesting, may bring suit of ejectment in the district court of the county in which the mine or mining claim is situated for the recovery of the same, whether in or out of possession of such mine or claim, and the question as to who was in the possession of the mine or claim at the time when the application was made for patent, or when the suit was begun, shall not be considered by the court, except as it may be necessary in determining the interests of the respective claimants, and their right to the possession of said mine or claim.

SEC. 2291. **Special Verdict—Trespass.**—The court, in an action for the recovery of a mine or mining claim where a patent is applied for, and the contest is pending in the Land Office of the United States, may, upon motion of either party to the suit, require the jury to return a special verdict, if tried by a jury; if not, then the judge trying the same shall make a special finding as to the particular interest each party owns in the mine or claim in dispute, under and by virtue of the mining laws of the United States, which special verdict or finding shall be entered into the judgment and upon the record of the court trying the same: *Provided, however*, There shall be no special verdict by the court or jury, except where the evidence shows both parties to the suit to have a *bona-fide* interest in the mine or claim sued for: *And provided further*, That no third person who may have entered upon such mining claim or any part thereof, for the purpose of locating or claiming the same before or during such litigation in the district court growing out of any contest in any United States land office in this Territory, shall acquire any interest either at law or in equity in the claim or any part thereof in dispute, and shall be deemed and declared a trespasser or trespassers, unless he or they have been, or may, during the pendency of such litigation in the district court resulting from such contest in the United States Land Office, by a proper application to the court, be made party or parties to such suit adverse to either of such litigants, or both, or shall have taken such legal steps to assert his or their claim in a court of competent jurisdiction within six months after the commencement of such contest in the United States Land Office.

SEC. 2292. **Work During Pendency of Suit.**—That nothing herein shall prohibit the working and developing of a mine or mining claim by either party in interest who may be in possession of the mine or claim during the pendency of the suit, nor shall this act prohibit any one from bringing an action for damages or a suit in equity to prevent waste. This act shall apply to any and all suits for the recovery of a mine or mining claim which are now or are hereafter commenced.

SEC. 2293. **Measuring or Surveying During Suit.**—In all actions at law, or suits in equity, now pending in any of the district courts of this Territory, or hereafter commenced in such courts, wherein the title or right of possession to any mining claim, or ores and minerals is in dispute, or any party to such action or suit shall have the right to go upon or enter the workings of said mining claim for the purpose of measuring or surveying the same, either upon the surface or in the workings thereof, peaceably, and without molestation; the costs and expenses of such measurement or survey to be paid by the party for whose use and benefit the same was done.

SEC. 2294. **Who Shall Survey.**—The right to go upon and enter said mining claim shall be extended to the party applying therefor, as well as a surveyor and two chain carriers.

SEC. 2295. **Notice of Survey.**—Before any person may enter upon or go into the workings of such mine without the consent of the person or corporation in possession, he shall give not less than five days' notice in writing to such person in possession, or to his agent or manager, and if the possession is held by a corporation, said notice shall be served upon the president, agent or manager of such corporation, or upon the foreman in charge of the mine, that at a certain date, specified in said notice, he desires to enter upon or go into the workings of said mine, as the case may be, for the purpose of surveying and taking a measurement of the same, in order that he may be able to present the facts on the trial.

SEC. 2296. **Court Proceeding on Refusal of Survey.**—If such person or corporation shall not permit any party in interest in such suit or action to go upon or enter said mine, as contemplated in the preceding sections, after having been notified in the manner designated, the court may, upon proper showing, verified by affidavit or otherwise, exclude all evidence offered on the trial by the party so refusing, to (and) render judgment or decree in favor of the party giving such notice: *Provided*, That the court may, in its discretion, make an order directing the sheriff to go upon the ground with the party applying for the measurement and survey of such mine, and place the person so applying in possession, for the purpose of measuring and surveying the same, in which case the court may direct the payment of costs as may be just and proper.

SEC. 2297. **Survey as Evidence.**—The competency, relevancy and effect of such survey and measurement, as evidence, shall be governed by the ordinary rules of evidence in civil cases.

SEC. 2298. **Discovery Shaft or Equivalent.**—That the locator or locators of any mining claim, located after this act shall take effect, shall, within ninety days from the date of taking possession of the same, sink a discovery shaft upon such claim, to a depth of at least ten feet from the lowest part of the rim of such shaft at the surface, exposing mineral in place, or shall drive a tunnel, adit, or open cut upon such claim, to at least ten feet below the surface, exposing mineral in place.

SEC. 2299. **Boundaries—How Marked.**—The surface boundaries of mining claims hereafter located shall be marked by four substantial posts or monuments, one at each corner of such claim, on the ground, so that its boundaries can be readily traced, and shall otherwise conform to Section 2286.

SEC. 2300. **Relocation—How Made.**—The relocation of any mining ground, which is subject to relocation, shall be made in the same way as an original location is required by law to be made, except the relocator may either sink a new shaft upon the ground relocated to the depth of at least ten feet from the lowest part of the rim of such shaft at the surface, exposing mineral in place, or drive a new tunnel, adit, or open cut upon such ground, at least ten feet below the surface, exposing mineral in place, or the relocator may sink the original discovery shaft ten feet deeper than it is at the time of relocation, or drive the original tunnel, adit, or open cut upon such claim ten feet further.

SEC. 2301. **Amended or Additional Location.**—If at any time the owner of any mining claim heretofore or hereafter located, or his assigns, shall apprehend that the original notice of location is defective, erroneous or the requirement of law has not been complied with before filing; or shall be desirous of changing his surface boundaries or to take in any part of an overlapping claim which has been abandoned, or in case the original notice of location was made prior to the passage of this act and the owner shall be desirous of obtaining the benefits of this act, such owner may file in the office where notices of location are by law required to be filed, an amended or additional notice of location, subject to the provisions of this act: *Provided*, That such additional or amended notice of location does not interfere with the existing right of others at the time of filing such notice; and no such a nended or additional location, or record thereof, shall preclude the claimant or his assigns from proving any such title as he or they may have held under the previous location.

SEC. 2302. **Destroying Location Notices.**—Any person who shall take down, remove, alter or destroy any stake, post, monument or notice of location upon any mining claim without the consent of the owner or owners thereof, shall be deemed guilty of a misdemeanor, and on conviction, shall be punished by a fine not exceeding one hundred dollars or by imprisonment in the county jail not exceeding six months, or by both such fine and imprisonment.

SEC. 2303. **Abandonment, How Evidenced—Liens Protected.**—In addition to the provision of law now in force in respect to the abandonment of mining claims, they may be abandoned in the following manner: The owner or owners of any mining claim, wishing to abandon the same, may sign and acknowledge in the same manner provided by law for the acknowledgment of deeds, and file for record in the office of the county recorder, a certificate describing the same, stating when and by whom located, the name of the claim, the book and page where the notice of location of such claim is recorded; that he or they give up and abandon such claim, and that the same is open and subject to relocation. Upon the filing of such certificate, the mining claim therein described shall be considered abandoned and open to relocation as if the same had never been located, and the owner or owners thereof forever estopped from claiming any right or interest therein under the location mentioned in said certificate: *Provided*, That this provision for abandonment shall not apply to any claim or location upon which any mortgage, lien or other incumbrance exists.

SEC. 2304. **Liens—How Protected.**—When the owner or owners of any mining claim or claims now located or which may hereafter be located, upon which there shall exist any mortgage, miner's or mechanic's lien, or other encumbrance of any kind which may be hereafter made or incurred, shall refuse, neglect, or fail, up to the first day of December of any year, to perform thereon the annual labor or make thereon the annual expenditure required by law to be made in order to prevent the same from becoming open to re-location, in such case the holder or owner of such mortgage lien or encumbrance, may, upon the first day of December of such year or any time thereafter, before any such mining claim or claims shall have been relocated, enter with his or their workmen and employés upon the same and perform, or cause to be performed, the one hundred dollars' worth of labor or make the one hundred dollars' worth of improvements upon such claim or claims as by law required to be done or made each year in order to prevent such claim or claims from becoming open to relocation; that such work shall be done and improvements made in a workmanlike manner; that for the purpose of performing or causing to be performed such labor and improvements, the holder or holders of such mortgage, miner's or mechanic's lien, or other encumbrance, shall be considered the agent or the agents of the owner or owners of such mining claim or claims; that the owner or owners of such mining claim or claims, or any person or persons, shall not in any manner prevent, obstruct, hinder, or delay the performance of any labor or the making of such improvements, and may be restrained from so doing by an injunction; that upon the completion of the one hundred dollars' worth of labor or improvements by the holder or holders of any mortgage, miner's or mechanic's lien or other encumbrance as aforesaid, upon any mining claim, as herein provided, all sum or sums of money expended by him or them shall be and become a lien upon the said mining claim or claims, and from the date of the completion of the same, draw the same rate of interest as the principal sum of such mortgage, miner's or mechanic's lien, or other encumbrance, and may be foreclosed according to law.

SEC. 2305. **Punishment for Obstructing Certain Work.**—Any person or persons who shall prevent, obstruct, hinder or delay the performance of the labor or the making of the improvements mentioned in the last preceding section of this act, shall be deemed guilty of a misdemeanor, and upon conviction, shall be punished by a fine of not less than one hundred dollars, or over five hundred dollars, or by imprisonment in the county jail for a period not less than six months, nor more than one year, or by both fine and imprisonment.

SEC. 2306. **Rights of Stockholders.**—Any person owning stock in any corporation or company owning or operating mines in this Territory, shall at any time during the business hours of the day have the right to enter in and upon any and all mines of such corporation or company, and all underground workings connected therewith for the purpose of examining the same.

SEC. 2307. **Punishment for Refusal to Stockholder.**—Every

corporation or company or officer or agent of such corporation or company who shall refuse to allow upon demand any person owning in such corporation or company, to enter such mines, as provided in section two thousand three hundred and six, shall be guilty of a misdemeanor, and the corporation or company shall forfeit and pay to the party injured a penalty of one hundred dollars for every such refusal, and all damages resulting therefrom.

Sec. 2308. **Definition of Stockholder.**—Whenever the words Any person owning stock occur in the above section, they shall be taken and considered to mean stockholders whose names appear on the stock book of the company as owners of stock, and none others.

Sec. 2311. **Punishment for Defacing Location Notice.**—Any person or persons, or the manager, officer, agent or employé of any person, firm, corporation or association, who shall in any manner alter, deface or change the location notice of any mining claim in this Territory, located under the laws of the United States and of this Territory, or any local regulations in force in the district wherein such claim is situated thereby in any manner affecting the rights of any person, firm or corporation, to such claim or location, or the land covered thereby, shall be deemed guilty of a misdemeanor, and upon conviction thereof before any court of competent jurisdiction, shall be fined in a sum not less than one hundred dollars, nor more than five hundred dollars, or imprisoned in the county jail for not less than sixty days, nor more than one year, or by both such fine and imprisonment in the discretion of the court trying the case. Nothing herein contained shall affect the rights of such locator or locators, and his or their assigns, to correct errors in such notice and file amended location notices as provided in section two thousand three hundred and one, and the laws of the United States: *Provided*, Such change shall not affect or change the date of such location notice, or affect the rights of any other person.

Sec. 2312. **Punishment of Certain Persons for Fraudulent Relocation.**—Any person or persons, or the manager, officer, agent or employé of any person, firm or corporation, who shall, either by himself or acting in collusion with others, relocate or attempt to relocate, or procure, or become interested, directly or indirectly in, and the relocation of, or in any manner attempt to hold possession of any forfeited mining claim, contrary to the provisions of this act, or who shall locate, or in any manner become interested in the location of any other claim which shall include the whole, or any portion of the ground covered by such forfeited claim, contrary to this act, shall be deemed guilty of a misdemeanor, and upon conviction thereof before any court of competent jurisdiction shall be subject to the same penalty and punishment as provided in section two thousand three hundred and eleven.

SEC. 2313. **Trespass—Court Proceedings.**—When any person, firm or corporation shall be lawfully and peaceably in possession of any mining claim in this Territory, and shall have complied with all the requirements of law and regulations in force in the district in which said mining claim is situated, such persons, firm or corporation shall be deemed to be the rightful possessor of such mining claim and of the land included therein; and any person or the officer, agent or employé of any corporation who shall by force, intimidation, fraud, or stealth, or in the temporary absence of the rightful possessor, enter upon such mining claim with intent to hold the same, or any part thereof, against the rightful possessor, shall be considered a trespasser, and the judge of the district court for the district in which such claim is situated shall, upon the proper showing of such facts made by affidavit or by oral testimony upon a hearing ordered for that purpose, and upon the filing with the clerk of said district court of a good and sufficient bond, grant an order to show cause why a writ of injunction should not issue, enjoining and restraining such trespasser, his servants, agents and employés, and any person associated with him, from in any manner interfering with the rightful possessor in the possession of such claim until the final disposition of said cause.

SEC. 2314. The owner or owners of lands within this Territory, the title to which has been vested by letters patent from the United States Government, may make and file in the office of the county clerk of the county in which such lands are situated, such rules and regulations, not inconsistent with the laws of the United States and of this Territory, as they may see fit, governing the location and acquisition of mining claims thereon, which rules and regulations when so filed shall be binding upon all parties, and a copy thereof duly certified by the county recorder shall be received and admitted as evidence in any suit or proceedings relating to such mining claims; such rules and regulations may be changed and supplemented from time to time by other rules and regulations filed in like manner, providing that such change shall not affect rights acquired prior thereto.

SEC. 2315. **Affidavit of Work Done.**—The owner or owners of any unpatented mining claim in this Territory, located under the laws of the United States and of this Territory, shall, within sixty days from and after the time within which the assessment work required by law to be done upon such claim should have been done and performed, cause to be filed with the recorder of the county in which such mining claim is situated an affidavit setting forth the time when such work was done, and the amount, character and actual cost thereof, together with the name or names of the person or persons who performed such work; and such affidavit, when made and filed as herein provided, shall be *prima facie* evidence of the facts therein stated. The failure to make and file such affidavit as herein provided shall, in any contest, suit or proceedings touching the title to such claim, throw the burden of proof upon the owner or owners of such claim to show that such work has been done according to law.

SEC. 2316. **Stealing Ores.**—Any person wrongfully extracting or carrying away or concealing or selling or attempting to sell ores from any mine, being the property of another, shall be deemed guilty of felony, and on conviction thereof shall be punished as for grand larceny, and the defendant or defendants shall be liable to the owner or owners of said ore for the value thereof recoverable by an action at law.

SEC. 2317. **Purchase of Stolen Ore.**—Any person or persons who shall knowingly purchase, or contract to purchase or make any payment for, or on account of, any ore which shall have been wrongfully extracted or stolen from any mine, shall be considered an accessory after the fact to the unlawful extracting or stealing of such ore, and upon conviction, shall be subjected to the same punishment to which the principals may be liable.

SEC. 2318. **Record of Ores Delivered.**—That every person, association or corporation that shall be engaged in the business of milling, sampling, concentrating, reducing, shipping or purchasing ores in the Territory of New Mexico, shall keep and preserve a book, in which shall be entered at the time of the delivery of each lot of ore: 1st, the name of the party on whose behalf such ore is delivered as stated; 2d, the name of the teamster, packer or other persons actually delivering such ore, and the name of the owner of the team or pack train delivering such ore; 3d, the weight or amount of each lot of ore; 4th, the name and location of the mine or claim from which it shall be stated that the same had been mined or procured; 5th, the date of delivery of any and all lots or parcels of ore.

SEC. 2319. **Access to Record of Delivery.**—Whenever affidavit shall have been made before any justice of the peace or notary public in any county in this Territory by any person, that ore has been stolen from him, stating as near as may be the amount and value of the ore stolen, such person, upon presentation of a certified copy of such affidavit, shall have access to such books, and may examine the entries which may have been made therein during a period of twelve months next preceding the filing of such affidavit

SEC. 2320. **Failure to Keep Record and Allow Access.**—Every person, association or corporation that shall fail or refuse to keep the book required by the terms of section two thousand three hundred and eighteen, or shall fail or refuse to make any proper entry therein, or who shall refuse to any person who may be entitled to the same, as provided by section two thousand three hundred and nineteen, the right of inspection thereof, shall forfeit and pay for each and every violation of the provisions of said section, a penalty of not less than fifty, nor more than three hundred, dollars, to be collected by action of debt at the suit of any person who may have made the necessary affidavit provided for in section two thousand three hundred and nineteen to entitle such person to access to such books. In addition to said penalty, any person, association or corporation violating the provisions of the said section two thousand three hundred and eighteen, shall be liable at the suit of the party or person aggrieved, in the proper form of action, for all damages which may accrue to any party or person by reason of any such violation. And in all actions the fact that a false entry has been made shall be *prima facie* evidence that the same was made wilfully or knowingly.

SEC. 2321. **Failure to Keep Proper Record.**—If any person, association or corporation shall fail or neglect to make the inquiries necessary to the making of the proper entries in said book as provided by section two thousand three hundred and eighteen, or shall so negligently make entries therein that any lot of ore cannot be particularly identified, or so negligently that it cannot be perceived therefrom what person delivered any lot of ore or received the proceeds of the same when purchased, or shall fail to keep such book or shall wilfully suffer the same to be lost or mislaid, so that the same cannot be produced for inspection, such failure or neglect shall not excuse any party defendant in any suit brought under the preceding section from judgment for any penalties prescribed by said section.

SEC. 2322. **Assessory to Unlawful Holding.**—Any person, association or corporation, or the agent of any person, association or corporation who shall knowingly purchase or contract to purchase, or shall make any payment for or on account of any ore which shall have been taken from any mine or claim, by any person or persons who have taken or may be holding possession of any such mine or claim contrary to law, shall be considered as accessory after the fact to the unlawful holding or taking of such mine or claim, and upon conviction shall be subjected to the same punishment to which the principals may be liable.

SEC. 2323. **False Weights.**—Any person, association or corporation, or the agent of any person, association or corporation engaged in the business of milling, sampling, concentrating, reducing, shipping or purchasing ores, as aforesaid, who shall keep or use any false or fraudulent scales or weights for weighing ore, or who shall keep or use any false or fraudulent assay scales or weights for ascertaining the assay value of ore, knowing them to be false, every person so offending shall be deemed guilty of a misdemeanor, and on conviction thereof shall be fined in a sum not exceeding one thousand dollars, nor less than one hundred dollars, or imprisonment not more than one year, or both, at the discretion of the court.

SEC. 2324. **Changing True Value of Ores.**—Any person, corporation or association, or the agent of any person, corporation or association engaged in the milling, sampling, concentrating, reducing, shipping or purchasing of ores in this Territory, who shall in any manner knowingly alter or change the true value of any ores delivered to him or them, so as to deprive the seller of the result of the correct value of the same, or who shall substitute other ores for that delivered to him or them, or who shall issue any bill of sale or certificate of purchase that does not exactly and truthfully state the actual weight, assay value and total amount paid for any lot or lots of ore purchased, or who, by any secret understanding or agreement with another, shall issue a bill of sale or certificate of purchase that does not truthfully and correctly set forth the weight, assay value and total amount paid for any lot or lots of ore purchased by him or them, shall be deemed guilty of a misdemeanor, and on conviction thereof shall be fined in a sum not exceeding one thousand dollars, nor less than one hundred dollars, or imprisonment not more than one year, or both, at the discretion of the court.

SEC. 2325. **Felony.**—If any person, lessee, licensee or employé in or about any mine in this Territory, shall break and sever, with intent to steal, the ore or mineral from any mine, lode, ledge or deposit, in this Territory, or shall take, remove or conceal the ore or mineral from any mine, lode, ledge or deposit, with intent to defraud the person or persons rightfully entitled to any such mine, lode, ledge or deposit, such offender shall be deemed guilty of felony, and on conviction shall be punished as for grand larceny.

SEC. 2326. **Fraudulent Misrepresentation.**—Any person or persons who shall falsely or fraudulently misrepresent the character or quality of any mine or the ores, minerals or deposits therein with fraudulent intent to injure the owner or owners of such mine or to depreciate the value of the same, or to prevent a sale thereof, shall be deemed guilty of blackmail, and upon conviction thereof shall be fined in a sum not to exceed one thousand dollars, nor less than five hundred, or to be imprisoned in the county jail not exceeding ninety days, or with both such fine and imprisonment, in the discretion of the court.

SEC. 2327. **Damage by Live Stock.**—Hereafter the owner of any live stock in this Territory shall not be liable to the owner or his agent of any mining or mineral claim or mill site for damages done by way of trespass upon the same by said live stock other than for actual damage done to buildings, tents, mining supplies or other personal property situated thereon: *Provided*, That nothing in this Act shall be construed as abridging or curtailing any of the existing rights of any such owner whenever any such mining or mineral claim or mill site may be used by the owners thereof, his tenant or lessee, as a live stock ranch.

SEC. 2328. **Right of Way.**—That any mine owner or mine owners of any mining corporation, for the purpose of transporting ores to a mill or reduction works of any sort for the reduction of ores, shall have a right of way for a tramway or railway across lands of other persons by condemnation and payment of damages.

[Sections 2329 to 2336 inclusive provide the method of procedure.]

SEC. 2337. **Disability of Employe of Smelting Works.**—Whenever any employé of any corporation, person or persons engaged in the management and operation of any smelting works in the Territory of New Mexico, shall become disabled and rendered unfitted for labor by reason of lead poisoning, which said lead poisoning shall be the result and consequence of said employé's performance and proper discharge of said employé's duties in and about said smelting works, said employé shall be provided with and receive all proper medical attendance, medicines and sustenance during such disability, at the expense of said corporation, person or persons so employing him.

SEC. 2338. **Failure to Provide for Disabled Employe of Smelting Works.**—If any such corporation, person or persons engaged in the management and operation of any smelting works in the Territory of New Mexico shall fail to provide such employé with all proper medical attendance, medicines and sustenance during such disability of said employé, then the reasonable expense of providing such employé with all proper medical attendance, medicines and sustenance during such disability of said employé may be recovered from such corporation, person or persons so engaged in the management and operation of smelting works as aforesaid, in an action at law by and in the name of any person or persons rendering or providing such employé with the said medical attendance, medicines and sustenance.

SEC. 2358. **Termination of Mining Lease.**—Hereafter, any lease upon any mine, or portion of a mine, not given in writing, for a specified time, shall not be terminated until after notice of the date of such termination, given by the lessor to the lessee, not less than thirty days prior to such date of termination.

SEC. 2359. The lessor and the mine upon which any lease is terminated without thirty days' notice, as provided in section two thousand three hundred and fifty-eight, shall be liable to the lessee for all damages resulting from such termination : *Provided*, That nothing in this act shall prevent the forfeiture and termination of any such lease without such notice when the lessee is working the leased ground in such manner as to damage the property.

Extracts from Compiled Laws of 1897, as amended by act of March 16, 1899. Session Laws, 1899, p. 111.

An Act Relative to Mill-Ditches.

SECTION 1. **Course.**—That the course of any mill-ditch already constructed shall not be changed, unless it be through some irrigating ditch to the cultivated lands which shall have the preference.

SEC. 2. **Arbitrators.**—That whenever it may become necessary for the owner or owners of a mill to construct a mill-ditch, when the same is to be constructed in whole or in part over the land of another owner, and the said owner does not permit the construction of said ditch, then and in that event, the owner of the mill and the owner of the land over which the ditch is to pass shall apply to the justice of the peace of the precinct asking him to appoint three arbitrators or assessors, each party shall name one and the justice shall name the third but, if the land owner refuses to name one then the justice shall name two and the owner of the mill one.

SEC. 3. **Record Proceedings.**—That the justice of the peace shall make a record of the fact that the arbitrators or assessors were appointed and shall swear them to act faithfully and impartially, as such arbitrators and to report to the said justice of the peace the amount by them assessed in order that the same may be turned over to the justice of the peace and by him turned over to the owner or owners of the land over which said ditch passes, and the said amount shall be paid in cash.

SEC. 4. **Payment.**—That if the owner of the mill for which the ditch is desired pay the amount assessed against him, as above required, he may construct his ditch as the same may be designated by the arbitrators and according to the record of the justice of the peace of the report of the said arbitrators.

Approved March 16, 1899. Session Laws, 1899, p. 130.

An Act to Encourage the Development of Mineral Resources.

SECTION 1. **Taxation.**—That no tax shall be assessed, levied or collected upon any mining claim in this Territory, located under the mining laws of the United States, nor upon any shaft or workings therein, until after patent shall have been duly issued therefor by the United States; and for one year thereafter; but nothing herein contained shall be held or construed to exempt from taxation, as now provided by law, the improvements upon any such mining claim, other than the shafts and other workings as aforesaid, nor the net product of any such mining claim. Approved March 16, 1899—Session Laws, 1899, p. 130.

An Act in Relation to Mining Claims.

SECTION 1. **Failure To Do Annual Work.**—Whenever the locator or locators of any mining claim in this Territory, located under the laws of the United States and of this Territory, shall fail or neglect to do and to perform, or cause to be done and performed, upon such mining claim, the amount and character of work necessary to be done and performed thereon as required by section 1 of Chapter XXV of the Acts of the 28th Session of the Legislative Assembly of the Territory of New Mexico, within the ninety days from the date of such location as provided in said section, such locator, or locators, and his or her assigns, shall forfeit all right to such mining claim, and shall henceforth for a period of ninety days from and after the expiration of such ninety days, be debarred and prohibited from relocating or procuring, or becoming interested, directly or indirectly, except as a *bona fide* purchaser for value in the relocation of such claim, or the location of any other claim which will include any portion of the ground which was included in such forfeited claim.

SEC. 2. **Forfeited Claims.**—Whenever the locator or locators, or his or their assigns, of any lode or placer mining claim in this Territory, located under the laws of the United States and of this Territory, shall fail to do or cause to be done, the amount of the assessment work required by law to be done thereon, within the time prescribed by law, such claim shall be considered forfeited and abandoned, and such locator or locators, and his or their assigns, shall thenceforth for the period of ninety days from and after the expiration of the time within which such work should have been done, be debarred and prohibited from relocating such claim, or becoming interested directly or indirectly, except as a *bona fide* purchaser for value, in the location or relocation of any claim which shall include the land covered by such forfeited claim, or any part thereof. And the subsequent locator of such claim, or of any claim including the whole or any part of the land covered by such forfeited claim, shall not be entitled to credit for any work that may have been done thereon before the time of such forfeiture, nor shall the former owner of any such forfeited claim have any right to compensation therefor.

SEC. 3. **Altering or Defacing Mining Notices.**—Any person or persons, or the manager, officer, agent or employé of any person, firm, corporation or association, who shall in any manner alter, deface or change the location notice of any mining claim in this Territory located under the laws of the United States and of this Territory, or any local regulations in force in the district wherein such claim is situated, thereby in any manner affecting the rights of any person, firm or corporation, to such claim or location, or the land covered thereby, shall be deemed guilty of a misdemeanor, and upon conviction thereof before any court of competent jurisdiction, shall be fined in a sum not less than one hundred dollars, nor more than five hundred dollars, or imprisoned in the county jail for not less than sixty days, nor more than one year, or by both such fine and imprisonment, in the discretion of the court trying the case.

Nothing herein contained shall affect the rights of such locator or locators, and his or their assigns, to correct errors in such notice and file amended location notices as provided in Section 4 of said Chapter XXV of the Session Laws of 1889, and the laws of the United States; *Provided*, such change shall not affect or change the date of such location notice, or affect the rights of any other person.

SEC. 4. **Illegal Relocations.**—Any person or persons, or the manager, officer, agent or employé of any person, firm or corporation, who shall, either by himself, or acting in collusion with others, relocate or attempt to relocate, or procure, or become interested, directly or indirectly in, and the relocation of, or in any manner attempt to hold possession of, any forfeited mining claim, contrary to the provisions of this Act, or who shall locate or in any manner become interested in the location of any other claim which shall include the whole, or any portion, of the ground covered by such forfeited claim, contrary to this Act, shall be deemed guilty of a misdemeanor, and upon conviction thereof before any court of competent jurisdiction shall be subject to the same penalty and punishment as provided in Section 3 of this Act.

SEC. 5. **Possession—Trespass.**—When any person, firm or corporation shall be lawfully and peaceably in possession of any mining claim in this Territory, and shall have complied with all the requirements of law and regulations in force in the district in which said mining claim is situated, such persons, firm, or corporation, shall be deemed to be the rightful possessor of such mining claim and of the land included therein; and any person or the officer, agent or employé of any corporation who shall by force, intimidation, fraud or stealth, or in the temporary absence of the rightful possessor enter upon such mining claim with intent to hold the same, or any part thereof against the rightful possessor, shall be considered a trespasser; and the judge of the district court for the district in which such claim is situated shall, upon the proper showing of such facts made by affidavit or by oral testimony upon a hearing ordered for that purpose, and upon the filing with the clerk of said district court of a good and sufficient bond, grant an order to show cause why a writ of injunction should not issue, enjoining and restraining such trespasser, his servants, agents, and employés, and any persons associated with him, from in any manner interfering with the rightful possessor in the possession of such claim until the final disposition of said cause.

SEC. 6. **Boundaries, How Marked.**—That Section 2 of Chapter XXV of the Acts of the 28th Session of the Legislative Assembly of the Territory of New Mexico be, and the same is hereby, amended to read as follows:

"Within one hundred and twenty days from the date of locating any mining claim within this Territory, the locator or locators thereof shall cause the surface boundaries of such claim to be plainly marked by eight substantial posts or stone monuments, each projecting at least three feet above the surface of the ground, to wit: One at each corner of said claim, and one at the center of each end and side line thereof, each of which posts or monuments shall be plainly marked so as to show the name of such claim and the direction thereof from each post or monument."

SEC. 7. **Regulations Filed by Owners of Patented Land.**— The owner or owners of lands within this Territory, the title to which has been vested by letters-patent from the United States Government, may make and file in the office of the county clerk of the county in which such lands are situated, such rules and regulations, not inconsistent with the laws of the United States, and of this Territory, as they may see fit, governing the location and acquisition of mining claims thereon, which rules and regulations when so filed shall be binding upon all parties, and a copy thereof duly certified by the county recorder shall be received and admitted as evidence in any suit or proceedings relating to such mining claims; such rules and regulations may be changed and supplemented from time to time by other rules and regulations filed in like manner, providing that such change shall not affect rights acquired prior thereto.

SEC. 8. **Affidavit of Work Done.**—The owner or owners of any unpatented mining claim in this Territory, located under the laws of the United States and of this Territory, shall within sixty days from and after the time within which the assessment work required by law to be done upon such claim should have been done and performed, cause to be filed with the recorder of the county in which such mining claim is situated, an affidavit setting forth the time when such work was done, and the amount, character and actual cost thereof, together with the name or names of the person or persons who performed such work; and such affidavit when made and filed as herein provided shall be *prima facie* evidence of the facts therein stated. The failure to make and file such affidavit as herein provided shall, in any contest, suit or proceedings touching the title to such claim, throw the burden of proof upon the owner or owners of such claim to show that such work has been done according to law.

Approved March 18, 1897. Session Laws, 1897, p. 125.

Delinquent Co-Owners.

A lengthy law prescribing transfer of title from delinquent co-owners of mining claims is found on pages 326 to 330, Session Laws, 1903.

Approved February 26, 1903.

OREGON.

Liens on Mining Claims.

Work and Materials.—SEC. 1. Every person who shall do work or furnish materials for the working or development of any mine, lode, mining claim or deposit yielding metals or minerals of any kind, or for the working or development of any such mine, lode or deposit, in search of such metals or minerals; and to all persons who shall do work or furnish materials upon any shaft, tunnel, incline, adit, drift or other excavation designed or used for the purpose of draining or working any such mine, lode or deposit, shall have a lien upon the same to secure to him the payment of the work or labor done or materials furnished, etc.

[The claim must be filed with the county clerk within sixty days after completion of the labor or the furnishing of the material, and suit must be brought within six months.]

Approved February 20, 1891. Session Laws, 1891, p. 76.

An Act Relating to Mining Claims.

SECTION 1. **Vein Locations—How Made.**—Any person, a citizen of the United States, or one who has declared his intention to become such, who discovers a vein or lode of mineral bearing rock in place upon the unappropriated public domain of the United States within this State, may locate a claim upon such vein or lode so discovered, by posting thereon a notice of such discovery and location, which said notice shall contain: First, the name of the lode or claim; second, the name or names of the locator or locators; third, the date of the location; fourth, the number of linear feet claimed along the vein or lode each way from the point of discovery, with the width on each side of the said vein or lode; fifth, the general course or strike of the vein or lode as nearly as may be with reference to some natural object or permanent monument in the vicinity thereof, and by defining the boundaries upon the surface of each claim, so that the same may be readily traced. Such boundaries shall be marked within thirty days after posting of such notice by six substantial posts, projecting not less than three feet above the surface of the ground, and not less than four inches square or in diameter, or by substantial mounds of stone, or earth and stone, at least two feet in height, to wit: one such post or mound of rock at each corner and at the center ends of such claims.

SEC. 2. **Record of Locations.**—Such locator shall, within sixty days from and after the posting of the location notice by him upon the lode or claim, file for record with the recorder of conveyances, if there be one, who shall be the custodian of mining records and miners' liens, otherwise with the clerk of the county wherein the said claim is situate, a copy of the notice so posted by him upon the lode or claim, having attached thereto an affidavit showing that the work required to be done by Section 3 of this Act has been done and performed, and shall pay a fee of one dollar for such record thereof, which said sum the recorder or clerk shall immediately pay over to the treasurer of such county, and shall take his receipt therefor, as in case of other county funds coming into his possession as such officer. Such recorder or clerk shall immediately record such location notice and the affidavit annexed thereto. No location notice shall be entitled to record or recorded until the work required by Section 3 of this Act has been done and the affidavit or proof thereof is attached to the notice to be recorded.

SEC. 3. **Work on Discovery Shaft.**—Before the expiration of sixty days from the date of the posting of the notice of discovery upon his claim as aforesaid, and before recording the notice of location as required by section 2 of this Act the locator must sink a discovery shaft upon the claim located to a depth of at least ten feet from the lowest part of the rim of such shaft at the surface, or deeper if necessary, to show by such work a lode or vein of mineral deposit in place. A cut or cross-cut or tunnel which cuts the lode at a depth of ten feet, or an open cut at least six feet deep, four feet wide, and ten feet in length along the lode from the point where the same may be in any manner discovered, is equivalent to such discovery shaft. Such work shall not be deemed a part of the assessment work required by the Revised Statutes of the United States. The locator or some one for him who did work upon and has knowledge of the facts relating to the sinking of the discovery shaft shall make and attach to the copy of the notice of location to be recorded an affidavit showing the compliance by the locator with the provisions of this section, which affidavit shall be recorded with such copy of the location notice.

SEC. 4. **Abandoned Claims.**—Abandoned claims shall be deemed unappropriated mineral lands, and titles thereto shall be obtained as in this Act specified, without reference to any work previously done thereon.

SEC. 5. **Real Estate.**—Mining claims so located shall thereafter be deemed real estate, and the owner of the possessory right thereto shall have a legal estate therein, with the meaning of Section 316 of Hill's Code.

SEC. 6. **Exempt from Taxation.**—Prior to the obtaining of patent from the general Government of the United States to such claim, the same shall be exempt from taxation, except as to the improvements, machinery and buildings thereon.

SEC. 7. **Proceedings to Divest Title.**—All conveyances of mining claims, or of interests therein, either quartz or placer, shall be subject to the provisions governing transfers and mortgages of other realty as to execution, recordation, foreclosure, execution sale, and redemption thereunder, but such redemption by the judgment debtor must take place within sixty days from date of confirmation, or such right is lost.

SEC. 8. **Proceedings in Redemption.**—In case of redemption from sale under judgment or decree, the redemptioner shall pay such sum or sums as are now required by law for redemption under execution sale, and such additional sum as may have been expended upon the property so redeemed by the purchaser under execution, or his assigns, in order to keep alive the possessory right thereto after such execution sale, not exceeding the sum of one hundred dollars for each claim, with ten per centum interest thereon from date of such expenditure or expenditures.

SEC. 9. **Ditches are Real Estate.**—Ditches and mining flumes, permanently affixed to the soil, are hereby declared to be real estate; *Provided*, that whenever any person, company, or corporation, being the owner of any such ditch, flume, and the water right appurtenant thereto, shall cease to operate or exercise ownership over said ditch, flume or water right, for a period of five years, and every person, company, or corporation who shall remove from this State with the intent or purpose to change his or its residence, and shall remain absent one year without using or exercising ownership over such ditch, flume or water right, shall be deemed to have lost all title, claim, and interest therein.

SEC. 10. **Void Location.**—Any and all locations or attempted locations of quartz mining claims within the State subsequent to the thirty-first day of December, 1898, that shall not comply and be in accordance with the provisions of this Act shall be null and void.

SEC. 11. **Grub-staking.**—That all contracts of mining co-partnership commonly known as grub-staking shall be in writing, and filed for record with the recorder of conveyances of the county wherein locations thereunder are made. Such contracts must contain, first, the names of the parties thereto, and, second, the duration thereof. Otherwise such contracts shall be null and void.

SEC. 12. **Repeal.**—That Chapter XIII of the Code of Civil and Criminal Procedure in justices' courts, and sections 3827, 3828, 3830, 3831, 3832, 3833, 3834, 3835, and 3836 of Chapter LX, Hill's Annotated Laws of Oregon, be, and the same are hereby, repealed.

SEC. 13, **In Force January 1, 1899.**—Whereas, under existing laws there is great uncertainty as to mining titles, and the abuse of rights to locate thereunder is detrimental to the mining industry of this State, this Act shall be in force and take effect on and after the first day of January, 1899.

Approved October 14, 1898. Special Session Laws, 1898, p. 16.
Amended February 25, 1901. Session Laws, 1901, p. 139.

Mining Claims are Real Estate.

SECTION 5.—All mining claims whether quartz or placer shall be real estate, and the owner of the possessory right thereto shall have a legal estate therein within the meaning of section 316 of Hill's Code.

Approved February 17, 1899. Session Laws 1899, p. 62.

An Act to Regulate the Location of Mining Claims and to Define the Rights of Locators.

SECTION 1. **Debris.**—That any location of any mining claim made upon any natural stream, or contiguous or near to any placer mine, or upon or below the dump of any placer mine, shall be subject to the prior right of all mines in operation prior to the making of such location, to discharge débris, gravel, earth and slickens as the same was discharged, or may be discharged, at the time of making such subsequent location of mining claim or claims.

Approved February 25, 1901. Session Laws, 1901, p. 122.

An Act making it a Crime to Remove or Interfere with Mining Location Marks, and Prescribing the Penalty Therefor.

SECTION 1. **Misdemeanor—Punishment.**—If any person or persons shall wilfully and maliciously deface, remove, pull down, injure, or destroy any location stake, side post, corner post, landmark or monument, or any other legal land boundary monument in this State, designating, or intending to designate, the location boundary or name of any mining claim, lode or vein of mineral, or the name of the discoverer, or date of discovery thereof, the person or persons so offending shall be guilty of a misdemeanor, and on conviction thereof, shall be punishable by a fine of not more than five hundred dollars ($500), or by imprisonment in the county jail for a period of not more than six months, or by both, such fine and imprisonment in the discretion of the court; *Provided*, that this act shall not apply to abandoned property.

Approved February 27, 1901. Session Laws, 1901, p. 175.

SOUTH DAKOTA.

Location and Size of Mining Claim.

SECTION 2656. **Length of Claim.**—The length of any lode claim hereafter located within this State may equal but shall not exceed fifteen hundred feet along the vein or lode. [C. L., 1997]

SEC. 2657. **Width of Claim.**—The width of lode claims shall be one hundred and fifty feet on each side of the center of the vein or crevice; *Provided*, That any county may at any general election determine upon a less width not exceeding three hundred feet on each side of the center of the vein or lode, by a majority of the legal votes cast at said election, and any county, by such vote at such election, may determine upon a less width than above specified; *Provided*, That not less than twenty-five feet on each side of the vein or lode shall be prohibited. [C. L., 1998.]

SEC. 2658.—**Record.**—The discoverer of a lode shall within sixty days from the date of discovery record his claim in the office of the register of deeds of the county in which such lode is situated, by a location certificate, which shall contain: 1st, the name of the lode; 2d, the name of the locator, or locators; 3d, the date of location; 4th, the number of feet in length claimed on each side of the discovery shaft; 5th, the number of feet in width claimed on each side of the vein or lode; 6th, the general course of the lode as near as may be. [C. L., 1999.]

SEC. 2659. **Certificate, When Void.**—Any location certificate of a lode claim which shall not contain the name of the lode, the name of the locator, the date of location, the number of lineal feet drained on each side of the discovery shaft, the number of feet in width claimed, the general course of the lode, and such description as shall identify the claim with reasonable certainty, shall be void. [C. L. 2000.]

SEC. 2660. **Manner of Locating.**—Before filing such location certificate the discoverer shall locate his claim by first sinking a discovery shaft thereon sufficient to show a well-defined mineral vein or lode; second, by posting at the point of discovery, on the surface, a plain sign or notice containing the name of the lode, the name of the locator or locators and the date of discovery, the number of feet claimed in length on either side of the discovery, and the number of feet in width claimed on each side of the lode; third, by marking the surface boundaries of the claim. [C. L. 2001.]

SEC. 2661. **Marking Surface Boundaries.**—Such surface boundaries shall be marked by eight substantial posts, hewed or blazed on the side or sides facing the claim and plainly marked with the name of the lode and the corner, end or side of the claim that they respectively represent, and sunk in the ground, to wit: one at each corner and one at the center of each side line, and one at each end of the lode. When it is impracticable on account of rock or precipitous ground to sink such posts, they may be placed in a monument of stone. [C. L. 2002.]

SEC. 2662. **Requisites of a Location.**—Any open cut, crosscut or tunnel at a depth sufficient to disclose the mineral vein or lode, or an adit of at least ten feet in along the lode, from the point where the lode may be in any manner discovered, shall be equivalent to a discovery shaft. [C. L. 2003.]

SEC. 2663. **Time for Performing Labor.**—The discoverer shall have sixty days from the time of uncovering or disclosing a lode to sink a discovery shaft thereon. [C. L. 2004.]

SEC. 2664. **Certificate Construed.**—The location or location certificate of any lode claim shall be so construed to include all surface ground within the surface lines thereof and all lodes and ledges throughout their entire depth, the top or apex of which lie inside of such lines extended vertically, with such parts of all lodes or ledges as continue by dip beyond the side lines of the claim, but shall not include any portion of such lodes or ledges beyond the end lines of the claim or the end lines continued, whether by dip or otherwise, or beyond the side lines in any other manner than by the dip of the lode. [C. L. 2005.]

SEC. 2665. **Claim not to Extend Beyond Boundary Line.**—If the top or apex of the lode in its longitudinal course extends beyond the exterior lines of the claim at any point on the surface, or as extended vertically downward, such lode may not be followed in its longitudinal course beyond the point where it is intersected by the exterior. [C. L. 2006.]

SEC. 2666. **Security from Miner.**—When the right to mine is in any case separate from the ownership or right of occupancy to the surface, the owner or rightful occupant of the surface may demand satisfactory security from the miner, and if it be refused may enjoin such miner from working until such security is given. The order for injunction shall fix the amount of bond. [C. L. 2007.]

SEC. 2667. **Amended Certificate Filed.**—If at any time the locator of any mining claim heretofore or hereafter located, or his assigns, shall apprehend that his original certificate was defective, erroneous, or that the requirements of the law had not been complied with before filing, or shall be desirous of changing his surface boundaries, or of taking in any part of an overlapping claim which has been abandoned, or in case the original certificate was made prior to the passage of this law, and he shall be desirous of securing the benefits of this act, such locator or his assigns may file an additional certificate subject to the provisions of this act: *Provided*, That such relocation does not interfere with the existing rights of others at the time of such relocation; and no such relocation or the record thereof shall preclude the claimant or claimants from proving any such title or titles as he or they may have held under previous locations. [C. L. 2008.]

Sec. 2668. **Amount of Annual Work.**—The amount of work to be done or improvements made during each year to hold possession of a mining claim shall be that prescribed by the laws of the United States, to wit, one hundred dollars annually; *Provided*, That the period within which the work required to be done annually on all unpatented claims so located shall commence on the first day of January succeeding the date of location of such claim. [C. L. 2009.]

Sec. 2669. **Relocating Abandoned Claim.**—The relocation of abandoned lode claims shall be by sinking a new discovery shaft and fixing new boundaries in the same manner as if it were the location of a new claim, or the relocator may sink the original shaft, cut or adit to a sufficient depth to comply with sections twenty hundred and one and twenty hundred and three, and erect new or adopt the old boundaries, renewing the posts if removed or destroyed. In either case a new location stake shall be erected. In any case, whether the whole or part of an abandoned claim is taken, the location certificate must state that the whole or any part of the new location is located as abandoned property. [C. L., 2010.]

Sec. 2670. **Certificate Contains But One Location.**—No location certificate shall claim more than one location, whether the location be made by one or several locators, and if it purport to claim more than one location it shall be absolutely void, except as to the first location therein described; and if they are described together, or so that it cannot be told which location is first described, the certificate shall be void as to all. [C. L. 2011.]

Sec. 2671. **Recording Fee.**—The register of deeds shall be entitled to receive the sum of one dollar for each location certificate recorded and certified by him, and shall furnish the locator or locators with a certified copy of such certificate when demanded, for which he shall be entitled to receive fifty cents. [C. L. 2012.]

Right of Way.

Sec. 2674. **Owners of Mines Have Right of Way.**—The proprietor, owner or owners of mining claims, whether patented under the laws of the United States or held under the local laws and customs of this Territory, shall have a right of way for ingress for necessary purposes over and across the land or mining claim, patented or otherwise, of others as hereinafter provided. [C. L. 2016.]

Sec. 2675. **For Road or Ditch.**—Whenever any such mine or mining claim shall be so situated that it cannot be conveniently worked without a road thereto, or a ditch or a cut to convey the water therefrom, or without a flume to carry water and tailings therefrom, or without a shaft or tunnel thereto, which road, ditch, cut or tunnel shall necessarily pass over, under, through or across any lands or mining claims owned or occupied by others, either under a patent from the United States or otherwise, then shall such first mentioned owner or owners be entitled to a right of way for said road, ditch, flume, shaft or tunnel over, under, through and across such other lands or mining claims upon compliance with the provisions of this Act. [C. L. 2017.]

SEC. 2676. **Proceedings to Obtain.**—Whenever the owner or owners of any mining claim shall desire to work the same, and it is necessary to enable him or them to do so successfully and conveniently, that he or they shall have a right of way for any of the purposes in the foregoing section, and such right of way shall not have been acquired by agreement between him or them, and the claim over, under, across and upon which he, or they, seek to establish such right of way, it shall be lawful for him or them to present to the judge of the circuit court of the several counties and subdivisions of the State of South Dakota in which such right of way or some part thereof sought to be enforced is situated, a petition praying that such right of way be awarded to him or them. Such petition shall be verified and contain a particular description of the character and extent of the right sought, a description of the mine or claim of the petitioner, and the claim or claims on lands to be affected by such right or privilege, with the names of the occupants or owners thereof; it may also set forth any tender or offer hereinafter mentioned, and shall demand the relief sought. [C. L. 2018.]

SEC. 2677. **Proceedings before the Court.**—Upon the receipt of such petition and filing thereof with the clerk of such court, the judge shall direct a citation to issue, under the seal of such court, to the owners named in the petition, of mining claims and lands to be affected by the proceedings, directing them and each of them to appear before the judge on a day therein named, which shall not be less than ten days from the service thereof, and show cause why such right of way should not be allowed as prayed for. Such citation shall be served on each of the parties in the manner prescribed by law for serving summons in ordinary proceedings at law. [C. L. 2019.]

SEC. 2678. **Commissioners Appointed.**—Upon the return day of the citation, or upon any day to which the hearing shall be adjourned, the judge shall proceed to hear the allegations and proofs of the respective parties; and if upon such hearing he is satisfied that the claims of the petitioner should be worked by means of the privilege prayed for, he shall make an order adjudging and awarding to the petitioner such right of way, and shall appoint three commissioners who shall be disinterested parties and residents of the county to assess the damages resulting to the lands or claims affected by such order. [C. L. 2020.]

SEC. 2679. **Damages to Be Assessed.**—The commissioners so appointed shall be sworn or affirmed to faithfully and impartially discharge their duties and shall proceed without unreasonable delay to examine the premises, and shall assess the damage resulting from such right or privilege prayed for and report the amount to the judge appointing them, and if such right of way shall affect the property of more than one person or company, such report shall contain an assessment of damages to each company or person. [C. L. 2021.]

SEC. 2680. **Report May Be Set Aside.**—For good cause shown the judge may set aside the report of such commissioners and appoint three other commissioners, whose duties shall be the same as above mentioned. [C. L. 2022.]

SEC. 2681. **Petitioner Entitled to Right of Way, When.**—Upon the payment of the sum assessed as damages aforesaid to the persons to whom it shall be awarded, or a tender thereof to them, then the person petitioning aforesaid shall be entitled to the right of way pr yed for in their or his petition, and may immediately proceed to occupy the same and to erect thereon such work and structures, and make therein such excavations as may be necessary to the use and enjoyment of the right of way so awarded. [C. L. 2023.]

SEC. 2682. **Appeals.**—Appeals from the assessment of the commissioners may be made and prosecuted in the proper circuit court by any party interested, at any time within ten days after filing the report of the commissioners, and a written notice of such appeal shall be served upon the appellee in the same manner as summons are served in civil actions. The appellant shall file with the clerk of the court to which the appeal is made, a bond with sureties to be approved by the clerk, in the amount of the assessment appealed from, in favor of the appellee, conditioned that the appellant shall pay any costs that may be awarded to the appellee, and abide any judgment that may be rendered in the case. [C. L. 2024.]

SEC. 2683. **Trial of the Appeal.**—Appeals shall bring before the appellate court only the propriety of the amount of damages, and may be tried by the court or by a jury as other cases in court. [C. L. 2025.]

SEC. 2684. **Appeal Not to Hinder Work.**—The prosecution of any appeal shall not hinder, delay or prevent the appellee from exercising all the rights and privileges mentioned in section twenty hundred and twenty-three; *Provided*, That the appellee shall file with the clerk of the court in which the appeal is pending a bond with sufficient sureties to be approved by the clerk, in double the amount of the assessment appealed from, conditioned that the appellee shall pay to the appellant whatever amount he may recover in the action, not exceeding the amount of such bond. [C. L. 2026.]

SEC. 2685. **Appellee to Pay Certain Costs.**—If the appellant recover fifty dollars more damages than the commissioners shall have awarded, or the appellee shall offer to allow judgment against him to be taken, the appellee shall pay the costs of the appeal; otherwise the appellant shall pay the costs. [C. L. 2027.]

SEC. 2686. **Costs and Expenses, by Whom Paid.**—The costs and expenses under the provisions of this act, except as herein otherwise provided, shall be paid by the party making the application; *Provided, however,* That if the applicant shall before the commencement of such proceeding have tendered to the parties owning or occupying such lands or mining claims a sum equal to or more than the amount of damages assessed by the commissioners, then all of the costs and expenses shall be paid by the party or parties owning the lands or claims affected by such right of way, and who appeared and resisted the claims of the applicants. [C. L. 2028.]

Water Rights.

SEC. 2687. **Persons Holding Land Have Right to Water.**—Any person or persons, corporation or company, who may have or hold or possessory right or title to any mineral or agricultural lands within the limits of this State shall be entitled to the usual enjoyment of the waters of the streams or creeks in said State for mining, milling, agricultural or domestic purposes; *Provided,* That the right to such use shall not interfere with any prior right or claim to such waters when the law has been complied with in doing the necessary work. [C. L. 2029.]

SEC. 2688. **Right of Way for Conducting Water.**—When any persons, corporation or company owning or holding lands as provided in section twenty hundred and twenty nine shall have no available water facilities upon the same, or whenever such lands are too far removed from any stream or creek to so use the waters thereof as aforesaid, such person or persons, corporation or company shall have the right of way through and over any tract or piece of land for the purpose of conducting and conveying said water by means of ditches, dykes, flumes or canals, for the purpose aforesaid. [C. L. 2030.]

SEC. 2689 **Right of Way Limited.**—Such right to dig and construct such ditches, dykes, flumes and canals over and across the lands of another shall only extend to so much digging, cutting or excavation as may be necessary for the purposes required. [C. L. 2031.]

SEC. 2690. **Controversy—How Determined.**—In all controversies respecting rights to water under the provisions of this act, the same shall be determined by the date of appropriation as respectively made by the parties, whether for mining, milling, agricultural or domestic purposes. [C. L. 2032.]

SEC. 2691. **Deterioration Not to Be Considered.**—The waters of the streams or creek of the Territory may be available to the full extent of the capacity thereof for mining, milling, agricultural or domestic purposes, without regard to deterioration in quality or diminution in quantity, so that the same do not materially affect or impair the rights of the prior appropriator. [C. L. 2033.]

Sec. 2692. **Penalty for Damaging Lands.**—Any person or persons, corporation or company damaging or injuring the lands or possessions of another by reason of cutting or digging ditches or canals or erecting flumes as provided by section twenty hundred and thirty, the party so committing such injury or damage shall be liable to the party so injured for the actual damage occasioned thereby. [C. L., 2034.]

Sec. 2693. **Abandoned Water Right—Bridging Ditches.**—This act shall not be so construed as to impair or in any way or manner interfere with the rights of parties to the use of the waters of such streams or creeks acquired before the passage of this act; *Provided*, That all water rights or ditches that have not been used or worked upon for one year next prior to the passage of this act shall be deemed abandoned and forfeited and subject to appropriation anew. Any person or persons, corporation or company who may dig any ditch or canal, dyke or flume over or across any public road, trail or highway, or who use the waters of such ditch, dyke, flume or canal shall be required to bridge the same and keep the same in good repair at such crossing or other places where the water from any such ditch, dykes, flumes, or canals may flow over or in anywise injure any road, trail or highway, either by bridges or otherwise. [C. L. 2035.]

Sec. 2694. **Failure to Comply with Law.**—Any person or persons, corporation or company offending against section twenty hundred and thirty-five, on conviction thereof shall forfeit and pay for every such offense a penalty of not less than twenty-five dollars nor more than one hundred dollars, to be recovered with costs of suit in civil action in the name of the State of South Dakota, before any court having jurisdiction. One-half of the fine so collected shall be paid into the county treasury of the county in which the offense was committed, and the other half shall be paid to the person or persons informing the nearest magistrate that such offense has been committed. All such fines and costs shall be collected without stay of execution, and such defendant or defendants may by order of the court be confined in the county jail until such fine and costs have been paid. [C. L. 2036.]

Sec. 2695. **Manner of Locating Water Rights.**—Any person or persons, corporation or company appropriating the waters of any streams or creeks in this State, shall turn the water from the channel of such creek or stream and construct at least twenty feet of the ditch or flume within thirty days from the date of appropriation, and turn the water therein, and construct at least twenty rods of said ditch or flume, if needed, within six months from the date of such appropriation, and turn the water therein; and within twenty days from the date of location the locator or locators of such water right shall file a location certificate thereof with the register of deeds in the proper county within which such water right is situated. A copy of such certificate shall be posted at or near the head of such ditch, flume or canal, and shall contain the name or names of the locators, the date of location, number of inches of water claimed or appropriated, and the purpose of the appropriation; and in no case shall the number of inches of water exceed the conveying capacity of the first twenty feet of the flume or ditch, nor shall said ditch or flume be enlarged to the prejudice or injury of a subsequent appropriator before such enlargement. [C. L. 2037.]

SEC. 2696. **When Abandoned.**—On failure to commence the construction of such ditch or flume for sixty days after location, and prosecute such ditch, canal or flume to a final completion without unnecessary delay, such appropriation shall be deemed abandoned. [C. L. 2038.]

Extracts from Political Code, 1899.

Relating to Mining Claims.
AN ACT

To amend sections 1998, 2001, and 2003, chapter 19, of the Compiled Laws, relating to the amount of work to be done before filing a location certificate for a mining claim.

SECTION 1. **Amendment.**—That section 1998 shall be and is amended to read as follows:

"The width of lode claim shall be three hundred (300) feet on each side of the center of the vein or crevice, provided that any county may at any general election determine upon a less width than above specified, *Provided*, That not less than twenty-five (25) feet on each side of the vein or lode shall be prohibited."

SEC. 2. **Amendment.**—That section 2001 shall be and is amended to read as follows:

"Before filing such location certificate the discoverer shall locate his claim by first sinking a discovery shaft thereon sufficient to show a well-defined mineral vein or lode, and not less than ten (10) feet in depth on the lower side; second, by posting at the point of discovery, on the surface, a plain sign or notice containing the name of the lode, the name of the locator or locators and the date of discovery, the number of feet claimed in length on either side of the discovery, and the number of feet in width claimed on each side of the lode; third, by working [marking] the surface boundaries of the claim."

SEC. 3. **Amendment.** That section 2003 shall be and is amended to read as follows:

"Any open cut, at least ten-foot face, cross-cut, or tunnel, at a depth sufficient to disclose the mineral vein or lode, or an adit of at least ten feet in along the lode from the point where the lode may be in any manner discovered shall be equivalent to a discovery shaft."

SEC. 4. **Repeal.**—All acts or parts of acts in conflict with this act are hereby repealed.

Approved February 23, 1899. Session Laws 1899, p. 148.

Relating to Location of Mining Claims.
AN ACT

To amend section 3 of chapter 31 of the Political Code of South Dakota; and sections 1 and 2 of chapter 96 of the Session Laws of 1881, being Section 1999 of the Compiled Laws Relating to Location of Mining Claims.

SECTION 1. **Amendment.**—That section 3 of chapter 31 of the Political Code of South Dakota, and sections 1 and 2 of chapter 96 of the Session Laws of 1881 be, and the same is hereby, amended to read as follows:

"§ 1999. **Discoverer to Record Claim.**—The discoverer of a lode shall within sixty days from the date of discovery record his claim in the office of the register of deeds of the county in which such lode is situated, by a location certificate, which shall contain:

1st, the name of lode; 2d, the name of the locator, or locators; 3d, the date of location; 4th, the number of feet in length claimed on each side of the discovery shaft; 5th, the number of feet in width claimed on each side of the vein or lode; 6th, the general course of the lode, as near as may be; 7th, that when the location certificate is filed for record in the office of the register of deeds, the register of deeds shall immediately furnish to the locator or locators a certificate giving the name of the location; the name of the locator or locators; the date of filing in the office of the register of deeds; and the book and page where recorded, for which certificate the register of deeds shall receive the sum of ten cents in addition to the amount now allowed by law for filing and recording location certificates, which certificate shall be delivered to the locator or locators, who shall post the same, or a copy thereof, on the said claim on the same post or tree where the original notice is posted and in a conspicuous place. And if said certificate from said register of deeds or a copy thereof is not so posted within ninety days from the date of the original notice the said claim shall be deemed abandoned ground and be subject to re-location by any qualified locator. The said register of deeds shall, at the time of issuing said certificate, make a notation on the margin of the recorded certificate giving the date of the delivery of said certificate, which notation shall be *prima facie* evidence of the delivery and posting of the same as herein provided."

Approved March 6, 1899. Sessons Laws 1899, p. 146.

UTAH.

Mining Claims.

SECTION 1495. **Area of Mining Claim—End Lines Parallel.**—A mining claim, whether located by one or more persons, may equal, but shall not exceed, fifteen hundred feet in length along the vein or lode; but no location of a mining claim shall be made until the discovery of the vein or lode, within the limits of the claim located. Any lode mining claim may extend three hundred feet on each side of the middle of the vein at the surface, except where adverse rights render a lesser width necessary. The end lines of each claim must be parallel.

SEC. 1496. **Discovery Monument—Posting Notice of Location—Contents.**—The locator, at the time of making the discovery of such vein or lode, must erect a monument at the place of discovery, and must post thereon his notice of location, which notice shall contain:

1st, the name of the lode or claim; 2d, the name of the locator or locators; 3d, the date of the location; 4th, if a lode claim, the number of linear feet claimed in length along the course of the vein each way from the point of discovery, with the width on each side of the center of the vein, and the general course of the vein or lode, as near as may be, and such a description of the claim, located by reference to some natural object or permanent monument, as will identify the claim; 5th, if a placer or mill-site claim, the number of acres or superficial feet claimed, and such a description of the claim or mill site located by reference to some natural object or permanent monument as will identify the claim or mill site.

SEC. 1497. **Boundaries Must be Marked within Thirty Days—Monuments.**—Within thirty days from the date of discovery or establishment, the locator must mark the boundaries of his lode or placers, or mill-site claims by establishing on each corner thereof, and at any angle in the side lines, a monument marked with the name of the claim, and the corner or angle it represents. When from any cause a monument cannot be safely planted at the true corner or angle it must be placed as near thereto as practicable and so marked as to indicate the place of such corner or angle. Monuments may be made of any such material and in such form as will readily give notice; and when of posts or trees they must be hewn and marked upon the side facing toward the discovery, and must be at least four inches in diameter. Monuments must be at least four feet high above the ground, and trees must be so hewn as to readily attract attention. Monuments and stakes must be kept in such state of preservation as to notify persons of the boundaries of the mining claim.

Sec. 1498. **Copy of Location Notice Must be Recorded Within Thirty Days—Fee.**—Within thirty days from the date of posting the location notice upon the claim the locator or locators, or his or their assigns, must file for record in the office of the county recorder of the county in which such claim is situated a substantial copy of such notice of location. Such county recorder shall charge and collect a fee of one dollar for filing and recording such notice; *provided*, That such notice of location shall not be abstracted unless a subsequent conveyance affecting the same property be filed for record, when said notice shall be abstracted.

Sec. 1499. **Fifty Dollars' Worth of Work Performed Within Ninety Days' Notice.**—Within ninety days from the date of posting location notice upon the claim, the locator or locators, or his or their heirs or assigns, shall do at least fifty dollars' worth of work upon said claim. Every person or company owning a group of claims and doing the development work for said groups at one point, shall post a notice upon each claim at the discovery monument stating where such work is being done. [1897, p. 58.]

Sec. 1500. **Proof of Annual Labor—Form of Affidavit—Filing.**—The owner of any quartz lode or placer mining claim who shall do or perform, or cause to be done or performed, the annual labor or improvements required by the laws of the United States in order to prevent a forfeiture of the claim, must, either during the year or within thirty days after the completion of such work or improvements, if completed after the termination of said year in or for which said work was done or improvements were made, file in the office of the county recorder of the county in which such claim is situated an affidavit or affidavits of the person or persons who performed such labor or made such improvements, showing: 1st, the name of the claim and where situated; 2d, the number of days' work done and the character and value of the improvements placed thereon; 3d, the date or dates of performing said labor and making said improvements and number of cubic feet of earth or rock removed; 4th, at whose instance or request said work was done or improvements made; 5th, the actual amount paid for said labor and improvements, and by whom paid, when the same was not done by the owner or owners of said claim. Such affidavits or duly certified copies thereof shall be *prima facie* evidence of the facts therein stated. [1897, pp. 58-59.]

Sec. 1501. **County Recorder to Record Mining Rules Without Charge.**—It shall be the duty of each county recorder to record the mining rules and regulations of the several mining districts in his county without fee, and certified copies of such record shall be received in all tribunals and before all officers of this State as *prima facie* evidence of such rules and regulations. [1897, p. 59.]

Sec. 1502. **County Recorder to Perform Duties of District Recorder—Penalty for Failure.**—The county recorder of the respective counties shall perform the duties heretofore performed by the district mining recorders in such counties, respectively; and the district mining recorders of each county shall, within thirty days after this chapter shall take effect, deposit the books and records pertaining to their offices with the county recorder of the county in which the district or the greater part thereof is situated; *Provided*, That said books and records shall not be required to be abstracted by the county recorder. Any district mining recorder who shall fail to deposit as aforesaid the books and records pertaining to his office, shall be deemed guilty of a misdemeanor.

SEC. 1503. **Papers Heretofore Certified by Mining Records Receivable in Evidence.**—Copies of notices of location of mining claims, mill sites and tunnel sites, heretofore recorded in the records of the several mining districts, and of the mining rules and regulations in force in the several mining districts, in like manner recorded, heretofore duly certified by the mining recorder, shall be receivable in all tribunals and before all officers of this State as *prima facie* evidence.

SEC. 1504. **County Recorder to Certify Copies from Mining Records—Evidence.**—Where books, records, and documents pertaining to the office of district mining recorder have been or shall hereafter be deposited in the office of any county recorder of this State, such county recorder is authorized to make and certify copies therefrom, and such certified copies shall be receivable in all tribunals and before all officers of this State in the same manner and to the same effect as if such records had been originally filed or made in the office of the county recorder.

SEC. 1505. **Transportation Charges on Records Paid by County.**—The board of commissioners of each county shall provide ways and means for the transportation of all books and records pertaining to the office of the respective mining recorders, to the office of the respective county recorder. [1897, p. 60.]

SEC. 1506. **Upon Petition, Records to be Copied and Returned to Mining District.**—Upon receipt of a petition signed by not less than one hundred *bona fide* miners residing in any mining district, petitioning for the return of the records of such mining district, the board of county commissioners shall cause the records of such district to be copied by the county recorder with the joint assistance of the district recorder of such mining district if the said district recorder wishes to render such assistance, and shall cause the original records to be sent to such mining district recorder; the copy so made shall remain in the office of the county recorder and shall be considered the original record. One-half of the expenses of copying the said records shall be paid out of the county treasury and one-half shall be paid out of the State treasury.

SEC. 990. **Mining Recorder.**—Every mining recorder shall be allowed the same fees for recording and making copies of any record in his custody as may be allowed by the by-laws of the mining district in which the same is recorded or said copies are made; or if not provided for, such fees as are allowed by law to county recorders for similar services.

Trespasses.

SEC. 1535. **Interfering With Notices, Stakes, Persons in Possession, or Records.**—Any person or persons who shall wilfully or maliciously tear down or deface a notice posted on a mining claim, or take up or destroy any stake or monument marking any such claim, or interfere with any person lawfully in possession of such claim, or who shall alter, erase, deface, or destroy any record kept by a mining recorder, shall be guilty of a misdemeanor and upon conviction thereof shall be punished by a fine of not less than twenty-five nor more than one hundred dollars, or by imprisonment for not less than ten days nor more than six months, or by both such fine and imprisonment. Justices of the peace shall have jurisdiction of such offenses. [C. L. § 2791.]

Eminent Domain.

SECTION 3588. **Exercised in Behalf of What Uses.**—Subject to the provisions of this chapter, the right of eminent domain may be exercised in behalf of the following public uses: 1. All public uses authorized by the Government of the United States. 2. Public buildings and grounds for the use of the State, and all other public uses authorized by the Legislature. 3. Public buildings and grounds for the use of any county, incorporated city or town, or school district; reservoirs, canals, aqueducts, flumes, ditches, or pipes for conducting water for the use of the inhabitants of any county, or incorporated city or town, or for draining any county or incorporated city or town; for raising the banks of streams, removing obstructions therefrom, and widening, deepening, or straightening their channels; for roads, streets, and alleys, and all other public uses for the benefit of any county, incorporated city or town or the inhabitants thereof. 4. Wharves, docks, piers, chutes, booms, ferries, bridges, toll roads, by-roads, plank and turn-pike roads, roads for transportation by traction engines or road locomotives, roads for logging or lumbering purposes, and railroads and street railways for public transportation. 5. Reservoirs, dams, water-gates, canals, ditches, flumes, tunnels, aqueducts, and pipes for supplying persons, mines, mills, smelters, or other works for the reduction of ores, with water for domestic or other uses, or for irrigating purposes, or for draining and reclaiming lands, or for floating logs and lumber on streams not navigable. 6. Roads, railroads, tramways, tunnels, ditches, flumes, pipes, and dumping places to facilitate the milling, smelting, or other reduction of ores, or the working of mines; outlets, natural or otherwise, for the deposit or conduct of tailings, refuse, or water from mills, smelters, or other works for the reduction of ores, or from mines; mill-dams; natural gas or oil pipe lines, tanks, or reservoirs; also an occupancy in common by the owners or possessors of different mines, mills, smelters, or other places for the reduction of ores, of any place for the flow, deposit, or conduct of tailings or refuse matter. 7. By-roads leading from highways to residences and farms. 8. Telegraph, telephone, electric light, and electric power lines. 9. Sewerage of any city or town, or of any settlement of not less than ten families, or of any public building belonging to the State, or of any college or university.

[For proceedings see Sections 3589 to 3608.]

Lease of State Mineral Lands.

SECTION 2370. **Mineral Lands to be Leased.**—Any State lands upon which stone, coal, coal oil, gas, or any mineral may be found, whether such land has theretofore been leased for a term of years or not, may be leased for the purpose of obtaining therefrom such stone, coal, coal oil, gas, or any mineral, for such length of time and conditioned upon the payment to the State board of land commissioners of such royalty upon the product, as the State board of land commissioners may determine. [1897, p. 88].

SEC. 2371. **Rules Regarding Leasing.**—The State board of land commissioners is hereby authorized to make all necessary rules and regulations to carry the foregoing into effect.

Extracts from the Utah Revised Statutes, 1898.

SECTION 1. **Extent.—No Location to be Made Until Discovery of Vein.**—A mining claim, whether located by one or more persons, may equal, but shall not exceed, one thousand five hundred feet in length along the vein or lode; but no location of a mining claim shall be made until the discovery of the vein or lode within the limits of the claim located. Any lode mining claim may extend three hundred feet on each side of the middle of the vein at the surface, except where adverse rights render a lesser width necessary. The end lines of each claim must be parallel.

SEC. 2. **Monument—Notice.**—The locator, at the time of making the discovery of such vein or lode, must erect a monument at the place of discovery, and post thereon his notice of location, which notice shall contain: 1st, the name of the lode or claim; 2d, the name of the locator or locators; 3d, the date of the location; 4th, if a lode claim, the number of linear feet claimed in length along the course of the vein each way from the point of discovery, with the width on each side of the center of the vein, and the general course of the vein or lode, as near as may be, and such a description of the claim, located by reference to some natural object or permanent monument as will identify the claim; 5th, if a placer or mill-site claim, the number of acres or superficial feet claimed, and such a description of the claim or mill-site located by reference to some natural object or permanent monument as will identify the claim or mill-site.

SEC. 3. **Boundaries Marked.**—Mining claims and mill-sites must be distinctly marked on the ground so that the boundaries thereof can be readily traced.

SEC. 4. **Filing Copy of Notice—Fee.**—Within thirty days from the date of posting the location notice upon the claim, the locator or locators, or his or their assigns, must file for record in the office of the county recorder of the county in which such claim is situated, if said claim be situated without and beyond an original mining district, a substantial copy of such notice of location. Such county recorder shall charge and collect a fee of seventy-five cents for filing and recording and indexing and abstracting such notice; *Provided*, That such notice of location shall not be abstracted unless a subsequent conveyance affecting the same property be filed for record, when said notice shall be abstracted.

SEC. 5. **Notice of Assessment Work Being Done.**—Every person or company owning a group of claims and doing the development or assessment work for said group at one point, shall post a notice upon each claim, at the discovery monument, stating where such work is being done, and also post a notice at the entrance of the workings where said work is done, stating the name of the claims for which the work is done.

SEC. 6. **Filing Affidavit of Work Done.**—The owner of any quartz lode or placer mining claim who shall do or perform or cause to be done or performed the annual labor or improvements required by the laws of the United States, in order to prevent a forfeiture of the claim, must, within thirty days after the completion of such work or improvements, file in the office of the county recorder in which the greater part of the mining district in which such claim is located is situated, his affidavit or an affidavit or affidavits of the person or persons who performed or directed such labor, or made or directed such improvements, and shall file a duplicate thereof with the district mining recorder of the district in which said claim is situated, showing, 1st, the name of the claim and where situated; 2d, the number of days' work done and the character and value of the improvements placed thereon; 3d, the date or dates of performing said labor and making said improvements and number of cubic feet of earth or rock removed; 4th, at whose instance or request said work was done or improvements made; 5th, the actual amount paid for said labor and improvements, and by whom paid when the same was not done by the owner or owners of said claim.

SEC. 7.—**Reorganization of Mining Districts.**—Mining districts may be organized, and all existing districts may be reorganized and the rules and regulations of the said mining district shall govern the said district according to the laws of the United States, in cases where a district organization is desired; *Provided*,

That the nearest boundary line of any mining district shall not be within ten miles from the county recorder's office of any county.

SEC. 8—**Copying Records—Expense.**—Upon application of the district mining recorder of any mining district to the board of county commissioners of the county having in custody the records of the said mining district, the said board of county commissioners shall cause the records of such district to be copied by the county recorder and shall cause all records of documents pertaining to district mining records, recorded since June 4th, 1896, up to the time of delivery, to be recorded in the original records of the mining district in which the property is situated, and the original records, when so amended, shall be delivered to such district mining recorder. The copy so made shall remain in the office of the county recorder, and shall be considered as the original record. One-half of the expense of copying such records shall be paid out of the county treasury and one-half shall be paid out of the State treasury.

SEC. 9. **Duplicate Notice of Location—Fee—Penalty.**—It shall be the duty of every district mining recorder to require every person depositing for record a notice of location to make a duplicate copy thereof, which copy said mining recorder shall carefully compare with the original and mark "duplicate," and endorse thereon his name, and the date and hour and fact of filing in his office of the original. He shall, at the time of filing the duplicate notice with the original, collect, in addition to his own fee, the sum of seventy-five cents, which shall be the fee for the county recorder for recording such duplicate. He shall immediately deposit the duplicate copy with the county recorder of the county in which the greater part of the said mining district is located for record, or forward the same to him by mail or express, or in such other manner as will ensure safe transit and delivery. The fee of seventy-five cents shall accompany the duplicate. The county recorder shall record said duplicate with the endorsements thereon for the said fee. The record of said duplicate notice in the office of the county recorder shall be considered an original record. Every person neglecting or refusing to comply with any of the provisions of this section shall be deemed guilty of a misdemeanor, and, upon conviction thereof, shall be punished by a fine not exceeding five hundred dollars or by imprisonment in the county jail not exceeding six months, or by both such fine and imprisonment.

SEC. 10. **Copies of Notices to Be Received as Evidence.**—Copies of notices of mining claims, mill sites and tunnel sites, heretofore recorded in the records of the several mining districts, and copies of the mining rules and regulations in force in the several mining districts, in like manner recorded, heretofore duly certified by the mining recorder, shall be receivable in all tribunals and before all officers of this State as *prima facie* evidence.

SEC. 11. Where books, records and documents pertaining to the office of district mining recorder have been or shall hereafter be deposited in the office of any county recorder of this State, such county recorder is authorized to make and certify copies therefrom, and such certified copies shall be receivable in all tribunals and before all officers of this State in the same manner and to the same effect as if such records had been originally filed or made in the office of the county recorder.

SEC. 12. **County Recorder to Record Rules—Certified Copies.**—It shall be the duty of each county recorder to record the mining rules and regulations of the several mining districts in his county without fee, and certified copies of such records shall be received in all tribunals and before all officers of this State as *prima facie* evidence of such rules and regulations, and it shall be his duty to record, index and abstract, all mining location notices presented for record, for a fee not to exceed seventy-five cents for each notice, and to file and index all affidavits of labor presented for filing affecting one mining claim for a fee not to exceed twenty-five cents; provided, that when an affidavit of labor contains the name of more than one mining claim, an additional fee of ten cents shall be charged for each additional claim named therein.

SEC. 13. **Recorder of Mining District to Give Bond.**—The recorder of each mining district shall take the oath of office and give bond with sureties in the penal sum of one thousand dollars. Such bond must be approved by the district judge and filed in the office of the county clerk of the county in which the greater part of the said mining district is located. Where the recorder of any mining district appoints a deputy, the recorder and his bondsmen shall be responsible for the official acts of such deputy.

SEC. 14. **District Recorder to Make Copies.**—It shall be the duty of the recorder of a mining district upon request and payment, or tender of the fees therefor, to make and deliver to any person requesting the same, duly certified copies of any records in his custody and for a failure so to do, or for receiving larger fees for any such service than those provided he shall be deemed guilty of a misdemeanor.

SEC. 15. **Vacancy—County Recorder to Receive Records.**—Whenever there is a vacancy in the office of the recorder of any mining district, or the person holding such office shall remove from the district, leaving therein no qualified successor in office; or whenever from any cause there is no person in such district authorized to retain the custody and give certified copies of the records, it shall be the duty of the person having custody of the records to deposit the same in the office of the county recorder of the county in which such mining district or the greater part thereof is situated, and the county recorder shall receive such records, and is hereby authorized to make and certify copies therefrom, and such certified copies shall be received in evidence in all courts and before all officers and tribunals. The production of a certified copy so made shall be, without other proof, evidence that such records were properly in the custody of the county recorder.

SEC. 16. **Fees of Mining Recorder.**—Every mining recorder shall be allowed the same fees for recording and making copies of any record in his custody as are allowed by law to county recorders for similar services; *Provided*, That fees for recording location notices may equal but shall not exceed one dollar for each notice.

SEC. 17. **Sections Repealed.**—Sections 1495 and 1496 and 1497 and 1498 and 1499 and 1500 and 1501 and 1502 and 1503 and 1504 and 1505 and 1506 and 1537 and 990 of the Revised Statutes of Utah are hereby repealed.

Approved March 3, 1899. Session Laws of 1899, p. 26.

Assessment Work on Mining Claims.

Section 1499 of the Revised Statutes of Utah, 1898, is hereby repealed.

Approved March 3, 1899. Session Laws of 1899, p. 30.

WASHINGTON.

Mining Claims and Rules of Mining Districts.

SECTION 1. **Location Record.**—The discoverer of a lode shall within ninety (90) days from the date of discovery record in the office of the audit r of the county in which such lode is found a notice containing the name or names of the locators, the date of the location, the number of feet in length claimed on each side of the discovery, the general course of the lode, and such a description of the claim or claims located by reference to some natural object or permanent monument as will identify the claim.

SEC. 2. **Location and Marking of Claims.**—Before filing such notice for record the discoverer shall locate his claim by first sinking a discovery shaft upon the lode, to the depth of ten (10) feet from the lowest part of the rim of such shaft at the surface, and shall post at the discovery at the time of discovery a notice containing the name of the lode, the name of the locator or locators, and the date of discovery, and shall mark the surface boundaries of the claim by placing substantial posts or stone monuments bearing the name of the lode and date of location ; one post or monument must appear at each corner of such claim ; such posts or monuments must be not less than three (3) feet high ; if posts are used, they shall be not less than four inches in diameter, and shall be set in the ground in a substantial manner. If any such claim be located on ground that is covered wholly or in part with brush or trees, such brush shall be cut and trees be marked or blazed along the lines of such claim to indicate the location of of such lines.

SEC. 3. **Discovery.**—Any open cut or tunnel having a length of ten (10) feet, which shall cut a lode at the depth of ten (10) feet below the surface, shall hold such lode the same as if a discovery shaft were sunk thereon, and shall be equivalent thereto,

SEC. 4. **Definition.**—The term "lode" as used in this Act shall be construed to mean ledge, vein or deposit.

SEC. 5. **Amendment.**—If at any time the locator of any quartz or lode mining claim heretofore or hereafter located, or his assigns, shall learn that his original certificate was defective, or that the requirements of the law had not been complied with before filing, or shall be desirous of changing his surface boundaries, or of taking in any additional ground which is subject to location, or in any case the original certificate was made prior to the passage of this law, and he shall be desirous of securing the benefits of this act, such locator or his assigns may file an amended certificate of location, subject to the provisions of this act, regarding the making of new locations.

SEC. 6. **Affidavit of Labor.**—Within thirty (30) days after the expiration of the period of time fixed for the performance of annual labor, or the making of improvements upon any quartz or lode mining claim or premises, the person in whose behalf such work or improvement was made, or some person for him knowing the facts, shall make and record in the office of the county auditor of the county wherein such claims are situate an affidavit or oath of labor performed on such claim. Such affidavit shall state the exact amount and kind of labor, including the number of feet of shaft, tunnel or open cut made on such claim, or any other kind of improvements allowed by law or by rules of mining districts made thereon.

SEC. 7. **Evidence.**—Such affidavit when so recorded shall be *prima facie* evidence of the performance of such labor or the making of such improvements, and such original affidavit after it has been recorded, or a certified copy of record of same, shall be received as evidence accordingly by all the courts of this State.

SEC. 8. **Relocation.**—The relocation of forfeited or abandoned quartz or lode claims shall only be made by sinking a new discovery shaft and fixing new boundaries in the same manner and to the same extent as is required in making a new location, or the relocator may sink the original discovery shaft ten feet deeper than it was at the date of commencement of such relocation, and shall erect new, or make the old monuments the same as originally required; in either case a new location monument shall be erected, and the location certificate shall state if the whole or any part of the new location is located as abandoned property.

SEC. 9. **Cascade Mountains.**—The provision herein relating to discovery shafts shall not apply to any mining location west of the summit of the Cascade Mountains.

SEC. 10. **Placers.**—The discoverer of placer or other forms of deposit subject to location and appropriation under mining laws applicable to placers shall locate his claim in the following manner:

First. He must immediately post in a conspicuous place at the point of discovery thereon a notice or certificate of location thereof, containing (*a*) the name of the claim; (*b*) the name of the locator or locators; (*c*) the date of the discovery and posting of the notice hereinbefore provided for, which shall be considered as the date of the location; (*d*) a description of the claim by reference to legal subdivisions of sections, if the location is made in conformity with the public surveys, otherwise a description with reference to some natural object or permanent monument as will identify the claim, and where such claim is located by legal subdivisions of the public surveys, such location shall, notwithstanding that fact, be marked by the locator upon the ground the same as the other locations.

Second. Within thirty (30) days from the date of such discovery, he must record such notice or certificate of location in the office of the auditor of the county in which such discovery is made, and so distinctly mark his location on the ground that its boundaries may be readily traced.

Third. Within sixty (60) days from the date of the discovery, the discoverer shall perform labor upon such location or claim in developing the same to an amount which shall be equivalent in the aggregate to at least ten (10) dollars' worth of such labor for each twenty acres, or fractional part thereof contained in such location or claim.

Fourth. Such locator shall, upon the performance of such labor, file with the auditor of the county an affidavit showing such performance, and generally the nature and kind of work so done.

SEC. 11.—**Evidence.**—The affidavit provided for in the last section, and the aforesaid placer notice or certificate of location, when filed for record shall be *prima facie* evidence of the facts therein recited. A copy of such certificate, notice or affidavit certified by the county auditor shall be admitted in evidence in all actions or proceeding with the same effect as the original, and the provisions of sections six (6) and seven (7) of this Act shall apply to placer claims as well as lode claims.

SEC. 12.—**Future Locations.**—All locations of quartz or placer formations or deposits hereafter made shall conform to the requirements of this Act in so far as the same are respectively applicable thereto.

SEC. 13.—**Mining Districts.**—Any mining district organized in the State of Washington in accordance with the laws of the United States, shall have power to make rules and regulations for such mining district, providing such rules and regulations do not conflict with the laws of the State of Washington or of the United States.

SEC. 14. **Road Building.**—Any mining district shall have the power to make road building to mining claims within such district applicable as assessment work, or improvement upon such claims: *Provided*, That rules pertaining to such road building shall be made only at a public meeting of the miners of such district regularly called by the mining recorder of such district: *Provided further*, That such meeting shall be attended by at least twelve (12) property holders of such district, and that no such rule can be made without the assent of the majority of the property holders of such district, who are present at such meeting. Such meeting to designate where, when and how such road work shall be done, and shall designate some one of their number who shall superintend such road building or construction, and who shall receipt for such labor to the performer thereof such receipts to be filed with the county auditor of the county in which such work is performed by the holder or holders of such receipts, and shall be received as *prima facie* evidence of labor performed as annual assessment work upon such claim or claims, as may be designated by an affidavit or oath of labor as provided for in section six (6) of this Act: *Provided*, That nothing in this Act can be construed as being mandatory upon any owner or holder of mining property to perform labor upon any such road.

Approved March 8, 1899. Session Laws 1899, p. 69.

Location and Possession of Mining Lodes.

SECTION 2427. **Governed How.**—All mining claims upon veins or lodes of quartz, or other rock in place, bearing gold, silver, or other valuable mineral deposits heretofore located, shall be governed as to length along the vein or lode by the customs, regulations, and laws in force at the date of such location.—1888, 160, 1; 1 H., 2210.

SEC. 2428. **Extent—Restrictions.**—A mining claim located upon any vein or lode of quartz, or other rock in place, bearing gold, silver, or other valuable mineral deposits, after the approval of this act by the Governor, whether located by one or more persons, may equal but shall not exceed one thousand five hundred feet in length along the vein or lode; but no location of a mining claim shall be made until the discovery of the vein or lode within the limits of the claims located. No claims shall extend more than three hundred feet on each side of the middle of the vein at the surface, nor shall any claims be limited by any mining regulations to less than fifty feet of surface, on each side of the middle of such vein or lode at the surface, excepting where adverse rights, existing at the date of the approval of this act, shall make such limitation necessary. The end lines of each claim shall be parallel to each other.—1888, 160, 2; 1 H., 2211.

SEC. 2429.—**Exclusive Right to What.**—The locators of all mining locations heretofore made, or hereafter made under the provisions of this act, on any mineral vein, lode or ledge on the public domain, and their heirs or assigns, so long as they comply with the laws of the United States, and the territorial and local laws relating thereto, shall have the exclusive right to the possession and enjoyment of all surface included within the lines of their location, and of all veins, lodes, or ledges throughout their entire depth, and the top or apex of which lies within the surface lines of such location, extending downward vertically, although such veins, lodes, or ledges may so far depart from the perpendicular in their course downward as to extend outside of the vertical side line of said surface location.—1888, 160, 3; 1 H., 2212.

SEC. 2430.—**Conditions for Holding.**—In order to hold the possessory right to a location of a mine not less than one hundred dollars' worth of work must be performed or improvements made thereon annually: *Provided*, That the period within which the work required to be done annually on all unpatented claims so located shall commence on the first day of January succeeding the date of location of such claim.—1893, 75, 1.

SEC. 2431.—**Recorder.**—The miners of each mining district may elect a recorder of the said district. When so elected, such recorder shall provide books of record, in which it shall be his duty to record all notices of locations or transfers, bonds, conveyances or assignments of mining claims within his district, when the same shall be presented to him for record. Such records are hereby declared to be public records open to inspection, and shall have the same force and effect, so far as notice is concerned, as the records of deeds and mortgages in this State.—1888, 161, 5: 1 H., 2214.

SEC. 2432. **Term—Oath—Fees.**—When a recorder shall be elected as provided in section 5 of this act [2431], he shall hold his office for a term of one year from the date of his election, and until his successor is elected and qualified. He shall, immediately after his election, file with the county auditor, of the county within which his district is situated, an oath to the effect that he will faithfully discharge the duties of his office. He shall be a certifying officer, and certified copies of his records shall have the same force and effect as similar papers certified by other officers of this State. His fees shall be the same as those of the county auditor for similar work; and should the office of recorder in any mining district at any time become vacant, it shall be the duty of the person last holding said office, and of any person into whose possession the same may come, to forthwith transmit all the records, papers and files of the said office to the auditor of the county in which such district is located, and such auditor shall thereafter keep the same as part of the records and files of his office.—1888, 161, 6; 1 H., 2215.

SEC. 2433. **Where Recorded.**—Inasmuch as sections five and six of this act [2431, 2432] leave the election of a recorder for a mining district optional with the miners thereof, all location notices, bonds, assignments and transfers of mining claims hall be recorded in the office of the county auditor of the county where the same is situated within thirty days after the execution thereof; *Provided,* That all records of mining claims and of assignments, deeds, bonds and transfers heretofore made by any recorder of any mining district, or by any county auditor, are hereby declared to be valid and to have the same force and effect as records made in pursuance of the provisions of this act.—1888, 161, 7; 1 H., 2216.

Code, 1896, pp. 424, 425.

For inspection and working of Coal Mines, Boring for Oil and Minerals, and to prevent accidents from excavation, see sections 2434 to 2483, Code, 1896.

Relating to Monuments and Notices on Mining Claims.

SEC. 1. **Mining Monuments.**—Any person who shall wilfully and maliciously deface, remove, injure or destroy any location stake, side post, corner post, landmark or monument, or any other land boundary monument, the same having been erected or implanted for the purpose of designating the location, boundary or name of any mining claim, lode or vein of mineral, or for posting the name of the discoverer, locator or owner or date of discovery thereon ; or any person who shall so deface, obliterate, remove or destroy any notice having been placed or posted upon any mining claim for the purpose of marking or identifying the the same, shall be deemed guilty of a misdemeanor, and upon conviction thereof shall be punished by a fine not less than one hundred dollars ($100) nor more than five hundred dollars ($500), or by imprisonment in the county jail not exceeding one year; *Provided, however,* That the provisions of this act shall not apply to abandoned mining claims.

Approved March 16, 1897.

To Permit Indians to Sell Property.

SECTION 1. **Alienation of Real Estate.**—Any Indian who owns within this State any land or real estate allotted to him by the Government of the United States, may, with the consent of Congress, either special or general, sell and convey by deed made, executed and acknowledged before any officer authorized to take acknowledgments to deeds within this State, any stone, mineral, petroleum or timber contained on said land, or the fee thereof, and such conveyance shall have the same effect as a deed of any other person or persons within this State ; it being the intention of this Act to remove from Indians residing in this State all existing disabilities relating to alienation of their real estate.

Approved March 13, 1899. Session Laws 1899, p. 155.

Right of Way for Ditches, Canals and Flumes.

SECTION 1. **Water—Public Use.**—That any person, corporation or association of persons is entitled to take from the natural streams or lakes in this State water for the purposes of irrigation and mining, not theretofore appropriated or subject to rights existing at the time of the adoption of the constitution of this State, subject to the conditions and regulations imposed by law : *Provided,* That the use of water at all times shall be deemed a public use, and subject to condemnation as may from time to time be provided for by the Legislature of this State.

SEC. 2. **Riparian Owners.**—All persons who claim, own or hold possessory right or title to any land, or parcel of land, or mining claim, within the boundaries of the State of Washington, when such lands, mining claims or any part of the same are on the banks of any natural stream of water, shall be entitled to the use of any water of said stream not otherwi-e appropriated for the purposes of mining and irrigation to the full extent of the soil for agricultural purposes.

SEC. 3. **Right of Way.**—When any person owning claims, lands or mining claims, as specified in the foregoing section, is not a riparian proprietor, or being such has not sufficient frontage on said stream, lake, artificial stream, ditch or reservoir, to obtain a sufficient flow of water to irrigate his land or use on his mining claim, he shall be entitled to the right of way through the farms or tracts of lands or other mining claims which lie between him and said stream, lake, artificial stream, ditch or reservoir, or the farms, tracts of lands or mining claims which lie above and below him on said stream, lake, artificial stream, ditch or reservoir.

SEC. 4. **Extent of Right of Way.**—Such right of way shall extend only to a ditch sufficient for the purpose required together with the right of ingress and egress to construct, maintain and repair the same; and whenever any person or persons find it necessary to convey water for the purposes of irrigation or mining through the improved or occupied lands of another, he or they shall select for the line of such ditch through such property the shortest and most direct route practicable upon which can be constructed with uniform or nearly uniform grade, and discharging the water at a point where it can be conveyed to and used upon the land or lands or mining claim of the person or persons constructing such ditch, canal or works.

SEC. 5. **Condemnation of Right of Way.**—Upon the refusal of the owner of the lands, lessees, or those in possession, through which it is proposed to run said canal, ditch or works to permit the passage of the same through their property, the person or persons desiring the right of way for such ditch, canal or works, may proceed to condemn and take the right of way therefor as hereinafter provided.

SEC. 6. **Condemnation Proceeding.**—In case of the refusal of the owners or claimants of any lands or mining claims through which such ditch, canal or other works are proposed to be made or constructed, to allow the right of way or the passage thereof, the persons, company or corporation desiring the right of way shall file in the superior court of the county a complaint describing the land or mining claim to be crossed, the size of the ditch, canal or works, the quantity of land required to be taken, and the value of the land and damages to the property, setting forth the names of the owners or reputed owners or parties interested in the lands to be crossed, and praying that the right of way be granted. A summons shall issue and be served upon all parties interested, as in all other cases of civil nature. In case the defendant fails to appear, the court shall, when the cause shall come on to be heard, impanel a jury in the cause, and they shall determine the value of the land occupied by said ditch, canal or works and the damages, and, upon the return of the verdict, the court shall enter a decree, directing that the right of way for the ditch, canal or works be established according to the description in the complaint, and that the plaintiff shall pay to the clerk of the court the full amount of the value of the land and damages found by the jury, before the plaintiff shall begin work on said ditch, canal or works.

SEC. 7. **Defendant's Allegations.**—That whenever the defendant shall appear in the cause, he shall allege in his answer the value of the land proposed to be used by said ditch, canal or works, and the jury shall determine the value, and the proceedings shall be had as in the preceding sections: *Provided*, That plaintiff shall not be required to reply to the answer of the defendant, but the sole issue to be determined by the jury shall be the value of the land to be occupied by said ditch, canal or works, and the damages thereto.

SEC. 8. **Definitions.**—The word person, whenever used in this act, shall be construed to mean either a natural person, an association, or corporation, and the word he shall be construed to mean she, it, or they, and the word ditch shall be construed to include and mean dike, flume-way and irrigating canal.

SEC. 9. **Liberal Construction.**—The provisions of this act shall be liberally construed so that the ultimate object and the intent of this act shall be fully carried out.

Approved March 14, 1899. Session Laws 1899, p. 261.

Relating to the Mineral Lands of the State.

SECTION 1. **Mining Leases.**—The commissioner of public lands of the State of Washington is hereby authorized to execute leases and contracts for the mining of gold, silver, copper, lead, cinnabar or other valuable minerals, except coal, from any land now belonging to the State or from any lands to which the State may hereafter acquire title, subject to the conditions hereinafter provided.

SEC. 2. **Proceeding to Secure Lease.**—Any citizen of the United States finding precious minerals upon any lands belonging to the State of Washington may apply to the commissioner of public lands for a lease of any amount of land not to exceed the amount of land allowed by the United States mining laws for locating and recording mining claims, and same dimensions.

SEC. 3.—**Mining Locations.**—The manner of locating a mineral claim upon State land shall be similar to the State law regulating locations of mineral claims on government land: *Provided*, That any citizens that have found minerals on State lands previous to the passage of this act, and have posted up notice setting forth the dimensions according to the mining law of the United States and the State of Washington, shall have prior right to lease the same, and shall have ninety (90) days after the passage of this act to make application to the commissioner of public lands for a lease.

SEC. 4.—**Timber.**—The lessee may cut and use the timber found upon said premises for fuel and construction of buildings, required in the operation of any mine or mines on the premises; also the timber necessary for drains, tramways and supports for such mine or mines, and for no other purpose.

SEC. 5. **Payment—Prospecting.**—Before any lease shall be granted, the applicant shall pay to the State Treasurer the sum of five dollars ($5). The holder of a mineral lease, secured as above, shall have two years to develop said mine or mines: *Provided*, That no more than five tons of ore shall be removed therefrom, for assaying or testing purposes, until a contract as hereinafter provided shall have been executed.

SEC. 6. **Contract.**—At any time prior to the expiration of said lease, the lease holder, or any assignee thereof, shall have the right to obtain from the said commissioner of public lands a contract which shall bind the State of Washington, as the party of the first part, and the person, persons or corporation to whom said contract shall issue, as the party of the second part, in a mutual observance of the obligation and conditions as specified therein.

SEC. 7. **Royalty.**—The terms and conditions on which the same may be mined shall be agreed upon by the commissioner of public lands and the lessee: *Provided*, That the royalty or tax to be paid by the lessee shall be graduated. All claims or mines that do not yield a net income of more than $2,000 shall pay a tax of ten dollars per year; over $2,000 and not to exceed $10,000, shall pay fifty dollars; from $10,000 to $100,000, five per cent.; all above $100,000, ten per cent. Where the lessee commits fraud, the penalty shall be the forfeit of the mine or mines and all property pertaining thereto.

Approved March 17, 1897.

Leasing of Mineral Lands Belonging to the State.

SECTION 1. **Contract.**—That section 6 of an act entitled "An act to regulate the leasing of mineral lands belonging to the State of Washington, and declaring an emergency," approved March 17, 1897, be amended to read as follows:

Section 6. At any time prior to the expiration of said lease, the lease holder, or any assignee thereof, shall have the right to obtain from the said commissioner of public lands a contract which shall bind the State of Washington, as the party of the first part, and the person, persons or corporations to whom said contract shall issue as the party of the second part, in a mutual observance of the obligations and conditions as specifie therein. (The contract provided for in this act shall be as follows:)

This indenture, made this...day of......, A. D. one thousand eight hundred and......, by and between the State of Washington, party of the first part, and ...., party of the second part,

Witnesseth, that the party of the first part, in consideration of the sum of ten dollars to it in hand paid by the party of the second part, being the first annual payment as provided for in chapter 102, Section 7, of the Session Laws of 1897, the receipt whereof is hereby acknowledged, and in further consideration of the covenants and conditions herein contained, to be kept and performed by the part... of the second part, does hereby contract, lease and demise to the part... of the second part for a term of thirty years from and after the...day of......., one thousand eight hundred and......., the following described land situated in the county of.........., in the State of Washington, viz. : ...., which premises are leased to the part... of the second part for the purposes of exploring for, mining, taking out and removing therefrom, the merchantable shipping ore, containing ore, lead, silver, gold and other minerals, which is or which hereafter may be found on, in or under said land, together with the right to construct all buildings, make all excavations, openings, ditches, drains, railroads, wagon roads, smelters and other improvements upon said premises, which are or may become necessary or suitable for the mining or removal of ore containing copper, lead, silver, gold or other minerals from said premises, with the right, during the existence of this lease, to cut and use the timber found upon said premises for fuel, and so far also as may be necessary for the construction of buildings required in the operation of any mine or mines, on the premises hereby leased, as also the timber necessary for drains, tramways and supports for such mine or mines; *Provided, however*, That the part...of the second part shall have the right at any time to terminate this agreement in so far as it requires the part...of the second part to mine ore on said lands or to pay a royalty therefor, by giving written notice to the party of the first [part], which shall be served by leaving the same with the Commissioner of Public Lands, who shall officially, in writing, acknowledge the receipt of said notice, and the foregoing lease shall terminate sixty days thereafter, and all arrearages and sums which may be due under the same up to the time of its termination as set forth in said notice, shall be paid upon settlement and adjustment thereof. The party of the first part further agrees that the part... of the second part shall have the right under this agreement to contract with others to work such mine or mines, or any part thereof, or to sub contract the same, and the use of the said land or any part thereof, for the purpose of mining for ore, with the same rights and privileges as are herein granted to the said part... of the second part."

Approved March 18, 1899. Session Laws 1899, p. 337.

For another law about leasing State Mineral Lands, see page 313, Session Laws of 1901.

AMENDMENT.

By Act approved March 18, 1901, Session Laws of 1901, p. 292, the following words were added to the third subdivision of Section 10, Act of March 8, 1899, top of page 160—" provided, however, that nothing in this subdivision shall be held to apply to lands located under the laws of the United States as placer claims for the purpose of the development of petroleum and natural gas and other natural oil products."

WYOMING.

General State Law.

SECTION 2533. **Organization of Mining District.**—In any mining district, or in mining field of discovery of veins, leads, lodes or ledges, or of gold placers, petroleum fields, soluble salt deposits, or of any mineral lands whatever, or of any lands that are or may be hereafter opened to location under the laws governing mineral deposits, the miners may meet and organize and el ct a recorder and make regulations not in conflict with the laws of the United States, or with the laws of this Territory governing the location, manner of recording, and amount of annual work necessary to hol l possession of a mining claim within the district, subject to the following requirements:

First. That any five miners, having locations, or owning in part or in whole, claims within the proposed district, shall give notice by at least three written or printed, or partially written and partially printed notices, posted in prominent places within the proposed district, of a meeting called by them for organizing such district, at a date at least ten days subsequent to the posting of such notices.

Second. That the meeting thus called shall be attended by at least ten persons, all having locations or owning, in part or in whole, claims within the proposed district.

Third. That the recorder elected for such an organized district, shall hold his office until his successor is elected and qualified according to law. Such recorder is required to give bonds with at least two sureties, to the people of Wyoming, in the penal sum of not less than one thousand dollars, for the faithful performance of his duties, and for the turning over of all books, papers, records, etc., of his office to his duly elected and qualified successor, which bond shall be approved by the probate judge, and filed in the office of the county clerk and recorder. The recorder of such a mining district may appoint a deputy, for whose official acts he shall be responsible.

Fourth. That no district need be organized if the majority at the meeting as hereinbefore provided so desire; but when a district is once organized, it cannot be subdivided except in accordance with the local laws of the district, enacted at the regular or special meetings, or by action of the Legislature of this Territory. In case of the abandonment of any district for any cause whatever, it shall be the duty of the district recorder, as soon as practicable thereafter, to deposit all records and other papers pertaining to his office in the office of the recorder and register of deeds of the county in which said district is located.

Fifth. Each mining district may regulate the fees to be charged by the local recorder for recording location certificates, affidavits of labor, and all other instruments to be filed in the said recorder's office.

SEC. 2534. **Copy of Laws and Proceedings to be Filed.**—A copy of all the laws and proceedings of each mining district shall be filed in the office of the recorder of deeds of the county in which the district is situated, which shall be taken as evidence in any court having jurisdiction in the matter concerned under such laws or proceedings; and all such laws or proceedings of any mining district heretofore filed in the recorder's office of the proper county, and transcripts thereof duly certified, shall have the like effect in evidence. Such copies of laws and proceedings shall be filed in the office of the said recorder of deeds by the recorder of each mining district within sixty days after the organization of each new mining district, or within sixty days after new laws were adopted or proceedings had.

SEC. 2535. **Use of Water.**—Whenever any person, persons, or corporation shall be engaged in mining or milling in this State and in the prosecution of such business shall hoist or bring water from mines or natural water courses, such person, persons or corporation shall have the right to use such water in such manner, and direct it into such natural course or gulch as their busines interests may require: *Provided*, That such diversion shall not infringe on vested rights. The provisions of this section shall not be construed to apply to new or undeveloped mines, but to those only which shall have been open and require drainage or other direction of water.

SEC. 2536. **Right of Way.**—All mining claims or property now located, or which may hereafter be located within this Territory, shall be subject to the right of way of any ditch or flume for mining purposes, or of any tramway, pack-trail or wagon road, whether now in use or which may hereafter be laid out across any such location, claim or property: *Provided always*, That such right of way shall not be exercised against any mining location, claim or property duly made and recorded as herein required, and not abandoned prior to the establishment of any such ditch, flume, tramway, pack-trail or wagon road, without the consent of the owner or owners, except in condemnation, as in the case of land taken for public highways. Consent to the location of the easements above enumerated over any mineral claim, location or property, shall be in writing: *and provided further*, that any such ditch or flume shall be so constructed that water therefrom shall not injure vested rights by flooding or otherwise.

SEC. 2537. **Protection of Surface Proprietors.**—Where a mining right exists in any case and is separate from the ownership and right of occupancy to the surface, such owner or rightful occupant of the said surface may demand satisfactory security from the miner or miners, and if such security is refused, such owner or occupant of the surface may enjoin the miner or miners from working such mine until such security is given. The order of such injunction shall fix the amount of the bond therefor.

SEC. 2538. **Relocation.**—Whenever it shall be apprehended by the locator or his assignees, of any mining claims or property heretofore or hereafter located, that his or their original location certificate was defective, erroneous, or that the requirements of the law had not been complied with before the filing thereof, or shall be desirous of changing the surface boundaries of his or her original claim or location, or of taking away part of an overlapping claim or location which has been abandoned, or in case the original certificate was made prior to the approval of this act, and he or they shall be desirous of securing the benefit of this law, such locator or locators, or his or their assigns, may file an additional location certifictate in compliance with and subject to this act : *Provided, however*, That such relocation shall not infringe upon the rights of others existing at the time of such relocation, and that no such relocation or other record thereof shall preclude the claimant or claimants from proving any such title or titles as he or they may have held under any previous location.

SEC. 2539. **Location Certificate.**—No location certificate shall contain more than one claim or location, whether the location be made by one or more locators, and any location certificate that contains upon its face more than one location claim shall be absolutely void, except as to the first location named and described therein, and in case more than one claim or location is described together, so that the first one cannot be distinguished from the others, the certificate of location shall be void as an entirety.

SEC. 2540. **Stealing Mining Clams—Penalty—Evidence.**—In all cases where two or more persons shall, through collusion or otherwise, associate themselves together for the purpose of obtaining possession of any lode, gulch, or placer or other mineral claim or mining property within this Territory, then in the actual possession of another or others, by force or violence, or threats of violence, or by stealth, and shall proceed to carry out such purpose by making threats to and against the party or parties in possession, or who shall enter upon such lode, gulch, placer or other mineral claim or mining property for the purposes aforesaid, or who shall enter into any mineral claim or mining property ; or, not being on such mining claim or mineral property, but within hearing of the same, shall make any threats or any use of any language signs, gestures, intended to intimidate any person or persons in possession or at work on the said claim or claims of mineral property of whatever kind or nature, from continuing such possession or work thereon or therein, or to intimidate others from engaging to be employed thereon or therein, every such person or persons so engaging shall be guilty of a misdemeanor, and, upon conviction thereof, shall be fined a penal sum not exceeding $250, and be imprisoned in the county jail for not less than thirty days nor more than six months, or by both such fine and imprisonment. On trial of any person or persons charged with any of the offenses enumerated in this section, the proof of a common purpose of two or more persons to unlawfully secure possession of any mining claim or mineral property within the Territory, or to intimidate any one in the possession of or laborers at work on any mining claim or mineral property aforesaid, accompanied or followed by any acts or utterances of such person or persons herein enumerated, shall be sufficient evidence to convict any one committing such acts, although such parties may not be associating or acting together at the time of the commission of such offenses.

SEC. 2541. **Destroying Mining Property—Penalty.**—Any person or persons who shall unlawfully cut down, break down, level, demolish, destroy, injure, remove or carry away any sign, notice, post, mark, monument or fence upon or around any shaft, pit, hole, incline or tunnel, or any building, structure, machinery, implements or other property, on any mining claim or mineral property, ground or premises, shall be guilty of a misdemeanor, and, upon conviction thereof, shall be fined a penal sum of money no less than fifty dollars nor more than one thousand dollars, or be imprisoned for not less than thirty days nor more than one year, or by both such fine and imprisonment, in the discretion of the court.

SEC. 2542. **Mining Swindles.**—Any person or persons who shall defraud, cheat, swindle or deceive any party or parties, in relation to any mine or mining properties by "salting," or by placing or causing to be placed in any lode, placer or other mine, any genuine metals, or material representing genuine mineral, which are designed to cheat and deceive others, for the purpose of gain, whereby others shall be deceived and injured by such, shall be guilty of a felony, and, upon conviction thereof, shall be fined in a penal sum of not less than fifty dollars and not more than five thousand dollars, or imprisonment in a penitentiary for not less than thirty days or more than three years, or both fine and imprisonment, in the discretion of the court.

SEC. 2543.—**Live Stock.**—Every person or persons, company or corporation, who have already sunk mining shafts, pits, holes, inclines, upon any mining claim or on any mineral property, ground or premises, or who may hereafter sink such opening aforesaid, shall forthwith secure such shafts and openings against the injury or destruction of live stock running at large upon the public domain, by securely covering such shafts and other openings, as aforesaid, in a manner to render them safe against the possibility of live stock falling into them, or in any manner becoming injured or destroyed thereby; or by forthwith making a strong, secure and ample fence around such shafts and other openings aforesaid. Any person, persons, corporation or company that shall fail or refuse to fully comply with the provisions of this section shall be guilty of a misdemeanor, and on conviction thereof, shall be liable for any damages sustained by injury or loss of live stock thereby.

SEC. 2544.—**Length of Lode Claims.**—The length of any lode mining claim located within Wyoming Territory shall not exceed fifteen hundred feet, measured horizontally along such lode or vein. Nor can the regulations of any mining district limit a locator to less than this length.

SEC. 2545.—**Width of Lode Claims.**—The width of any lode claim located within Wyoming Territory shall not exceed three hundred feet on each side of the discovery shaft, the discovery shaft being always equally distant from the side lines of the claims. Nor can a mining district limit the location to a width less than one hundred and fifty feet on either side of the discovery shaft.

SEC. 2546.—**Recording Mining Claims.—Requisites of Certificates.**—A discoverer of any mineral lead, lode, ledge or vein shall, within sixty days from the date of discovery, cause such claim to be recorded in the office of the county clerk and *ex officio* register of deeds of the county within which such claim may exist, by a location certificate which shall contain the following facts:

First. The name of the lode claim.

Second. The name or names of the locator or locators.

Third. The date of location.

Fourth. The length of the claim along the vein, measured each way from the center of the discovery shaft, and the general course of the vein as far as it is known.

Fifth. The amount of surface ground claimed on either side of the center of the discovery shaft, or discovery workings.

Sixth. A description of the claim by such designation of natural or fixed objects, or if upon ground surveyed by the United States system of land survey, by reference to section or quarter-section corners, as shall identify the claim beyond question.

SEC. 2547. **Imperfect Certificates Void.**—Any certificate of the location of a lode claim which shall not fully contain all the requirements named in the preceeding section, together with such other description as shall identify the lode or claim with reasonable certainty, shall be void.

SEC. 2548. **Prerequisites to Filing Location Certificate.**—Before the filing of a location certificate in the office of the county clerk, and *ex officio* register of deeds, the discoverer of any lode, vein or fissure shall designate the location thereof, as follows:

First. By sinking a shaft upon the discovered lode or fissure to the depth of ten feet from the lowest part of the rim of such shaft at the surface.

Second. By posting at the point of discovery, on the surface, a plain sign or notice, containing the name of the lode or claim, the name of the discoverer or locator, and the date of such discovery.

Third. By marking the surface boundaries of the claim, which shall be marked by six substantial monuments of stone or posts, hewed or marked on the side or sides, which face is toward the claim and sunk in the ground, one at each corner, and one at the center of each side line, and when thus marking the boundaries of a claim, if any one or more of such posts or monuments of stone shall fall by necessity upon precipitous ground, where proper placing of it is impracticable, or dangerous to life or limb, it shall be lawful to place any such post or monument of stone at the nearest point, properly marked to designate its right place; *Provided*, That no right to such lode or claim, or its possession or enjoyment, shall be given to any person or persons, unless such person or persons shall discover in said claim mineral bearing rock in place.

SEC. 2549. **Open Cut, Tunnel.**—Any open cut which shall cut the vein ten feet in length, and with face ten feet in height, or any cross-cut tunnel, or tunnel on the vein ten feet in length, which shall cut the vein ten feet below the surface, measured from the bottom of such tunnel, shall hold such lode the same as if a discovery shaft were sunk thereon.

SEC. 2550.—**Discovery Shaft.**—The discoverer of any mineral lode or vein in this State shall have the period of sixty days from the date of discovering such vein or lode, in which to sink a discovery shaft thereon.

SEC. 2551.—**Mineral Boundaries Defined.**—The locators of all mining locations heretofore made, or which shall hereafter be made, on any mineral vein, lode or ledge, situated on the public domain, their heirs and assigns, shall have the exclusive right of possession and enjoyment of all the surface included within the lines of their locations, and of all veins, lodes and ledges throughout their entire depth, the top or apex of which lies inside of such surface lines extended downward vertically, although such veins, lodes and ledges may so far depart from a perpendicular in their course downward as to extend outside the vertical lines of such surface locations. But their right of possession to such outside parts of such veins or ledges shall be confined to such portions thereof as lie between vertical planes drawn downward as above described through the end lines of their locations, so continued in their own direction that such planes will intersect such exterior parts of such veins or ledges. And nothing in this section shall authorize a locator or possessor of a vein or lode which extends in its downward course beyond the vertical lines of his claim, to enter upon the surface of a claim owned or possessed by another.

SEC. 5552.—**Relocation.**—Any abandoned lode, vein or strata claim may be relocated, and such relocation shall be perfected by sinking a new discovery shaft, and by fixing new boundaries in the same manner as provided for in the location of a new claim; or the relocator may sink the original discovery shaft ten feet deeper than it was at the time of its abandonment, and erect new, or adopt the old boundaries, renewing the posts or monuments of stone if removed or destroyed. In either event, a new location stake shall be fixed. The location certificate of an abandoned claim may state that the whole or any part of the new location is located as an abandoned claim.

SEC. 2553.—**Placer Record.**—That hereafter the discoverer of any placer claim shall, within thirty days of the date of discovery, record such claim with the recorder of the mining district in which it is situated, if such district be organized; and shall, within ninety days from the date of discovery, cause to be recorded such claim within the office of the recorder of deeds of the county within which such claim may exist, by a location certificate, which shall contain in either or both cases, the following facts:

First. The name of the claim, designating it as a placer claim.
Second. The name or names of the locator or locators thereof.
Third. The date of location.
Fourth. The number of feet or acres thus claimed.
Fifth. A description of the claim by such designation of natural or fixed objects as shall identify the claim beyond question. Before filing such location certificate, the discoverer shall locate his claim; first, by securely fixing upon such claim a notice in plain, painted, printed or written letters, containing the name of the claim, the name of the locator or locators, the date of discovery, and the number of feet or acres claimed; second, by designating the surface boundaries by substantial posts or stone monuments at each corner of the claim.

SEC. 2554. **Placer Expenditure.**—For every placer claim, assessment work as hereinafter provided shall be done during each and every calendar year after the first day of January following the date of location. Such assessment work shall consist in manual labor, permanent improvements made on the claim in buildings, roads, or ditches made for the benefit of working such claim, or after any manner, so long as the work done accrues to the improvement of the claim, or shows good faith and intention on the part of the owner or owners, and their intention to hold possession of said claim.

SEC. 2555. **Amount of Assessment Work.**—On a placer claim of an area of one hundred and sixty acres heretofore or hereafter located in this Territory and not situated in an organized district, not less than one hundred dollars' worth of assessment work shall be performed during each calendar year, from the first day of January after the date of location. On every placer mining claim so located, of less than one hundred and sixty acres, the amount of annual assessment work shall be at the rate of sixty-two and one-half cents per acre for each and every acre and fraction thereof: *Provided*, That the total amount to be annually expended be in no case less than fifteen dollars.

SEC. 2556. **Assessment Work on Contiguous Claims.**—When two or more placer mining claims lie contiguously, and are owned by the same person, persons, company or corporation, the yearly expenditure of labor and improvements required on each of such claims may be made upon any one of such contiguous claims if the owner or owners shall thus prefer.

SEC. 2557. **Regulation of Amount of Assessment Work.**—Where such placer claims are situated in an organized mining district, or if they are finally embraced in such a district, then the amount of assessment work and the manner of its accomplishment shall be regulated entirely by the district laws, whether the amount of work required annually be greater or less than the amount hereinbefore set forth as required of placer claims not located in such districts.

SEC. 2558. **Failure to do Assessment Work.**—Upon the failure of the owners to do or have done the assessment work required within the time above stated, such claim or claims upon which such work has not been completed shall thereafter be opened to re-location on or after the first day of January of any year after such labor or improvements should have been done, in the same manner and on the same terms as if no location thereof had ever been made: *Provided*, That the original locators, their heirs, assigns or legal representatives, have not resumed work upon such claim or claims after failure, and before any subsequent location had been made.

SEC. 2559. **Affidavit of Work Done.**—Upon completion of the required assessment work of any mining claim, the owner or owners or agent of said owner or owners shall cause to be made by some person engaged in performing the work, an affidavit setting forth that the required amount of work was performed, which affidavit shall within thirty days after the completion of the work be recorded in the office of the recorder of the district in which such claim is situated, if such be organized, or if such district be not organized, such affidavit shall within sixty days of completion of the work be filed for record in the office of the recorder and register of deeds of the county in which such claim is located.

SEC. 2560. **Patent.**—When any person, persons or association, they and their grantors, have held and worked their placer claims in conformance with the laws of this Territory and the regulations of the mining district in which such claim exists, if such be organized, for five successive years after the first day of January succeeding the date of location, then such person, persons or association, they and their grantors, shall be entitled to proceed to obtain a patent for their claims from the United States without performing further work; but where such person, persons or association, they or their grantors, desire to obtain a United States patent before the expiration of five years from the date hereinbefore mentioned, they shall be required to expend at least five hundred dollars' worth of work upon a placer claim.

SEC. 2561. Coal Mines.—Nothing in this act shall apply to the working of coal mines.

Extracts from the Revised Statutes, 1899.

Miners' Liens.

SECTION 1. When Created.—That every miner or other person, who, at the request of the owner of any ledge or lode of quartz bearing gold silver, cinnabar, or copper, or of any coal bank or mine, shall work in upon such mine or bank, shall have a lien upon such vein or lode, mine or bank, to the amount due at any time when a demand shall be made upon such owner, or his or their agent, for money due for such labor, and payment shall be refused.

SEC. 2. Materials.—That any person who shall labor as a mechanic, or otherwise, or who shall furnish timber, lumber, rope, nails, or any other material for timbering shafts [or] levels for the mine, who shall furnish any kind of materials for erecting windlass, whim, or other hoisting apparatus upon any vein, mine, or coal bank, referred to in the first section, shall also have a lien upon the mine or coal bank for which he furnished such materials, or upon which he performed such labor.

SEC. 3. Manner of Proceeding.—The party seeking a lien shall proceed, so far as the proceedings are applicable in the same manner, to enforce a lien as by law required in the case of mechanics and other persons seeking to enforce a lien upon dwelling-houses and other buildings, except when other provisions are made by this act.

SEC. 4. Notice How and When Filed.—When any sum exceeding ten dollars for labor performed by any miner or other person upon or in any mine or coal bank specified in section one of this act, shall be due and unpaid for ten days, it shall be competent for the person or persons to whom such sum of money shall be due, to file a notice in the office of county recorder in the county where such mine is situated, at any time within thirty days after the last day upon which work was done by him; which said notice shall in substance set forth the fact that the party performed labor (naming the kind) for a party or company (naming the party or company), that such labor was performed under a contract (stating the substance); also, the time when the party commenced and when he ceased to work, the amount still due and unpaid, together with a description of the mine or coal bank upon which such work was performed, which statement shall be verified by the affidavit of the party so filing it, and when filed, the county recorder shall record the same in a "lien book," the same as required in the case of mechanics' notices of liens.

SEC. 5. **Materials Furnished.**—The provisions of the next preceding section shall apply to persons who shall furnish materials or work upon any shaft, whim, or other hoisting works, who, by complying with the general provisions of such section, shall have a like lien.

SEC. 6. **Lien Holds Against Purchasers.**—When notices as provided in the next two preceding sections shall be filed, the lien shall hold not only against the owner of the mine or bank, from the time when the miner or other person began work, but against all persons or company who shall have purchased such mine or coal bank while such miner or other person was employed therein, or furnished materials used therein or thereon.

SEC. 7. **When Suit May Be Commenced.**—Suit to enforce such lien may be commenced at any time within one year after filing such notice.

SEC. 8. **Oil Well or Spring.**—Any owner of any oil well or spring who shall employ any person to perform any work of any kind around or about any oil well or spring, either in building derricks, buildings, or any kind of machinery, or in boring or drilling, shall be deemed within the provisions of the act; and all persons performing labor or furnishing materials, shall have like liens upon oil territory upon which he labored, or for which he furnished materials or the improvements thereon, as miners or other laborers upon or in mines as provided in this act, and shall proceed in the same manner to enforce a lien.

Approved December 2, 1869. Session Laws of 1869, p. 404.

Placer Claim.

AN ACT *to amend and re-enact Sections 2553, 2555, and 2559 Revised Statutes.*

SECTION 2553. **Location Certificate.**—Hereafter the discoverer of any placer claim shall, within ninety days after the date of discovery, cause such claim to be recorded in the office of the county clerk and *ex officio* register of deeds of the county within which such claim may exist, by filing therein a location certificate, which shall contain the following:

1st, the name of the claim, designating it as a placer claim; 2d the name or names of the locator or locators thereof; 3d the date of location; 4th the number of feet or acres thus claimed; 5th a description of the claim by such designation of natural or fixed objects as shall identify the claim beyond question. Before filing such location certificate, the discoverer shall locate his claim: First, by securely fixing upon such claim a notice in plain painted, printed or written letters, containing the name of the claim, the name of the locator or locators, the date of the discovery, and the number of feet or acres claimed; second, by designating the surface boundaries by substantial posts or stone monuments at each corner of the claim.

SEC. 2555. **Assessment Work.**—On all placer claims heretofore or hereafter located in this State not less than one hundred dollars' worth of assessment work shall be performed during each calendar year from the first day of January after the date of location.

SEC. 2559. **Affidavit of Assessment Work.**—Upon completion of the required assessment work for any mining claim, the owner or owners or agent of such owner or owners shall cause to be made by some person cognizant of the facts, an affidavit setting forth that the required amount of work was done, which affidavit shall within sixty days of the completion of the work, be filed for record, and shall thereafter be recorded in the office of the county clerk and *ex officio* register of deeds of the county in which the said claim is located. [Usual repeal and take effect sections.]

Approved February 19, 1901. Session Laws 1901, pp. 104 and 105.

Placer Mines.

AN ACT *to Repeal Section 2557 Revised Statutes.*

That Section 2557 of the Revised Statutes of the State of Wyoming relating to the regulating by mining districts of the amount of assessment work that may be done upon placer mining claims in an organized district be, and the same is hereby, repealed. [Usual repeal and take effect sections.]

Approved February 14, 1901. Session Laws 1901, p. 39.

CANADA AND NORTHWEST TERRITORY.

Revised and Amended Regulations Approved by the Lieutenant-Governor in Council, April 7th, 1899.

1. Any person may explore for minerals on any Crown Lands not for the time being marked or staked out and occupied, except on such lands as by the Lieutenant-Governor in Council may have been withdrawn from sale, location or exploration as being valuable for their pine timber or for any other reason.

2. Where Crown Lands are situated within a Mining Division they may be occupied as Mining Claims under miners' licenses.

3. The Lieutenant-Governor may appoint for every Mining Division or for any part thereof an Inspector, who shall be an officer of the Bureau of Mines.

4. Every Inspector shall have power to enter, inspect and examine any mine or portion thereof or works connected therewith relating to the health and safety of the persons employed in or about the mines or works, and to give notice to the owner or agent in writing of any particulars in which he considers such mine or works, or any portion thereof, or any matter, thing or practice, to be dangerous or defective, and to require the same to be remedied within the period of time named in such notice; and on the occasion of any examination or inspection of a mine the owner shall produce to the Inspector, if required so to do, an accurate plan of the workings thereof up to the time of such inspection, and also shall permit the Inspector to take a copy or tracing thereof.

5. Every Inspector shall be *ex officio* a Justice of the Peace of the county or united counties, district or districts which a mining Division comprehends or includes, in whole or in part, or in which or in any portion of which a Mining Division lies.

6. Every Inspector shall have power, within the Mining Division for which he has been appointed, to settle summarily all disputes between licensees as to the existence or forfeiture of mining claims, and the extent and boundary thereof, and as to the use of water and access thereto, and generally to settle all difficulties, matters or questions which may arise between licensees; and the decisions of the Inspector in all such cases shall be final, except where otherwise provided by the Mines Act, or where another tribunal is appointed under authority of the Act; and no case under the Act shall be removed into any Court by *certiorari*.

7. Every Inspector of a Mining Division appointed under the Mines Act may appoint any number of constables not exceeding four; and the persons so appointed shall be constituted constables and peace officers for the purposes of the Act for and during the terms and within the Mining Divisions for which they are appointed.

8. No person shall be appointed or authorized to act as an Inspector who practices, or acts, or is a partner of any person who acts as a mining agent, or who is employed by the owners of or is interested in any mine.

9. The Director of the Bureau of Mines shall have all the powers, rights and authority throughout the Province which an Inspector has or may exercise in any Mining Division, and such other powers, rights and authority for the carrying out of the provisions of the Mines Act as shall be assigned to him by regulation.

10. No Director, Inspector or other officer appointed under the Mines Act shall directly or indirectly purchase or become interested in any Crown lands or mining claim; and any such purchase or interest shall be void; and if any officer violates this regulation he shall forfeit his office and be

liable in addition to a penalty of $500 for every such offence, to be recovered in an action by any person who sues for the same.

11. The Lieutenant-Governor in Council may by Order declare any tract of country therein described to be a Mining Division; and by any subsequent Order in Council may add to or diminish the limits of the Division, or may otherwise amend any such Order, or may cancel the same.

12. On payment of a fee of $10, or such other sum as may be fixed by regulation, the Director of the Bureau of Mines (or the Inspector, of a Division when so authorized by the Commissioner of Crown Lands) may grant to any person, registered partnership, or mining company incorporated under the laws of the Province applying therefor a license to be called a "miner's license," which shall be in force for one year from the date thereof, and shall not be transferable except with the consent of the Director of the Bureau or the Inspector of the Division upon payment of a fee of $5.

13. The person, partnership or company named in a license shall be called the "licensee," and upon payment of the fee fixed by law or regulation, such licensee shall have the right to renewal if application is made therefor before the expiration of the license or within ten days thereafter.

14. Every licensee shall produce and exhibit his license to the Inspector for the Division, and prove to the satisfaction of the Inspector that it is in force, at the time of recording his claim, and at any other time when required by the Inspector so to do.

15. A miner's license shall authorize the licensee to explore any portion of the Mining Division named in his license, and to mine during one year from the date of the license on any mining claim marked or staked out by such licensee on Crown lands, and he may employ any person to assist him in working such claim, or may organize a company to work the same, but no licensee shall have the right to cut down or use any timber which may be upon his claim except for purposes of building, fencing or fuel, or other purposes necessary for working the mine upon the said claim.

16. A licensee who discovers a vein, lode or other deposit of ore or mineral in place within the Division mentioned in his license shall have the right to mark or stake out thereon a mining claim, providing that it is not included in a claim occupied by another licensee, or is not on Crown lands withdrawn from location or exploration, or on lands the minerals and mining rights whereof have been reserved by the Crown; and he shall have the right to work the same, or he may transfer his interest therein to another licensee upon payment of a fee of $5 to the Inspector of the Division, who shall record the transfer in his book.

17. If the working conditions have been complied with as hereinafter required for a period of four years on a claim of twenty chains square, or for three years on a claim of fifteen chains square or less, or when the equivalent of such working conditions has been complied with in a less period of time in the respective cases, the licensee may apply for and obtain a certificate of full performance of the working conditions for the claim free from any further working conditions, renewal fee or miner's license to work the same, and also a patent or lease for the land embraced in the claim, free from any further working conditions and miner's license to work the same, upon a survey thereof being made and filed according to section 27 of *The Mines Act*, R. S. O. 1897, the boundary lines in each survey to follow the courses of the lines of the claim as originally staked out and recorded, or as the lines may have subsequently been altered, changed or corrected by the Inspector, and upon payment therefor to the Department of Crown Lands of the purchase price of first year's rental at rate per acre as provided in sections 31 and 35 respectively of the said Act; and the time when the royalties may begin to be imposed or collected upon ores or minerals mined, wrought or taken from a claim so patented or leased shall be reckoned from the date of recording such claim in the Inspector's office. The commissioner of Crown Lands in granting patents under this regulation may grant at the

same price to the owner of a claim any contiguous fraction or piece of land not staked of a less size than ten acres if surrounded by staked claims.

18. A mining claim shall be marked or staked out by planting a discovery post of wood or iron (on which is written or stamped the name of the licensee, number of his license, and date of his discovery) upon an outcropping or show of ore or mineral in place within the boundaries of the claim, and by planting at each of the four corners a post of wood or iron in the order following, viz: No. I. at the northeast corner, No. II. at the Southeast corner, No. III. at the southwest corner, and No. IV. at the northwest corner, the number in each case to be on the side of the post towards the post which follows it in the order in which they are named.

19. If one or more corners of a claim fall in any situation where the nature or shape of the ground renders the planting of a post or posts impracticable, such corner or corners may be indicated by placing at the nearest suitable point a witness post, which in that case shall contain the same marks as those prescribed for corner posts, together with the letters "W. P." (witness post) and an indication of the bearing and distance of the site of the true corner from such witness post.

20. Where there are standing trees upon a mining claim so staked out, the licensee shall be required to blaze the trees and cut the underbrush along the boundary lines of the claim, and also along a line from the first corner post to the discovery post.

21. A mining claim shall be a square of fifteen chains or 990 feet, horizontal measurement, containing twenty-two and one-half acres or of such other extent, greater or less, but so as not to exceed a square of twenty chains or 1,320 feet, containing forty acres, and shall be laid out with boundary lines running north and south and east and west astronomically, and the ground included in each claim shall be deemed to be bounded under the surface by lines vertical to the horizon; but an irregular portion of land lying between two or more claims may be staked out with boundaries conterminous thereto, provided that its area shall not exceed forty acres. A valuable water-power lying within the limits of a claim shall not be deemed as part of it for the uses of the licensee.

22. No more than one claim shall be staked out by any individual licensee upon the same vein, lode or deposit of ore or mineral, unless such claim is distant at least sixty chains from the nearest known mine, claim or discovery on the same vein, lode or deposit, but no licensee shall stake out and record in the same Mining Division, within a radius of fifteen miles, more than four claims in one calendar year.

23. For each additional mining claim after the first marked or staked out by a licensee, whether upon the same vein, lode or deposit, or upon another, he shall pay to the Inspector of the Division a fee of $10 a year in advance when recording the same if the area is more than twenty-two and one-half acres, and $6 if it is twenty-two and one-half acres or less, and a like fee in each case shall be paid for every additional claim so held at the time of renewal of the license.

24. Every Inspector of a Mining Division shall keep a book for recording of mining claims therein, and such book shall be open to inspection by any person on payment of a fee of twenty cents.

25. Every licensee who has marked or staked out a mining claim shall, within thirty days thereafter, supply under oath to the Inspector of the Division an outline sketch or plan thereof, showing the discovery post and corner posts, and the witness posts (if any), and their distances from each other in feet, together with a notice in writing setting forth under oath the name of the licensee and the number of his license, the name (if any) of the claim and its locality as indicated by some general description or statement, the length of the boundary lines if for any cause they are not regular, and the nature of such cause, the situation of the discovery post as indicated by distance and direction from the first corner post, the time when

discovery of ore or mineral was made, and when the claim was marked or staked out, and the date of the said notice ; and every licensee shall accompany his sketch or plan and notice with an affidavit showing the discovery of valuable ore or mineral upon the claim by or on behalf of such licensee, and that he has no knowledge and has never heard of any adverse claim by reason of prior discovery or otherwise.

26. The Inspector shall forthwith enter in his book the particulars of the notice of claim presented by every licensee, and shall file the notice, sketch or plan and affidavit with the records of his office, and if there is no dispute as to the rights of the licensee to the claim by reason of prior discovery or otherwise, the Inspector may at the expiration of ninety days from date of the record thereof grant to the licensee a certificate of such record.

27. If the licensee fails to comply with the provisions of Regulation 25 so far as they relate to him, or if, having complied with them, he or any person in his behalf shall remove any post for the purpose of changing the boundaries after the plan and notice have been filed, the mining claim marked or staked out by him shall be deemed to be forfeited and abandoned, and all right of the licensee therein shall cease.

28. A mining claim shall also be deemed to be forfeited and abandoned, and all right of licensee therein shall cease in case the miner's license has run out and has not been renewed, or if the annual fee for a claim has not been prepaid, or if $150 has not been expended upon each claim taken up except as hereinafter provided in stripping, or in opening up mines, in sinking shafts, or in other actual mining operations, exclusive of all houses, roads and other like improvements in every calendar year, and the said expenditure shall consist of labor actually performed by grown men to be computed at the rate of $2 per man per day. Nevertheless it shall be competent for the licensee to prove that during one or more preceding years the extent of mining operations carried on has been adequate to cover the requirements for the year in default, in which case the claim shall not be cancelled, and the licensee may also defeat forfeiture by an undertaking with satisfactory security to expend the full amount of labor required for working conditions within the next succeeding year, including the operations in default.

29. For every five claims or less held by the same licensee or by different persons agreeing to combine their mining operations within a radius of one mile, all such mining operations may be carried on upon one of the claims ; but notice of an intention to carry on such operations must be filed with the Inspector, and a record of all mining operations carried on by a licensee during his license year verified by oath shall be filed with the Inspector, who shall enter an abstract thereof in his book.

30. A licensee may at any time abandon a mining claim by giving notice in writing to the Inspector of the Mining Division of his intention so to do, and from the date of the record of such notice in the Inspector's book all interest of the licensee in such claim shall cease.

31. A party wall at least fifteen feet thick (seven and one-half feet on each side of the boundary lines) shall be left between adjoining claims on Crown lands, which shall be used in common by all parties as a roadway for all purposes, and shall not be obstructed by any person throwing soil, stone or other material thereon ; and if it is found necessary or expedient to remove such party wall the person so removing it shall, if required, construct a new roadway in nowise more difficult of approach than the one destroyed by the removal of the party wall ; and every person obstructing a party wall or failing to construct a new roadway in place of the one destroyed shall be liable to a fine of not more than $5 and costs, or in default to be imprisoned for any period not exceeding one month.

32. No person mining upon Crown lands shall cause damage or injury to the holder of another claim by throwing earth, clay, stones or other material thereon, or by causing or allowing water to flow into or upon such other claim from his own, under a penalty of not more than $5 and costs, and in

default of payment he may be imprisoned for any period not more than one month.

33. Any person who removes or disturbs with intent to remove any stake, picket or other mark placed under the provisions of the Mines Act shall forfeit and pay a sum not exceeding $20 and costs; and in default of payment may be imprisoned for any period not exceeding one month.

34. Any person contravening Part III. of the Mines Act or any rule or regulation made under it, in any case where no other penalty or punishment is imposed, shall for every day on which such contraventions occurs, or continues, or is repeated, incur a fine of not more than $20 and costs; and in default of payment may be imprisoned for a period not exceeding one month.

35. Every person who pulls down, injures or defaces any rules, notice or abstract posted up by the owner or agent of a mine shall be guilty of an offence against the Mines Act.

36. Every person who wilfully obstructs an Inspector in the execution of his duty under the Mines Act, and every owner or agent of a mine who refuses or neglects to furnish to the Inspector the means necessary for making an entry, inspection, examination or enquiry under the Mines Act in relation to such mine shall be deemed to be guilty of an offence against the Act.

37. Every Inspector of a Mining Division may convict upon view of any of the offences punishable under the provisions of Part III of the Mines Act or any regulations made thereunder.

38. The Lieutenant-Governor in Council may, as often as occasion requires, declare by proclamation that he deems it necessary that the Act respecting Riots near Public Works (R. S. O. 1897, chap. 38) shall, so far as the provisions therein are applicable, be in force within any Mining Division; and upon and after the day to be named in any such proclamation, section 1 and sections 3 to 11, inclusive, of said Act, so far as the provisions thereof can be applied therein, shall take effect within the Mining Division designated in the proclamation; and the provisions of the said Act shall apply to all persons employed in any mines, or in mining within the limits of such Division, as fully and effectually to all intents and purposes as if the persons so employed had been specially mentioned and referred to in the said Act.

39. All the provisions of Part IV. of the Mines Act, R. S. O., 1897, being the Part under the heading of Mining Regulations, shall apply in every particular to all mines and other openings from which ore or mineral of any kind or class is raised or taken, and to all works of smelting, milling or otherwise treating ores or minerals for any economic objects, which are situated within the limits of a mining division.

ARE YOU POSTED?

Is it Wise Economy to Save a Few Dollars

And, by so doing, drive the business of your section of country into the hands of your well-posted rivals?

COPP'S PUBLIC LAND LAWS,

DECISIONS, OPINIONS AND INSTRUCTIONS.

Nearly 1,400 Pages. Two Volumes.

TWO EDITIONS:
- Full Law Binding, Extra Paper, only - - - $4.50
- Half Law Binding, Medium Paper, only - - - 3.00

☞ One case won by the knowledge it imparts will more than pay for the work.

IT IS THE LATEST WORK ON THE SUBJECT EXTANT PUBLISHED IN 1890.

No respectable land attorney can afford to be without this valuable publication. Address,

HENRY N. COPP,
President, Copp and Company, (Incorporated)
WASHINGTON, D. C.

Do You Want to Strike it Rich?

An old-time Colorado miner has suggested to H. N. Copp, of Washington, a new book, with details of what it should contain, and how each chapter should be treated.

THE PROSPECTOR'S MANUAL

is the result of this advice, and it is hoped by the editor that the book, having such an inception, will prove useful to the wealth producers of the mining regions.

The work does not profess to be a scientific treatise on assaying or mineralogy, but is intended as an elementary, concise guide for practical men. It contains numerous tests for various ores; full description of gold, silver, copper and other metals and their compounds, gems and paints, with tables for determining minerals, together with valuable suggestions to prospectors.

IT CONTAINS ALSO

1. **The United States Mining Laws and Land Office Instructions Thereunder.**—Each section of the Law is immediately followed by the Land Office instructions relating thereto. This is a convenient arrangement, as it avoids turning several pages when the instructions are consulted in connection with the law.
2. **Local Laws.**—Embracing the State and Territorial Laws relating to lode and placer mines, water rights, etc.
3. **New and Improved Forms** for making the various proofs, from the location of a claim, miner's lien, notice to delinquent co-owners, etc., down to issuance of patent. **Price, 50 Cents.**

Address, **HENRY N. COPP,** Washington, D. C.

Land Office Blanks. The Cheapest and Best.

If you do not wish to keep an office supply of these blanks, ask your bookseller to keep them on hand for you and for all interested.

FOLLOW DIRECTIONS FOR ORDERING.

In ordering, give "Office Number" (*sure*) and "Title of Blank" (*sure*), with quantity of each blank wanted. Put only one blank on a line, to avoid mistakes. Many errors have occurred through not observing the above directions.

MONEY MUST INVARIABLY ACCOMPANY THE ORDER.

In view of the low prices of these blanks, the additional expense of book-keeping and sending out bills cannot be afforded   Address,

HENRY N. COPP,
President, Copp and Co. (Incorporated), Washington, D. C.

Office No.	Title of Blank.	By the Doz.	By the 50.	By the 100.
	Applications to Enter.			
4-001	Cash System	$0 12	$0 40	$0 75
4-007	Homestead Law	12	40	75
4-015	Soldiers' and Sailors' Homestead	12	40	75
4-018	Additional Homestead	12	40	75
	Affidavits.			
4-059	Affidavit of Service of Contest by Mail	12	40	75
4-060	Affidavit of Notice Posted on Land	12	40	75
4-062	Non-Mineral	15	50	90
4-062a	Non-Saline	15	50	90
4-063	Homestead Entry	12	40	75
4-065	Soldiers' and Sailors' Homestead	12	40	75
4-066	Adjoining Farm Homestead	15	50	90
4-067	Adjoining Farm, Final	15	50	90
4-069	Affidavit in Commuted Homestead	12	40	75
4-070	Final Homestead Affidavit	12	40	75
4-072	Contest, Homestead (Land Office)	15	50	90
4-072a	Contest, Homestead (not at Land Office)	15	50	90
4-074	Desert Lands, Witness	15	50	90
4-074a	Assignees of Entrymen	12	40	75
4-074b	Desert, Yearly Proof, Claimant	12	40	75
4-074c	Desert, Yearly Proof, Witnesses	12	40	75
4-086	Additional Homestead	12	40	75
4-102b	Entries since August 30, 1890	12	40	75
4-107	Nearest Office	12	40	75
4-628	Affidavit and Order for Publication of Notice of Contest Against Non-Resident Entryman	15	50	90
	Notices.			
4-345	Contest, Homestead Law	12	40	75
4-347	For Publication	12	40	75
4-348	Intention to make Final Proof, Homestead	12	40	75
4-356	Desert Lands, Intention to Make Proof	12	40	75
	Notices.			
4-357	Timber-land Act, June 3, 1878—Publication	$0 12	$0 40	$0 75
4-358	Desert Land—Final Proof—Publication	12	40	75
	Proofs.			
4-369	Homestead — Claimant and Witnesses	25	85	1 50
4-370	Timber and Stone Lands—Claimant	25	85	1 50
4-370a	Timber and Stone—Cross-Examination of Claimant	12	40	75
4-371	Timber and Stone Lands—Witness	25	85	1 50
4-371a	Timber and Stone—Cross-Examination of Witness	12	40	75
4-372a	Desert Lands—Deposition of Applicant	25	85	1 50
4-373	Desert Lands—Deposition of Witness	25	85	1 50
4-376	*Ex Parte*, Contested Homestead	15	85	1 50
	Statements.			
4-537	Timber and Stone Lands	15	50	90
4-545	Soldier's Declaratory and Affidavit	15	50	90
4-546	Soldier's Declaratory	15	50	90
	Miscellaneous.			
4-109	Repayment of Purchase Money	15	50	90
4-274	Desert Lands, Declaration of Applicant	15	50	90
4-518	Reservoir Declaratory Statements	25	85	1 50
4-590	Township Plats, sections one inch square	10	30	50
4-590a	Township Plats, sections 1¼ inch square	10	30	50
4-592	Township Plats, sections two inches square	25	85	1 50
4-597	Relinquishment of Homestead	12	40	75
4-598	Soldier's Discharge	12	40	75
	Combination Appearance Blank	12	40	75
	General Power of Attorney	12	40	75

Fortunes Await Inventors.

Isaac M. Singer, the sewing machine inventor, who started life a poor boy, left $13,000,000 to his heirs. Elias Howe passed his first years in poverty, but had an income in later life of half a million dollars annually from royalties on his sewing machine patents. Charles Goodyear accidentally mixed sulphur and india rubber on a red-hot stove. His royalties on his vulcanization patents gave him a princely income. The Westinghouse Air-brake has produced $20,000,000 for its inventor's company. The McCormick and other harvester patents have poured millions of dollars into the pockets of their owners. Edison and the other inventors in the field of telegraphy and electricity have piled up enormous wealth. Alexander Graham Bell started life as an impecunious teacher. His telephone invention has blessed the world and made him rich. The barbed wire patents, covering a simple idea, have earned immense profits. Dr. Higgins invented the sliding thimble for umbrellas. He took out patents in England, France, Germany and elsewhere at small cost, and says he has received $100,000 in royalties. A Washington clerk, riding in the cars on his way home, bent a piece of brass and invented a paper fastener. He is said to have had an income of $30,000 annually for a considerable period. The inventor of the puzzle known as "Pigs in Clover" is reported to have cleared more than $100,000. The Hoe Printing Press patents have been very remunerative. Hundreds of patents could be mentioned that have made their owners wealthy.

Pointers for Inventors Sent Free.

A booklet entitled, "Pointers for Inventors," will be sent free to any address on request. It tells the expense of procuring American and Foreign Patents. What may be the subject-matter of a Patent. How to proceed to procure a Patent. Requirements of the Patent Office as to drawings and models. Assignments. Patents for Compounds and Medicines. Trade-marks, Prints and Labels. Design Patents. Copyrights. How to invent. How to sell patent articles and territorial patent rights. Caveats. Infringements. The importance of employing a Washington attorney, and gives suggestions to correspondents and much valuable information.

HAVE YOU AN IDEA?

Do not drop it because you cannot pay for a patent. We may suggest a way to help you. Fortunes are often made on the simplest things and on slight improvements of existing machines and tools. A successful toy was patented in 1891 by a six year-old Canadian boy. Many valuable patents have been issued to women.
Address,

COPP & CO., Patent Attorneys,
WASHINGTON, D. C.

www.ingramcontent.com/pod-product-compliance
Lightning Source LLC
Chambersburg PA
CBHW062351220526
45472CB00008B/1772